Dear Reader:

The book you are about to read is the latest bestseller from the St. Martin's True Crime Library, the imprint *The New York Times* calls "the leader in true crime!" The True Crime Library offers you fascinating accounts of the latest, most sensational crimes that have captured the national attention. St. Martin's is the publisher of John Glatt's riveting and horrifying SECRETS IN THE CELLAR, which shines a light on the man who shocked the world when it was revealed that he had kept his daughter locked in his hidden basement for 24 years. In the Edgar-nominated WRITTEN IN BLOOD, Diane Fanning looks at Michael Petersen, a Marine-turned-novelist found guilty of beating his wife to death and pushing her down the stairs of their home—only to reveal another similar death from his past. In the book you now hold, AT ANY COST, Rebecca Rosenberg and Selim Algar reconstruct a frenzied case of greed, obsession, and murder.

St. Martin's True Crime Library gives you the stories behind the headlines. Our authors take you right to the scene of the crime and into the minds of the most notorious murderers to show you what really makes them tick. St. Martin's True Crime Library paperbacks are better than the most terrifying thriller, because it's all true! The next time you want a crackling good read, make sure it's got the St. Martin's True Crime Library logo on the spine—you'll be up all night!

Charles E Spicer

Charles E. Spicer, Jr.
Executive Editor, St. Martin's True Crime Library

AT
ANY
COST

A FATHER'S BETRAYAL,
A WIFE'S MURDER,
AND A TEN-YEAR
WAR FOR JUSTICE

REBECCA ROSENBERG
AND SELIM ALGAR

St. Martin's Paperbacks

Published in the United States by St. Martin's Paperbacks, an imprint of St. Martin's Publishing Group.

AT ANY COST

For information, address St. Martin's Publishing Group, 120 Broadway, New York, NY 10271.

www.stmartins.com

ISBN: 978-1-250-26458-9

Our books may be purchased in bulk for promotional, educational, or business use. Please contact your local bookseller or the Macmillan Corporate and Premium Sales Department at 1-800-221-7945, ext. 5442, or by email at MacmillanSpecialMarkets@macmillan.com.

Printed in the United States of America

St. Martin's Press hardcover edition published 2021
St. Martin's Paperbacks edition / February 2022

10 9 8 7 6 5 4 3 2

For Ayla and Henry

Authors' Note

While much of the dialogue in this book stems directly from court transcripts and audio recordings, in some instances conversations have been reconstructed based on interviews and legal documents.

Passages and statements set off by quotations come from interviews, court documents and trial testimony, and we often do not indicate the source in order to preserve the narrative's flow.

In cases where people have divergent recollections of the same event, we have used the version that we believe is the most accurate.

CHAPTER ONE

New Year's Eve

In the snow-dappled early morning hours of New Year's Eve, 2009, little Anna Covlin blinked herself out of slumber. The sound of running water had slowly awakened the 9-year-old girl, and her eyes flickered open in the blackness of her mother's bedroom. Anna had nestled beside her the prior evening and was still cocooned in a tangle of covers. Her 3-year-old brother, Myles, remained suspended in dreamland a few feet away. But there was a rumpled depression where she had expected to see her mother's form. Straining her ears, Anna detected the faint cascade of water from a nearby bathroom.

She planted her bare feet on the carpeted floor and advanced to the bathroom door. Myles awoke and joined her.

Peering inside, Anna saw her mother, Shele Covlin, seated in the tub with her bare back exposed and her thick blond mane flipped forward. Anna assumed that she was indulging in a nocturnal soak and washing her hair. Anna guided Myles back to bed and they burrowed beneath the comforter.

A few hours later, a piercing winter sun now fully aloft over Manhattan, Myles suddenly shook his sister awake.

"Where is Mommy?" the little boy asked.

Anna inventoried the room once again. She and her brother remained the bed's only occupants.

It was now 7 in the morning. Five floors below, the city began issuing the opening notes of its daily cacophony—the stray bleat of a cabby's horn, the plaintive bellow of a reveler parrying the admonitions of daylight.

The Dorchester Towers, a regal if slightly dated 34-story apartment building, stood just three blocks from famed Lincoln Center, home to the New York Philharmonic, the Metropolitan Opera and the New York City Ballet.

Anna again walked toward the bathroom in search of her mother—only this time with a surging dread. Inside, she saw Shele bobbing facedown in reddened bathwater.

The chilling scene would initiate a nearly decade-long mystery that baffled veteran New York City investigators, leveled two families and captivated hardened New Yorkers like few tragedies before it.

Barely able to make sense of the atrocity before her, Anna rushed to the apartment's landline phone and dialed her father, Rod Covlin. He had recently separated from Shele after more than a decade of marriage and had moved into a studio apartment directly across the hall. The familiar number flashed on Rod's phone at 7:04 A.M.

"Something is wrong with Mommy!" Anna wailed. "Something is wrong with Mommy!"

The broad-shouldered 36-year-old, who stood 6-foot-2, darted across the hall and told Anna to unlock the front door of apartment 515. He hurried to the master bathroom and saw his wife in the bloodied tub. Hoping to shield his children from the grisly scene, Rod shepherded them into Anna's bedroom and ordered them to stay there. He returned to the bathroom, hoisted Shele's petite body out of the sloshing tub and placed her faceup on the white-tiled bathroom floor. There was no movement. Shele's shimmering blond hair was now soaked crimson. Rod frantically performed CPR before calling 911 at 7:14 A.M. An operator then guided him through a few more attempts at resuscitation before he surrendered.

As he waited for emergency crews to arrive, Rod snatched a beige comforter and pink blanket off of Shele's bed and draped them over her nude body. New York City Fire Department EMS Lt. Matthew Casey and four members of his team were the first to trundle into 155 West 68th Street at 7:18 A.M., making their way past a startled doorman and into an elevator. Casey knocked on the door and lowered his gaze to meet Anna's. Instinctively softening his tone as the child peered up at him, he asked if her mother was home.

"She just pointed down the dark hallway," he later remembered.

Casey and his men walked down the corridor. "FDNY!" the troop announced as they advanced into the silent gloom. "FDNY!"

Casey reached the master bathroom, the only lighted area in the house, and saw Rod sitting beside his estranged wife. Her head was resting at the base of the toilet, her mouth slightly agape and her eyes shut. Shele's left arm covered her left breast and her right hand lay near her navel. There were bright red scratches on the lower half of her face and a deep purple contusion, the size of a dime, on the left side of her lower lip.

The freshly manicured nails on her hands and feet were aflame with red polish—a jarring counterpoint to her inert state. The medics remained silent, immediately recognizing death in her rigid limbs and alien pallor.

"Do something! Do something!" Rod barked at them.

A medic escorted him from the bathroom before checking Shele's vital signs. There were none.

Firefighter William Rix crouched beside her to check for

rigor mortis, the setting of joints and muscles that occurs a few hours after death.

"I pulled out her arm and noticed that it was completely stiff," he said. "I grabbed her by the wrist to try to pull them away and they were locked." Her limbs had already curled into a pose of death.

At 7:20 A.M., paramedic Bobby Wong entered the apartment and made his way down the long hallway to document the conclusion of Shele's life and declared her dead at 7:25 A.M. In the living room, Wong saw Rod and his daughter weeping softly on a sofa. Unaware of the calamity that had just befallen him, Myles cheerfully played with toys. Rod, wearing a clean white T-shirt and dark gray sweatpants, received the stream of NYPD officers who began appearing at the front door. He directed them to the bathroom and pointed to a cabinet above the bathtub faucet that had been partially ripped from its hinges.

"I think that she may have grabbed a piece of wood, the wooden cabinet, and fell and hit the back of her head, and slipped under the water," the husband told police. Overcome by the unfolding horror, Rod began retching at one point and rushed to a secondary bathroom to gather himself.

"I can't believe this is happening," he later told a female sergeant as he extended his arms for a consolatory embrace. The unemployed Ivy League graduate told officers that he and his wife were separated and mired in a divorce proceeding. She had taken out a restraining order against him, but he lived across the hall to stay close to their children, he explained.

Shele, a thriving wealth manager at UBS, had long been the primary breadwinner, earning nearly half a million dollars a year. Well-regarded for both her professional successes and her exuberant charms, she worked alongside her brother, Philip Danishefsky, and her doting father, Joel Danishefsky, at the finance giant.

At just 47, Shele's sudden death had arrived in the midst of a personal revival. She had wielded a Midas touch at work, and business was more profitable than ever. With her split from Rod nearly resolved, she had begun to entertain an expanding pool of suitors.

Shele often remarked on her budding optimism to the family's longtime nanny, Hyacinth Reid. Like many working Manhattan mothers, Shele was reliant on a caregiver to help manage her domestic and professional demands. A native of Jamaica, Reid had swaddled Anna as an infant and worked for the family for nearly a decade. Rose, as she preferred to be called, became a maternal surrogate for the children and adored them deeply. As Shele's relationship with Rod worsened, her dependence on Rose became critical. Her tasks included cleaning the house and taking Anna and Myles to school while Shele applied her makeup and hurried out the door to work in Midtown, just a few blocks from Rockefeller Center. Anna attended Manhattan Day School, an exclusive private Jewish school, while Myles was enrolled in a nearby day care.

That morning, the nanny took a subway train from her modest home in Brooklyn to the Dorchester Towers. Bundled up against the sharp winter chill and gripping a cup of McDonald's coffee, Rose arrived at 7:57 A.M., with her grandson, J.J., in tow. She would occasionally bring him with her to work, and Shele's kids delighted in playing with the boy.

Rose immediately noticed that the apartment door was open and heard several hushed voices murmuring within. Her unease mounting, she walked in and saw two grim-faced police officers silently flipping through notepads. Rod was seated on the sofa. The three men said nothing as she entered.

"Where are the children?" she asked.

The officers pointed across the hall to Rod's apartment.

"Where is Shele?" she asked.

Again, silence.

"Where is Shele?" she asked two more times, her Jamaican brogue losing its melodic lilt and growing urgent.

Rod finally spoke, his eyes affixed to the floor. "Shele had an accident in the bathroom," he said.

"How bad is it?" Rose asked, her voice now quivering. "Where is she?"

"She's dead," Rod replied, his words shooting through Rose's body like an electric current.

Her hands went limp, and the McDonald's coffee she was clutching fell to the floor and splattered across a wall. Rose followed in its path and collapsed, sobbing.

She had been with Shele and the kids the night before. Rose was inconsolable, crying hysterically and begging to see Shele. When the officers refused, she fell silent for several moments.

"No," she said. "No! She did not have an accident! She did not have an accident!"

CHAPTER TWO

Daddy's Girl

While Shele's life came to an abrupt end in middle age, the extraordinary circumstances of her death—and the tortured investigation that followed—can be traced to the contours of her youth.

Shele Minna Danishefsky was born in Elizabeth, New Jersey, on July 13, 1962, to a young butcher, Joel Danishefsky, and his homemaker wife, Jaelene. The son of Polish immigrants, Joel spent his early years in a teeming Jewish enclave in Brooklyn. His father, Jacob Danishefsky, a rabbi, yearned to escape the lurid aggravations of urban life and eventually relocated his growing clan to the placid town of Bayonne, New Jersey.

Immersed in Judaica as a boy, Joel adopted his father's piety and soon sought to emulate him as a rabbi. He enrolled in Yeshiva University, a prestigious Orthodox Jewish college in Manhattan, where he earned a degree in math along with rabbinical ordination.

Joel married Jaelene in 1956 and the young couple initially settled in Elizabeth, New Jersey, an austere working-class town roughly 15 miles from Manhattan. Joel pursued regular positions at local houses of worship but was only able to wrangle sporadic assignments and was often compelled to seek work back in Brooklyn.

Joel would travel to the borough on weekends to offer his services for the Jewish Sabbath. From sundown on Friday to nightfall on Saturday, observant Jews are expected to suspend many routine activities to rest, just as God rested on the seventh day after creation. Prohibitions range from cooking and driving to the active use of electricity. Instead, Jews devote the period to gathering with family and friends for festive meals and prayer.

But Joel found a steady position elusive. Relatives suggested that he become a *schochet*—a Jewish butcher—to help make ends meet. A *schochet*—which means "slaughterer" in Hebrew—must master a precise cut to an animal's throat so that both the esophagus and trachea are severed in a single blade movement. The slightest deviation from the ancient practice renders the carcass unfit for Jewish consumption. Joel eventually acquired the necessary skills and would soon spend his early mornings executing animals with rote precision.

While the pay was good, Joel tired of the monotonous carnage and bloodied smocks. The day's labors would end in the early afternoon, giving him time to roam the streets of downtown Elizabeth. He would often stop outside banks during these strolls and ponder the rushing procession of stock ticker letters and digits inside their offices. While Joel had a vague familiarity with finance and a facility with numbers, he struggled to make sense of the torrent that built and toppled fortunes each day.

He vowed to decode the ticker—a sidewalk resolution that would eventually rescue him from the slaughterhouse and deposit him on Wall Street.

"He knew that he loved finance," his daughter, Eve Danishefsky, recalled. "He loved it. That's where he wanted to position his career. His mind, just the way he used numbers, was unbelievable. He was brilliant."

Soon after the birth of his first son, Joel pivoted to finance and enrolled in a Merrill Lynch training program to become a broker. Joel's natural business acumen, command of figures and tireless work ethic soon vaulted him to a position as a wealth manager with the firm, where he would at one point manage more than $1 billion in client assets.

As their prospects glistened, Joel and Jaelene expanded their family. In addition to the eldest, Fred, they welcomed three more children: Shele, followed by Eve and finally Philip. The kids were each separated by two years.

Meanwhile, Joel's equally talented siblings were mirroring his successes. The Danishefskys all displayed a penchant for math and science. His brother Sam Danishefsky would eventually become a pioneering cancer researcher after earning a Ph.D. from Harvard University. He currently leads a lab at Memorial Sloan Kettering Cancer Center in Manhattan and is on the faculty at Columbia University.

Joel had realized his dream of a sprawling, prosperous and spiritually grounded family. While often moored to his office late into the night, the patriarch ensured that he and Jaelene devoted ample time to their children on weekends. Without fail, the family would gather for meals on the Sabbath to review the week and wax hopeful about the future. They would pile into a car for modest excursions sweetened by familial harmony. With the advent of cheap air travel still a few years off, the Danishefskys contented themselves with road trips to Niagara Falls, Washington, D.C., and Disney World.

The family eventually settled into a tranquil Elizabeth neighborhood marked by tree-shaded streets, sensibly sized two-story homes and prim lawns that radiated communal pride. In keeping with Orthodox Jewish modesty, Joel shunned garish displays of affluence and instilled that sensibility into his own children. Rather than lavish them with material luxuries, Joel instead stressed industry, piety and loyalty.

"For us, family was everything," Eve said.

But in the midst of this easy childhood contentment, tragedy struck. Shele suffered a cruel injury at just 3 years old that would physically and emotionally scar her for the rest of her life.

Every Sabbath, the Danishefskys gathered at the home of Shele's maternal grandmother for a traditional Jewish meal. They would happily dine on matzoh-ball soup, kugel and roast chicken. After eating, the adults repaired to a separate room to enjoy a cup of hot tea while the children played nearby.

Since all cooking is prohibited during the Sabbath, Jewish families often keep a large urn of hot water—known as a samovar—heated for the duration of the holiday. Shele's grandmother kept her ornamented brass pot in a cabinet above a small drawer containing cutlery. While the adults chatted, little Shele made her way over to the tea station and noted that the drawer—slightly above her head—was ajar. Hoping to get a better look at its contents, the curious child grabbed it and tried to hoist herself up to peer inside. But the force brought down the entire cabinet and tipped over the samovar. Scalding water splashed across her chest, lower neck and upper arms like lava. Shele screamed in agony as her panicked parents rushed over. The scorching water had melted her skin.

Joel scooped up his little girl and sped to the nearest hospital. Doctors immediately recognized that Shele had suffered severe third-degree burns and began a series of ex-cruciating skin grafts. She would remain bedridden in the hospital for six weeks, undergoing a seemingly endless series of procedures as her parents and relatives looked on in guilt-ridden despair. While her face was spared, the scarring to her chest and neck was expansive and permanent. The skin on her upper torso was irreversibly deformed, exhibiting a rough texture that varied in color from pale to bright red. Joel was crestfallen, feeling responsible for not having protected her.

"My father always blamed himself for that," her sister, Eve, recalled. "He always felt a certain guilt, that he could have prevented it from happening." It was a lament that would shadow him for the next four decades. While Shele had no recollection of the accident, she was reminded of it each time she glimpsed her reflection. As she became a teenager, Shele noticed little else. Her family said she insisted on wearing long sleeves and high necklines even on the hottest days of summer to hide her injuries. When other kids squealed with delight at the prospect of a swim, Shele shriveled.

"It had a very dramatic effect on her," said Eve's husband, Marc Karstaedt. "She became very self-conscious about it." Joel and Jaelene sought out corrective treatments all over the world, desperate to restore their daughter's skin. Jaelene and Shele once journeyed to Brazil for a series of experimental procedures—but the scarring remained. As a teen, Shele sought to compensate for her discomfort by binge-eating, and the weight gain compounded her damaged self-esteem. Wracked with guilt and unwilling to interfere with her means of solace, Joel and Jaelene quietly accepted Shele's coping mechanisms. They would become far more permissive with their suffering daughter than their other children. "I used to get hand-me-downs from my cousins," Eve recalled. "I fit into their clothing, but Shele didn't. So my mother used to take her to the city to go to Lane Bryant. She could get whatever she wanted."

Shele was unusually accident-prone. At 10 years old, while attending a Jewish summer camp, she fell into a large pit and bashed her head. Doctors had to shave her scalp to stitch up the wound. Six years later, Shele was playing with the family dog, Sasha, teasing her with a treat. The Siberian Husky suddenly became enraged and locked her jaws onto her face. Shele again needed stitches, Eve said.

Just a year later, Shele was running with a friend at a pool party to celebrate her high school graduation when misfortune struck again. Unable to see a plate-glass window directly in front of her, she barreled through it. She was taken to the hospital to be sewn together once more.

Shele was especially close to Eve, with whom she shared a room growing up. The siblings collected an ever-growing legion of dolls and played with them whenever they had a spare moment. "We had the Barbie dolls, we had the Dawn dolls," recalled Eve. "Oh my gosh, we had so many different dolls."

As the little girls grew into teenagers, their attention veered away from playthings toward their romantic futures. Eve recalled Shele rhapsodizing about her future betrothal and doting husband.

"We loved watching 'Cinderella,'" Eve said. "We had these ideas of these big, beautiful weddings and Prince Charming. We used to talk about it all the time."

Eve and Shele attended Bruriah High School for Girls in Elizabeth, roughly a mile from their home. The religious school was part of the Jewish Educational Center, where the family also attended synagogue every Saturday.

Joel ensured that his family kept a kosher home and adhered to Jewish dietary restrictions. Pork and shellfish were strictly forbidden, and dairy products and meat could not be cooked or eaten together. Some scholars posit that the ancient dictate stems from a biblical passage that warns worshippers not to "boil a kid in its mother's milk." While specific interpretations vary, one theory holds that early rabbinical authorities thought it unholy to mingle the flesh of dead animals with the life-sustaining staple of milk. Kosher homes have separate sets of dishes and cutlery for dairy and carnivorous meals. After eating meat, a person must wait six hours before consuming dairy, according to Jewish law.

Jaelene developed a chronic circulatory condition when Shele was 10 and would seek relief in Florida for weeks at a time. As the oldest female child in the house, Shele was expected to assume many of her mother's domestic duties during these absences. Her maternal instincts revealed themselves even at this young age, Eve recalled. "Shele was very nurturing," she said. "She had to jump into mom mode and just take care of us. My mom would leave partially cooked meals in the freezers, but it was Shele who would take them out and add spices."

Eve and her older sister became inseparable. While still in high school, the siblings took a trip to Israel together to visit the burial sites of several relatives. They visited the Tomb of Rachel in Bethlehem and the Mount of Olives in Jerusalem, a 3,000-year-old cemetery overlooking the old city, where some of their family members were laid to rest.

But, perhaps due in part to her fragile self-esteem and social unease, Shele's family began to note an uneven performance in school. While her brothers and sisters returned home with sterling grades, Shele's marks were mediocre. Teachers questioned her diligence and engagement. "She was a poor student," Marc said of his sister-in-law. "She just did not apply herself."

While Joel and Jaelene expected and demanded academic excellence of Eve, Fred and Philip, they were reluctant to harangue Shele about her teenage lassitude. Still shouldering the blame for her childhood accident, Joel coddled his daughter—often to her detriment. "My in-laws never pushed her," Marc said.

Her academic shortcomings were mirrored by social frustrations. Hampered by her weight and unsightly scars, Shele couldn't penetrate the elite school cliques and would often confide her sorrows to Eve. Classmates whom she had taken for friends would often exclude her from major social occasions, cruelly confirming her sense of inadequacy.

While all of her siblings were admitted to the highly competitive New York University after graduating from high school, Shele settled on the less prestigious Pace University in Manhattan. She majored in marketing and opted to live in a dorm on campus, her first taste of independence. Like most teens liberated from the binds of parental scrutiny, Shele was exhilarated by her newfound freedom. Once she was set loose in Manhattan, Shele's social anxieties began to dissolve—as did her weight. She grew increasingly meticulous about her appearance and accepted her scarring as an unwelcome but manageable quirk. The bingeing ceased, and Shele dropped more than 30 pounds during her freshman year.

Newly emboldened and exuding confidence, Shele began to date casually. She graduated in 1984 but was uncertain as to a career path. Joel, then an established figure on Wall Street, suggested that she explore a career in finance. While he pushed Shele to pursue a vocation, Joel was beginning to yearn for grandchildren and was wary that a demanding position would delay Shele's childbearing. For this reason, he counseled against a conventional corporate path.

"He always felt that a broker was a perfect job for a woman," Eve said. "There was a flexibility, as it was easy to work from home or from an office, which was ideal for a woman who planned to have children." While still sensitive to Shele's insecurities, Joel no longer felt the need to serve as buffer between his daughter and the realities of adulthood. Rather than simply install her at his side in an entry-level post, Joel advised her to work with an associate to gauge her interest and aptitude. He connected her with another broker and Shele soon took a job as a sales assistant—her first taste of employment. Shele developed a zest for the glamorous grind of high finance and impressed her bosses with her dedication, instinctive business savvy and ease with numbers. Like her father years earlier, Shele found herself energized by the stock ticker.

Joel watched his daughter's maturation with pride and soon brought her on to his global wealth-management team at Merrill Lynch. Shele was ensconced at the finance giant's flagship location on Fifth Avenue, advising wealthy clients on their investment strategies. Philip joined his father and sister, and they formed a subsidiary under the Merrill umbrella called the Danishefsky Group. The family business filled Joel with joy and a sense of parental accomplishment. Shele soon moved into a one-bedroom apartment her father owned in the Dorchester Towers, while Eve took up residence in an adjoining studio. The two sisters were near-roommates yet again.

Prioritizing matrimony and kids, Shele began to tailor her dating practices accordingly. There were plenty of pursuers and Shele was in a position to be selective. Eve recalled her sister building up cautious hope in one particular relationship with a long-term boyfriend. They appeared to be enamored with each other, often inviting Eve over for group dinners at the Dorchester. But he would eventually come to dislike the demanding churn of New York City and told Shele that he wanted to move back to his native Florida. She held out hope for an invitation to join him—but it never arrived and the relationship disintegrated.

Still pursuing their respective Prince Charmings, the sisters would often attend Jewish singles events in Manhattan. They came to enjoy the religiously rooted but still rambunctious gatherings and would giddily review their prospects at the end of the night. "We had so much fun," Eve recalled wistfully. Much as they had done as doll-clutching children, the sisters would fantasize about their desired partners. Inevitably, they felt certain, these flawless specimens of masculinity would materialize.

Despite her immersion in the indulgent bacchanal of 1980s Wall Street, Shele managed to preserve her core religious beliefs. She would insist on a devout Jewish husband who was flexible enough in his piety to make room for a modern life. She also hoped he would earn enough money that she could stay home to raise their children.

While Shele became increasingly frustrated by a succession of dating disappointments, her little sister's daydreams became a reality. Eve began exulting to friends and family about a man named Marc, a tall financier who was raised in Zimbabwe and educated in South Africa, relocating to New York to work in finance. Eve, then 29, fell for her erudite suitor and the two married and soon had a young son.

Shele was joyous about her sister's marital success, but the union magnified her own solitude. She was 31. A creeping desperation began to infiltrate Shele's decision-making and manifested itself in a string of ill-advised dalliances, Eve recalled. Having loosened her qualifications, Shele was suddenly gravitating toward questionable partners.

"I can say, generally, Shele's choice in men was not good," Marc said of this period. "We went on double dates with some of these people, and some of the things they did were asinine." On one of these regrettable evenings, Marc said, Shele's date unexpectedly eschewed cutlery and consumed an entire plate of pasta by hand. Another abortive boyfriend had a troubling penchant for signaling his enthusiasm for a given topic with a canine bark. Men were flitting in and out of Shele's life to the point that her friends and family struggled to keep track. Despite their often-shaky credentials, Shele would present them to politely cautious friends as potential husbands.

Shele's choice of escort to Eve and Marc's wedding soon burnished himself in family lore for the wrong reasons. All but mute at the otherwise festive occasion, the taciturn mystery man somehow managed to appear in nearly every photo taken that day, staring vacantly at the camera amid the smiling faces. "People would ask who he was," Marc recalled. "Is he a family member? He's in all our wedding shots." The relationship perished a week later.

Painfully alone and advancing deeper into the thicket of her 30s, Shele's biological alarm began to blare. She spent more and more time with Eve and Marc, joining them for movies and dinners. As the years piled up, Eve could sense Shele's despair. Though she was profiting handsomely at work, Shele's romantic impoverishment was taking a toll. As an observant Jew, she was keenly aware of the societal premium placed on marriage and kids and knew that whispers about her single existence trailed her. "She wanted to have a family," Marc said. "There was a lot of self-imposed pressure, and then pressure from the environment, from society."

Two years after Eve married in 1993, both Philip and Fred found wives. Shele was now the only one of the Danishefsky children still single.

"She knew her clock was ticking," Eve recalled. "She knew it."

CHAPTER THREE

Shining Armor

The hallway phone inside Eve's Upper West Side home jangled unexpectedly well after 11 P.M. on February 15, 1998. She and Marc had moved to an apartment in the same neighborhood as Shele, just blocks from the Dorchester. Not wanting to disturb her sleeping husband, Eve gingerly arose from bed, entered the foyer and picked up the receiver. "It's Shele," her sister announced. Late-night calls from her sibling were a rarity and Eve was surprised.

She immediately detected a euphoric abandon in Shele's speech. She giddily announced that she was streaking across Manhattan in a cab with a man she had met earlier that same evening. Still groggy, Eve struggled to comprehend her breathless sister.

"I've met my soulmate," Shele told Eve. "We're on our way to the airport. We're catching a flight to Las Vegas. We're getting married!"

Shele was giggling. "He says he loves me, and he says we're going to have a happy life together," she gushed to her sister.

Shele, then 36, had met Roderick Covlin, 25, just a few hours prior at Le Bar Bat, a now-shuttered restaurant and music venue on West 57th Street near Columbus Circle. They were passing each other on a stairwell at the event when Shele lost her footing and nearly toppled over. Rod caught her before impact, looked up at her from a lower step and asked playfully, "Will you marry me?"

That act of chivalry—seemingly plucked from a trite romantic comedy—commanded Shele's attention. Rod blanketed the swooning older woman with attention and compliments for the remainder of the evening, never letting her veer more than a few feet away. Shele had become increasingly conscious of her advancing years, but Rod, more than a decade her junior, marveled at her glistening emerald eyes and thick natural brunette hair that fell to her shoulders in ringlets. Rod wasted no time in tantalizing Shele with fancies of marriage and a house ringing with the playful shrieks of children. The enraptured couple clambered into a cab together to plan their Vegas nuptials.

Staggered by the lunacy of it all, Eve had initially hoped that Shele was in the midst of some alcohol-induced mania that would soon pass. But as the sisters continued talking, Shele made it clear that she had every intention of formalizing a love that had coalesced in a matter of hours. Eve pleaded with Shele to adopt a more appropriate pace. "Shele, please don't do this, don't do this," she begged.

Eve realized she had to invoke her parents to snap the spell. "It will break Mom and Dad's heart if you do this. Please think of them."

The words instantly neutralized Shele's delirium. "Okay, okay, Eve, I've got to go," Shele said, reassuring her distressed sister that she wouldn't do anything rash.

Troubled by the erratic behavior—and curious about the man who had ignited it—Eve climbed back into bed.

She recounted the conversation to Marc the following morning. While Shele's dating selections were often suspect, the prior night's episode was acutely out of character. They knew that the man with whom Shele had shared a cab had had an immediate and unprecedented impact. "It was just the opposite of everything that she was," Marc recalled. "It was like another person."

Shele soon debriefed Eve about this promising new entrant into her life. She sheepishly relayed that he was 11 years her junior. A martial-arts enthusiast, he boasted a muscular 6-foot-2-inch frame and was blessed with a pair of steely blue eyes. Raised as a traditional Jew, Rod had educational and professional attributes nearly as impressive as his physical allure. He had earned an engineering degree from Columbia University in 2004 after transferring from Rensselaer Polytechnic Institute in Troy, in upstate New York. Rod had presented himself as a budding tech entrepreneur on the cusp of riches and renown. On the night of their meeting at Le Bar Bat, he had listened intently as Shele outlined her own impressive credentials and lucrative career in finance.

Rod's pursuit of Shele only accelerated in the days and weeks after their chance staircase encounter. He lavished her with chocolates, flowers and gifts almost daily, and constantly reiterated his desire for a large family. "Here was this nice-looking younger man giving her all this attention," Eve said of those early days. "It was intoxicating for her."

Although she had attained professional success, Shele was 36, and visions of indefinite isolation were bearing down. But Rod had pierced this gathering darkness like a streak of lightning. Her wants were his wants. Her needs were his needs. Shele had met her white knight. Six weeks later, they were engaged.

Rod grew up in the prim, affluent New York suburb of New Rochelle just 45 minutes north of Manhattan, in a simple two-story home at the end of a manicured cul-de-sac. His father, Dave Covlin, had a dry-cleaning business and later became a middling stockbroker, while his mother, Carol Covlin, worked as a pharmacist. He has only one sibling, an older sister, Aviva.

Carol grew up in New York, the daughter of Joe and Harriet Steinberg. Her mother was a homemaker and her father was also a stockbroker. Dave was born in 1948 in Bismarck, North Dakota, and raised as a Lutheran on a Native American reservation. As a white man, he felt that he had experienced reverse discrimination and, in a rejection of his Christian faith, converted to Orthodox Judaism and then married Carol. The Covlins attended a modern Orthodox synagogue, Young Israel, but Dave soon became offended by a perceived insult and the family began attending Magen David Sephardic Synagogue, for Jews of Middle Eastern descent. "He was always feeling slighted by some community or another," a friend recalled. The Covlins were minimally observant and did not keep kosher or the Sabbath in accordance with Orthodox tradition. But they enjoyed a strong cultural connection to the religion, celebrating holidays and attending synagogue regularly.

Despite these attempts to create spiritual structure for their children, Rod began to exhibit aberrant behavior as a young boy. At just 4 years old, he would catch frogs in the backyard, put firecrackers in their mouths and then gleefully look on as they were blown to pieces. "I knew then that I had a problem," Carol once confided to a friend. Alarmed by these bouts of sadism, Carol had the boy see a psychiatrist.

Although Rod would eventually grow into a hulking man, he was runty as a youth and became a favored target of local bullies. Violence, menace and confrontation soon became routine, and Rod often found himself exchanging punches.

When Carol married Dave, he was struggling to make ends meet with his small dry-cleaning business. In an attempt to help the young family, Carol's father, Joseph, invited Dave to work with him as a broker at Prudential Securities. But their personal relationship eventually soured and the partnership collapsed. Dave brazenly insisted that Joseph relinquish half of the client base he had worked decades to build. Disgusted by the demand, Joseph refused.

Feeling that his father was being mistreated, Rod leveled a shocking defamation in order to force his grandfather's surrender. He falsely accused Joseph of having sexually abused him as a child. The tactic achieved its aim and he relinquished the client list.

Dave moved on to Morgan Stanley after the ugly episode and established a modest investment-advisory business. But Rod's ruthless strategy created a permanent rift in the family, and he would confess to Shele and a later girlfriend that he had fabricated the accusation.

While she was cautiously optimistic about Shele's new love interest, Eve's first encounter with Rod was a peculiar one. The sisters were shopping for a gift for their mother at Fortunoff, a luxury Manhattan jeweler, when Shele excitedly said Rod was coming to pick her up for dinner. For days, Shele had gushed to Eve about Rod's qualifications as a future spouse. He was tall, handsome, attentive, educated and bright. "She was head over heels," Eve said.

But rather than greet the sisters with a beaming smile and open arms after finally arriving at the store, Rod stood expressionlessly near the front door and awaited their approach. "We were having a great time, laughing," Eve said. "It was just odd. Why wouldn't you come over to your girlfriend and your girlfriend's sister that you've never met and say hi? But, no, he waited at the front. He looked like a security guard just standing there."

Rod's cold demeanor was compounded by his odd clothing. "He had this hideous gray sweater. It was this long sweater with a hood," Eve recalled. The garment was especially notable because Shele was a stylish and meticulous dresser. Forced to walk over to Rod, Eve mustered a greeting. "We just said hello and that was pretty much it," she said. "There wasn't a dialogue—no 'Yeah, nice to meet you' or 'I've heard a lot about you.'"

Eve chalked up Rod's aloofness to shyness. She muzzled her concerns over the breakneck pace of the relationship and the age difference, instead focusing on Shele's jubilation. Preoccupied by her young son at the time, Eve didn't meet Rod again until the couple's engagement party. The festivities took place at his parents' New Rochelle home, where he was living at the time. Dave and Carol said years later in a TV interview that Rod was lovestruck with an intensity they had never seen.

The Covlins prepared a spread of food for the small gathering. Dave enthusiastically showed off his collection of Belgian beer bottles that lined the shelves in the living room and kitchen, while the respective clans got to know each other. In the midst of an otherwise subdued event, Rod's suddenly vexed voice carried from the kitchen, where he was chastising his mother. "I just remember he was very angry, and it was over something that wasn't a big deal," Marc said. "It didn't necessitate that reaction."

But Rod often balanced his unusual quirks with a natural charm. He was a smart conversationalist and exuded self-assurance that sometimes veered into arrogance. Joel focused on Rod's impressive credentials and promising career prospects. He was also deeply relieved that Shele was finally able to secure an engagement and hoped that grandchildren would soon follow. Joel enthusiastically offered to pay for their wedding. "We all had high hopes of a wonderful marriage," Marc said. "We thought he was a good guy."

But, as plans for the wedding took shape, tensions between

the Danishefskys and Covlins began to rise. The families had initially agreed that they would split the guest list in half to avoid any imbalances or perceived slights. But the Covlins soon began augmenting their side of the ledger to the point of offense.

"The Covlins would intermittently throw in another few people, so it was becoming much more weighted on the Covlins' side," recalled Marc. For the sake of peace, Joel grudgingly accommodated their additional guests. But relations hit another impasse over the amount and variety of alcohol to be served. Dave insisted on an expansive selection of beers, wine and spirits, while Joel lobbied for a more modest assortment. He was footing the final bill, after all.

Joel again acquiesced to pacify Shele, who was becoming increasingly distressed by the growing rancor. But that detente would also prove short-lived, as the two sides began warring over who would preside over the ceremony. Joel, an ordained and experienced rabbi, offered to perform the service himself. He had been the officiant for his other children and was hoping to do the same for Shele. But the Covlins strenuously objected and instead proposed their rabbi from Westchester.

Willing to placate the Covlins on the guest list and alcohol, Joel was now reaching his limit. He firmly objected to their final demand and the two sides were at loggerheads once again, just weeks before the wedding. Rod was relentless and pressured Shele to intervene. "Could you just accommodate the Covlins so we can have peace?" she pleaded with her father. Joel abandoned this last stand and gave in.

With the contentious negotiations finally settled, Shele was able to focus on selecting a dress. As always, she consulted with Eve. On the night before the wedding, Shele beckoned her sister into a room at their parents' home and unveiled a flowing, diaphanous gown.

"She had a beautiful dress," recalled Eve. The high neckline hit the clavicle and the sleeves extended to an elegant point at the back of each hand. "I hate my gown," Shele suddenly blurted, as Eve, taken aback, tried to reassure her. The younger sister wondered to herself whether the outburst was related to the self-doubt that had plagued her big sister since childhood.

The next day, on September 7, 1998, before 200 guests at the Marriott Hotel in suburban Teaneck, New Jersey, Rod and Shele were bound together by the Covlin family rabbi. Jewish tradition holds that every wedding serves as a reenactment of the marriage between God and the Jewish people that took place on Mount Sinai with the acceptance of the Ten Commandments. Traditionally, the bride and groom abstain from seeing each other before the wedding, some say to heighten anticipation. On the wedding day, both bride and groom are honored at separate receptions in nearby rooms. The bride sits atop a throne-like chair and is feted as a royal, with friends and family extending their good wishes. The groom is treated to boisterous singing by his attendants and Talmud recitations.

Then comes the *badeken,* known as the veiling ceremony, where a singing and dancing procession marches the groom to his awaiting bride. He covers her face with a veil and both sets of parents offer their heartfelt blessings. The groom's entourage then departs.

Flanked by escorts holding candles, the bride and groom then walk to the *chuppa,* a marriage canopy. With her face still shrouded, the bride slowly circles the groom seven times underneath the *chuppa.* Blessings are recited before they both sip from a cup of wine. The groom places the wedding band on the bride's right index finger and then breaks a ceremonial glass with his right foot in remembrance of an ancient Jewish temple that had been destroyed. After another blessing, the ceremony ends with collective shouts of "Mazel tov!"

"She was on cloud nine," Eve said with a smile. "I was so thrilled for her that she found her husband, her Mr. Right. It was Shele's day. It was such an exciting time, and she was so happy."

Beaming in wedding photos, Shele, her curly, shoulder-length brown hair framing her face, was a portrait of elation and hope. She wore a glittering 2.5-carat pear-cut diamond engagement ring, a triple string of pearls around her neck and matching earrings. Her new husband, in a dapper black suit and bow tie, smiled broadly next to his bride.

Rod moved in with Shele at her father's apartment at the Dorchester Towers, and the young couple, brimming with optimism, embarked on their new life together. They soon departed for their honeymoon. But, just five days into the planned vacation, Rod abruptly told Shele that they had to return to New York at once.

"I have to get back for my parents' anniversary," he told his confounded wife, only halfway into their trip. Shele was so deeply mortified by Rod's demand that she didn't reveal it to family members until many years later.

CHAPTER FOUR

Anna and Myles

Upon return from their truncated honeymoon, Shele and Rod settled into her apartment. Joel, who owned the unit along with an adjoining studio, combined the two residences to provide the newlyweds room for a family.

There was conflict almost instantly. As their primary wedding present, Rod's parents gave the new couple an oversized surrealist painting by obscure Polish artist Tomek Setowski titled "Queen of Spades Castle." The bizarre piece features a montage of sinister images, including a grinning man wearing a blindfold and horns, a set of winding steps leading into a distant turret and the disembodied head of a queen attached to a fishtail. While Rod found it exquisite, Shele's assessment was less glowing.

She grimaced each time she was forced to lay eyes on the garish piece and its ornate gold frame. Shele thought it a hideous crime against the arts. But in the spirit of marital compromise, she told Rod that they could perhaps display the work in a less prominent corner of their shared abode.

Shele also gently reminded her spouse that his parents had said they could exchange the expensive gift. "It's really not my style," she said with trepidation. "It's not what I like."

Rod was incensed. Not only would they keep the painting, it would be the centerpiece of their home. He hung it above the living-room sofa, and Shele was forced to lock eyes with the fishtailed queen on a daily basis.

Though a seemingly prosaic domestic skirmish, that early episode was a harbinger of things to come. There would be none of the balances and compromises that normally accompany a functional marriage. But while Rod's regime would be marked by authoritarian control, he could still dazzle Shele with charm and affection.

Shele did not let the painting squabble dampen her zeal for her new life. By all appearances, Rod was still on track to fulfill his destiny as a tech-world titan. With Shele bankrolling his degree, Rod soon earned his MBA from Fordham University's business school.

Already well established professionally, Shele was focused elsewhere. Now 37, the aspiring mother knew that a successful pregnancy was not to be taken for granted and that her reproductive viability was waning. Rod was equally ardent about having children, and they tried to get pregnant naturally for many months. But one pregnancy test after another produced disappointment and fear.

Growing impatient, Shele opted for in vitro fertilization, in which a woman's eggs are fertilized by the male's sperm in a laboratory dish before being transferred to her uterus. It is a time-consuming and costly procedure that dramatically increases the odds of conception. But there were no guarantees. When Shele learned that she was pregnant after just one round, she was jubilant.

For more than a decade, Shele had feared a barren future. Now, in a matter of months, she would be holding her newborn and gifting her father with a granddaughter. On October 12, 2000, the Covlins welcomed little Anna into the world. When the blinking, brown-haired cherub was finally placed

into Shele's weakened arms, she was overcome with gratitude and love.

"She was besotted," Marc said. "Anna was everything that
she wanted. Her joy overshadowed everything."

Like any new mother, Shele doted and cooed and hovered
over the delicate baby after the couple brought her home. Rod
was equally smitten, happily changing diapers, administering feedings and rising in the dead of night to soothe distur-
bances. So it shook Shele when Rod abruptly announced
that he would be leaving the apartment for a few days to play
in a backgammon tournament when Anna was just one month
old.

Shele was well acquainted with Rod's affinity for the
game. While her attention level varied, Rod could rapturously
discuss the game's unmatched appeal for hours. Stripped to
its essence, two opposing players race to maneuver their 15
"checkers" across 24 narrow triangles and off the board
completely. These movements are dictated by dice rolls and
the contestant who manages to guide all of their pieces
"home" first wins. Confident of his unique mastery, Rod even
insinuated that he could profit from playing professionally.

Although backgammon dates back more than 5,000 years,
its contemporary standing stems more from Ian Fleming
than the ancients. During a sudden burst of popularity in
the late 1970s, the glamorous classes were tumbling dice
from Monte Carlo to Manhattan. Wearing a white tuxedo
and black bow tie, Roger Moore plays a high-stakes game
of backgammon against a rakish Afghan prince in the 1983
James Bond film "Octopussy."

But that glitzy appeal would eventually fade like dated
casino carpeting. Though still widely popular across the
globe, backgammon is now viewed as the somewhat inferior
cousin to more cerebral pursuits like chess and poker. As
those games have grown in popularity, backgammon has

contracted to niche status and prize money at major tournaments has slimmed accordingly.

Even the most ardent backgammon booster will allow that much of the game hinges on the random physics of tossed dice. As a result, it's not uncommon for a master to be toppled by a novice. Superior talent is disclosed over the long haul rather than during single matches.

Victory and financial rewards often result from bursts of fortune and friendly dice rather than experience and skill. Backgammon mirrored Rod's own personality in this way, and perhaps explained his appetite for it. For Rod, backgammon glory was always at his fingertips and just out of reach at the same time. It was a seductive tension that would turn an affinity into an obsession. "Games are controlled violence," wrote legendary backgammon player Paul Magriel. "You take out your frustrations and hostilities over a backgammon set."

Shele had dismissed Rod's backgammon aspirations as little more than adolescent residue. She nodded and smiled and encouraged her husband to pursue whatever gave him contentment. Anna, after all, was still her obsession, and a quick weekend away for Rod was not an egregious request.

Eve, however, was dumbfounded by the departure, and seeds of worry about her sister's spouse had sprouted. "Are you kidding me?" she exclaimed when Shele sheepishly told her of his trip. But rather than express rage, Shele simply rolled her eyes and said, "Can you believe it?"

Whatever creeping concerns Shele had during those early months were offset by Rod's attentiveness to Anna. She looked on with deep satisfaction—and a measure of relief—whenever Rod held his bundled daughter close and peered into her eyes. Their tightening bond, she reasoned, would only strengthen her own relationship with him.

Shele soon returned to work at Merrill alongside her

father and brother. While Shele and Rod were financially comfortable, thanks to her earnings, he had yet to secure a permanent position after business school.

Shele hurried out the door each morning, and Rose, the family's trusted nanny, took Anna while Rod remained asleep in their bedroom. With each passing month, Shele began to question his commitment to gainful employment. Whenever she would gently question him as to his prospects, Rod would reassure her that the perfect opportunity was always imminent and that he would soon begin producing paychecks.

Lured by the tech boom taking place at the time, most of Rod's business plans revolved around the internet. One day he was buying up domain names, convinced that they would eventually soar in value and provide a life-altering windfall. On another, he was conjuring up a new online platform for stock trading. But while the plans sounded promising in the abstract, Shele—and her family—began to question Rod's ability to make them materialize.

They could no longer ignore the schism between his grand plans and their execution. The proportion of labor to languor began to warp in the wrong direction, with Rod spending an increasing portion of his waking hours locked in silent combat with an online backgammon opponent. He would also dedicate sizable portions of his day to the gym.

Shele had known she would be the sole breadwinner in the early stages of their marriage, but she had been confident that Rod, given his intellect, education and bombast, would eventually make it big. She would be able to become a homemaker. Shele even once dumped a sizable sum of cash into one of his projects. When that scheme withered, Shele's fears intensified. As time passed, the Danishefskys began to suspect that Rod was more parasite than partner. As their marriage progressed, there was a noticeable ebb in the chivalrous doting Shele had once found so irresistible. The flow of thoughtful gifts ceased.

Rod became stingy with his compliments and grew more critical. He began to regularly—and cruelly—denigrate Shele's appearance, even in public and around friends and family. There were cutting jibes about her advancing age. Rod, who had once meticulously rehabilitated Shele's damaged self-esteem, now seemed bent on dismantling it.

Resigned to her role as the home's only reliably employed adult, Shele was forced to keep long hours at her office, away from Anna. With a harried work week followed by the Sabbath, Sunday was Shele's only free day.

But that would soon change as Dave and Carol began arriving nearly every Sunday morning—always with gifts for Anna. They adored their new granddaughter and deluged her with toys and trinkets. The frequent and often-unannounced visits from Rod's parents did little to improve the tense climate inside the apartment. Shele gritted her teeth and invited her in-laws inside. But she could no longer hide her displeasure when Carol and Dave expanded their unsolicited visits to the work week.

Exacerbating matters, the Covlins began to disparage Shele's parents during these stays as Shele would silently fume. While the senior Covlins' grievances were varied, they always took exception when they weren't invited to a Danishefsky event—no matter how marginal.

Ever since shedding her excess weight in college, Shele had made exercise an integral part of her routine. In addition to gym sessions, she began running the New York City Marathon each year. To support her, the Danishefskys would often convene for a modest pasta meal on the eve of the race. It would eventually become a family ritual, with Shele's siblings and parents in attendance.

When the Covlins found out that the event took place

without them, they were infuriated. They expressed their outrage to Rod, who relayed this displeasure to Shele. The Danishefskys were mystified by the umbrage, reasoning that they were, on occasion, entitled to gather without them.

With friction mounting, familial rifts deepened.

Eve and Marc omitted the Covlins from a Thanksgiving at their apartment one year, while Philip and his wife, Peggy, failed to invite them to a Hanukkah party. The senior Covlins seemed to nurture these slights, bringing them up at every opportunity. Rod often chastised Shele for her relatives' behavior toward his parents, putting her in the crosshairs of the family feud.

Despite these collisions, Rod and Shele soldiered on. In 2004, four years after Anna's birth, Shele was eager for a second child. She began another round of IVF, but she was 42 and the odds of a successful second pregnancy were low.

Her whispered entreaties to God at synagogue ultimately paid off. Not only did she conceive, but this time she was bearing twins. Anna would have the siblings she begged for, and the Covlin clan would soon expand to five.

Doctors warned Shele that the pregnancy would be a difficult one, but she promised her two unborn children that she would do everything in her power to bring them safely into the world. The pregnancy was taxing, and she struggled with unexplained bouts of bleeding and intense pain during her first two trimesters. Her doctors ordered her on bed rest shortly before her final trimester, but her condition continued to worsen.

The lower portion of her uterus, the cervix, had begun to shorten and open dangerously early—putting her at risk of preterm labor. Doctors at Columbia Presbyterian/Weill Cornell Medical Center in Manhattan, considered one of the top facilities in the country, scheduled a simple procedure known as a cervical cerclage to sew her cervix closed and prevent their premature birth.

As the ob-gyn stitched her up, Shele began to hemorrhage and her blood pressure plummeted. Doctors scrambled to stabilize her vital signs, as the hearts of the two frail lives inside her pulsed weakly. The situation quickly grew dire. She suffered a placental abruption, in which the placenta detaches from the uterus, depriving the fetus of oxygen and nutrients. Shele suddenly went into labor, and now not only were her twins' lives in peril, but so was her own. Shele had to give birth knowing that at only six months, the twins may not survive.

One infant died 15 hours after emerging into the glare of hospital lights. Her sister persevered for a day and half before her heart went silent.

Shele was broken both physically and emotionally. Her family surrounded her bedside in stunned silence.

"She was devastated. Just devastated," Eve said. "And we almost lost her."

Doctors later concluded that Shele had suffered from a rare blood-clotting condition that caused the hemorrhaging and the placental abruption, setting off early labor.

Plunged into a paralytic sorrow, Shele could barely speak in the days after the deaths of her beloved twins. While Eve and other relatives sought to comfort her, Rod became consumed with the legal implications of what had taken place. With Shele still bedridden and deeply despondent, Rod wanted to file an immediate lawsuit against the hospital and badgered Shele to initiate it.

"She was very sick and trying to digest the fact that she lost the twins," Marc said. But after her discharge from the hospital, Rod dragged Shele to meetings with personal-injury lawyers. Bringing a potentially lucrative case against the famed medical facility became his new get-rich scheme.

"It was just weird," Marc said of Rod's preoccupation with legal action. Unable to muster even the slightest appetite for a litigious slog in the midst of her grief, Shele refused to participate.

As she recuperated, Rod grew frustrated that she had not shed the baby weight from the twins and often remarked on the perceived failure. She ignored the taunts and instead trained her focus on another pregnancy.

Less than a year after the devastating loss, Shele began another round of IVF treatments. It soon became apparent that Shele's eggs were no longer viable, and the couple opted to use a donor egg from a fertility clinic. It was fertilized with Rod's sperm and implanted in Shele's uterus. Seven months after burying her beloved twins, Shele's belly began to swell with new life. On September 26, 2006, she gave birth to a boy, Myles, without incident.

Euphoric over the new addition to the family, Shele failed to notice that Rod's darker impulses were bubbling to the surface.

CHAPTER FIVE

Sheep's Clothing

While Shele financed the family, Rod's enthusiasm for work continued to dissipate. Rose assumed most of the child-rearing duties for Anna and Myles while Shele kept long hours at the office. Liberated from both fatherly and professional obligations, Rod found himself with a surfeit of idle time.

Instead of blanketing the internet with his résumé, Rod was plastering his romantic qualifications across dating websites and other portals of infidelity. He set up new email accounts in order to correspond with women—including prostitutes.

Rod's intensifying zest for novel sexual encounters was rivaled only by his deepening obsession with backgammon. With no other demands on his time, he was constantly traveling to national tournaments, defending them to Shele as essential to his dream of board-game stardom.

He would often intermingle these twin lusts, setting up trysts with women at tournament locations. One week after establishing an email account under the handle 9grainsofsand, Rod feverishly searched for potential partners in Pittsburgh, Charlotte and Toledo, where his upcoming tournaments were located. In front of the blue-tinged glow of his computer, he searched for Brazilian and Polish escorts. But Rod's sprawling sexual appetite was also satisfied closer to home. He opened an account on Jdate, a popular dating site catering to Jewish singles. Rod used the alias James Early, in a likely nod to the American engineer who was considered a pioneer in the field of transistors.

Increasingly addicted to online prowls, Rod enhanced his adventures with marijuana and amphetamines. The latter would allow him to engage in marathon computer sessions while Shele and his two children slumbered nearby. On a typical night, Rod would engage in backgammon and cyber flirting from 10 P.M. until 5 A.M. He often clambered into bed just as Shele was rising to get the kids ready for school and prepare for work.

When she challenged his nighttime habits, Rod argued that backgammon wasn't just a casual hobby and that he would soon make a career of it. Although Shele disapproved, she generally swallowed her misgivings for the sake of domestic calm. She still loved Rod and made every effort to keep him content. Her raw physical attraction to him remained intact, and his biting wit kept her engaged. But Rod's behavior was now alarming her relatives. He was often dour and caustic at family functions, but he had graduated to open disrespect of Shele in front of her parents and siblings.

On one Jewish holiday, Rod and Shele joined Eve and Marc for a dinner at their synagogue along with other members of the congregation. Marc recalled Rod gratuitously demeaning Shele in front of horrified guests. "He was insulting her and thought it was funny," Marc said. "He was calling her ugly, fat, dirty, in front of us and other people." Rod worsened the spectacle by pouring salt and pepper into a water glass like a toddler. "There were strangers from the synagogue that we didn't even know and acquaintances that happened to be placed at our table, and he's behaving like this," Eve said.

Shele was becoming inured to the verbal abuse. While inwardly mortified, she once again brushed off Rod's adolescent and embarrassing behavior at the gathering. "She tried to make a joke of it," Eve recalled. "She said something like, 'Oh, there goes Rod again.'"

But her rationalizations would finally collapse one afternoon in 2008, as the couple approached their 10-year wedding anniversary. Rod was normally careful to shield his online activities, logging out of his accounts and maintaining rotating passwords. On this occasion, however, Shele noticed that his email account was fully exposed on his computer. She saw an opened correspondence: a sexually suggestive exchange with one of Rod's backgammon belles. Shele ingested the horror line by line, struggling to fully absorb the reality of Rod's betrayal. But her priority was to maintain their marital mirage for the sake of Anna and Myles, both of whom were still young and vulnerable. As a deeply religious woman, she viewed divorce as near taboo.

But the revelation began to burrow through Shele's brain like a virus, and, despite wanting to keep up appearances, she revealed the wretched truth to Eve.

The sisters were accompanying their mother to a doctor's appointment in Manhattan. While Jaelene was being X-rayed in another room, Shele relayed what had happened, her voice coated in bitterness. "What in the world do I get him for a 10-year anniversary gift knowing that he's cheating on me?" she asked. Eve was shocked.

But Shele decided not to immediately confront her husband, and Rod took her out for an anniversary dinner in September 2008. Rather than perpetuate the ruse of faithfulness or present his wife with a gift, Rod instead proposed an open marriage. He calmly discussed the plan as if proposing a kitchen renovation. "You could be with other people," he suggested. "I would no longer have to hide."

Shele had endured many indignities during their decade together, but Rod had outdone himself this time. "I can't believe you'd consider this," she said. The proposal left her reeling for days—and she would later realize that Rod had likely intended for her to discover his offending email to prepare her for the blow.

Still prioritizing the children, she insisted on trying to rescue the capsizing marriage. A few months after their anniversary, on New Year's Day, 2009, Rod arrived home after 6 A.M., reeking of an unfamiliar perfume. Rod, who had been hired at a financial-analysis firm in May 2008, claimed to have been at work all night and into the morning hours. Unwilling to dignify the charade, Shele scoffed. "Do you think I'm a fool?" she asked. She finally told Rod that she had seen his emails. In a sad formality, he confirmed the obvious, admitting to a series of lurid, fleeting affairs—but insisted that he still loved her.

They began to discuss divorce on a regular basis. Rod resented her refusal to let him pursue other sexual partners and she became a constant target of his spiraling furies. The mildest transgression would set Rod off. On a visit to a casual falafel restaurant, she accidentally poured tahini on her dish instead of yogurt sauce. She apologized to an employee and asked if she could replace the entree.

The condiment crime infuriated Rod. "What's the problem!" he barked in front of other patrons.

"He confronted me and said he was embarrassed and to explain right then and there why it was wrong," Shele later told her sister. "I didn't answer because we were in public. At the end of the day, I just anger and irritate him more than I'm able to make him happy."

Having abandoned any pretense of a healthy relationship with Rod, Shele now openly discussed her troubles with Eve. "He constantly picks fights and flies off the handle very easily, and when he does, his anger is out of control," she told her sister. "He is a highly critical and overanalytical person. That's just who he is. Frankly, I doubt he is capable of having a long-term relationship with anyone, because he finds fault with anyone who he's with."

Despite her misery, Shele continued to resist divorce. A separation could result in shared custody and less time with the children. "I haven't spent one night away from Myles since he was born," she told Eve. Anna, old enough to sense the acrimony between her parents, voiced her opposition to a split. "Anna said a week ago she doesn't want to be the daughter of divorced parents. I'm completely stuck and have no idea how to handle this," Shele said.

She was becoming hopeless. No matter what she did to sate Rod's needs or soothe his moods, his hatred of her was intensifying. "I feel like I am at my wits' end," she texted a friend a few days after Rod's admissions of cheating. "Scared if I stay with a person with this kind of temper then something very bad cud happen in the future 2 my kids or me."

Shele's texts and emails to friends revealed how quickly her marital goals shifted from satisfaction to survival. "I am concerned and very scared that at some point in the future all his anger and rage may result in something bad happening," she texted Eve. "Also with Rod's temper I am uneasy about leaving him with the kids . . . at least now when he goes crazy with anger I'm there for them and i comfort them or i'll tell anna that she really didn't do anything wrong (if that's the case) when he scolds her for stupidity. If we're not together and he blows up there will be no one there to protect them."

Though her home life was disintegrating, Shele still managed to shine professionally. Perhaps sensing that a split with Rod or some other calamity would drain her resources, she stiffened her resolve at the office and kept the revenue rushing. The partnership with her father and brother at Merrill had proven lucrative. Attracted by their consistent profitability and impeccable reputation, banking giant UBS coaxed the Danishefskys away from Merrill Lynch in early 2009, where they had managed nearly $600 million in client funds.

Rod, meanwhile, was barely clinging to his $93,000-a-year position with a Manhattan company called Pragma Securities as its vice president of operations. He would frequently vanish from the office for hours at a time, and, when he was present, supervisors would often notice him toggling between his official tasks and another online backgammon game.

Despite being married, Rod openly boasted about his extramarital conquests to friend and colleague Marshall Baron. They had met in 1999 while working at a financial-services company and would meet up with other staffers for drinks from time to time. When Baron had been looking for work, Rod helped him land a position at Pragma. He had met Shele more than a dozen times and had been in their home for social occasions.

Baron was fond of Rod's wife and found his infidelity distasteful. "There were times when we were discussing going out and he had explained that he was seeing other people," Baron recalled. "We were supposed to go to Atlantic City with a group of people we worked with, and he was talking about meeting women on a dating page, Backpage or something." The site was the largest online prostitution marketplace until federal authorities shut it down in 2018. "It's one of the points I have very little tolerance for, so I really didn't get into conversations," he said. The disclosures gave him pause. "If your wife and family can't trust you, why should I?" he would wonder.

One of Rod's preferred rendezvous spots was Lure Fishbar in Manhattan's fashionable SoHo district. The venue's interior is designed to resemble the inside of a luxury yacht, complete with porthole windows and gray leather booths.

Between 2008 and 2009, Rod met at least 14 different women at Lure, assuring several of them that the restaurant served "yummy" drinks to secure dates. Spending with abandon, Rod lavished them with neon cocktails until the wee hours, dropping $16 apiece on concoctions with campy names like Life Boat and Aperitif for Destruction. Thanks to Shele's income, the arrival of the bill was of little consequence.

Rather than hinder his conquests, Rod's marital strife only drove him out of the home and onto a barstool with increasing frequency. He coupled these local jaunts with backgammon tournaments across the map. During a three-month stretch beginning in March 2009, his itinerary included Chicago, Cleveland, Las Vegas, Atlanta and Washington, D.C. In an email message to himself, Rod enumerated the various women he would meet at each stop. Elly was booked for Chicago, Sari for Las Vegas, Kim in Atlanta. The note included a reminder that he still had to fill empty dating slots in Cleveland and D.C.

At a subsequent tournament in Los Angeles, Rod's black book referenced meetings with Maha and Christina. A later Maryland event slotted "Alycia for Wednesday, Stacee for Thursday, Beth for Friday, Kim for Saturday." In an April 26 entry, Rod listed an additional 13 women he planned to meet.

Rather than bristle at Rod's weekend trips, Shele now looked forward to them. The respites from his oppressive presence allowed Shele and the kids to sample normalcy for a few days. Once an unthinkable scenario, Shele began warming to the idea of a trial separation. She treasured these furloughs, even taking the time to note her happiness in a day planner, which she used as a diary.

"Been great without him—kids very happy!" she wrote during one of his trips.

The more forbidden fruit Rod gorged on, the less tolerance he had for the blander flavors of domestic life. When Rod returned to the apartment from his latest jaunt, he erupted at the dinner table. Enraged over some minor offense, he began screaming with the children looking on. "I'm so angry I have to put down my fork, because I feel like jamming it down your throat!" he ranted at Shele.

While her husband had always been prone to tantrums, Shele felt that his outbursts were becoming unhinged. She had long served as his primary target, but now many of Rod's rages were being directed at the children, and he would berate Anna for the slightest misdeed. One night in March, Shele returned home to find her daughter, then 8, visibly distraught. Normally hesitant to disparage her father, Anna confided that he had been on a shouting binge prior to her arrival. "She said Rod had been yelling at her & Myles," Shele wrote in her day planner. "I feel like I can't leave my children with their father b/c of his violent temper."

A few days later, Rod boiled over again while waiting for Anna to finish using the bathroom. "Anna taking too long in bathroom—Rod opened door grabbed her arm pulled her out of shower yelling at her," Shele wrote. "I came home later that night & she told me he yelled at her and slapped her shoulder."

The situation had become unbearable. Other than their cohabitation, Rod and Shele's union bore little resemblance to a marriage. His philandering and absences had become the norm—and Shele's capacity to care had been all but extinguished. While a public admission of marital defeat would be difficult, staying tethered to Rod seemed untenable.

Rod and Shele finally agreed that he would move out of the apartment and into a studio directly across the hall. The arrangement would perhaps minimize the disruption and trauma to the kids. He could come and go at his leisure, while Shele would no longer be captive to his abuse. Despite his flaws, Rod was often a doting father and always made time to help Anna with her homework or class projects. With Shele often stuck at work late, Rod could assist with the kids at a moment's notice. It was an imperfect stopgap.

But, as with any pursuit that required money, Rod needed Shele's assistance, and she cosigned the lease for apartment no. 510 at $2,200 a month. "She said it was for the benefit of the children," Eve recounted.

A few days after Rod's relocation, Shele decided to permanently split from Rod and met with divorce lawyer Lance Meyer inside the Ritz-Carlton on Central Park South.

"We sat down for an hour or two," Meyer recalled. "She was sure she wanted to do it, but she just wasn't sure how." He said that Shele struck him as a late bloomer whose beauty and confidence didn't develop fully until her 40s. Considering her assets and earning power, Shele knew that she needed pugnacious counsel to combat Rod in divorce court. Shele had served as his de facto ATM for years, funding everything from his Manhattan apartment to his extramarital dates. Rod knew that being financially cleaved from Shele would endanger his life of indolent decadence. "She wanted to move forward but was concerned about how Rod would react," Meyer said. "She was hesitant and scared."

After the meeting, Shele did not immediately follow up with Meyer and tried to maintain a veneer of family unity to ease the transition for Myles and Anna. That April she scheduled a Passover vacation with Rod and the kids to Princeton, New Jersey. They stayed in the same hotel but slept in separate rooms. "Two rooms at some Passover program at some hotel," he groused to a girlfriend at the time.

After a few excruciating days of family captivity, Rod had had enough and hopped on a flight to Las Vegas with a mistress to attend a backgammon tournament. When he returned to New York, Rod entered Shele's apartment as though it were still his own. He saw that Shele had not unpacked his suitcase or done his laundry after the Passover debacle. Seething, he grabbed Shele by her arms and threw her to the floor as Anna and Myles cowered tearfully nearby.

The episode erupted just as Rose was walking in at about 8 A.M. to begin her nannying shift. She saw Shele on the floor of the living room, distraught. "What happened?" she asked worriedly. Rod emerged from another room and demanded that Shele talk to him privately—out of Rose's earshot.

Shele resisted the order. "Rod, if you have something to say to me, you can say it in front of Rose," she hissed. Not wanting to become entangled in their dispute, Rose excused herself and went down to the building's laundry room. She told Shele to call her once she and Rod were done talking.

Roughly 15 minutes later, Shele summoned Rose back up to the apartment. When she entered, Rod immediately excoriated her for supposedly breaking a vase he had bought for Shele's birthday. The nanny denied the accusation and Rod left. Shele told Rose how sorry she was for his behavior.

"Stop apologizing for him. He's a grown man!" the nanny exclaimed.

Shele tried to stifle her emotions in front of Rose but finally surrendered, emitting loud, heaving sobs as tears streamed down her face. She remained crumpled on the floor, making no effort to rise. She told her that Rod had thrown her to the ground minutes before her arrival.

Engulfed in despair, Shele wrote an email to Rod pleading with him to control his temper—especially in front of the kids. "You came over after having left us during our family holiday vacation," she wrote. "You were full of anger. You crossed boundaries by grabbing and pushing me to the floor. It was not okay for our kids to witness that kind of behavior. Roderick, they see your behavior and they think it's okay to treat people like that or that it's ok to BE treated that way. They must not think that physical abuse is an option for handling anger! How would you feel if Anna was with a man who was physically abusive to her???"

But Rod was unmoved. Days later, he stopped by the apartment. Shele told him that she had put his remaining belongings in a plastic bag. Rod was irate, yelling and cursing at her while the kids quivered. He marched into her room and ransacked it like a home invader, ripping her clothes from hangers and throwing them to the ground. He then targeted her shoes, gathering them in armfuls from a closet and flinging them angrily to the floor. He repeated the destruction in the kitchen and the bathroom.

Later, Rod would deny ever physically abusing his wife. "I mean there was, you know, the two times that I put holes in the door, there was the time that, you know, Shele and I got into a heated argument/fight and she grabbed me and like bloodied my arm by grabbing it, but I mean I never—I never struck Shele, okay, I never—I mean, you know, one time we got into a tussle right before the divorce and you know, wound up on the floor," he said. "But I never beat Shele."

CHAPTER SIX

Battle Lines

Shele vacillated when it came to pressing for a divorce. The escalating physical and verbal abuse would often convince her that she had no alternative. But then there would be a lull in Rod's rage, when he would suddenly activate the charm and warmth that had initially drawn her to him. Anna and Myles still loved their father dearly, and his parenting, while inconsistent, was often tender and attentive. If Shele could somehow convince him to appreciate the gifts that God had bestowed upon him—children, a faithful wife, a comfortable home—perhaps he would abandon his self-destructive vices.

In what would be her final attempt to sew their tattered relationship back together, Shele organized two separate Mother's Day outings on May 10, 2009—one for the Danishefskys and another for the Covlins. The first leg consisted of a visit to the New York Botanical Garden with Rod, the kids and his parents. That evening, they would join Joel and Jaelene for dinner in Manhattan.

But the garden's tranquil scenery couldn't suppress another ugly public confrontation. Not long after their arrival, Rod angrily accused her of disrespecting his mother in some way. It was at this moment that Shele fully realized that reconciliation was impossible. Surrounded by Rod's parents, her two children and a sea of exotic plants and flowers, Shele finally unsheathed her dagger.

"Let's get a divorce," she blurted out. While Rod had often threatened the action as a means of control, it was the first time Shele made the demand.

The nearby crowds of parents, children and park staffers did nothing to curtail Rod's eruption. He shrieked at Shele at earsplitting volume. "You bitch!" he sneered. "You cunt!" Shele simply walked away, her Mother's Day in ruins.

Rod was apoplectic. "Your mother is divorcing me!" he told Anna, telling the terrified girl that Shele would try to separate them.

He soon bombarded Shele with bizarre texts, sending a single letter of the alphabet one after the other. He then moved on to digits, one number in each text. There was no coherent message—the meaningless onslaught was intended to terrorize her, to let her know she couldn't get rid of him so easily.

"Ur point???" she finally replied. There was no response.

Later that morning, Rod angrily called Jaelene, complaining that Shele had robbed his mother of a pleasant Mother's Day and vowing to demolish hers. Rod's texts to his wife took on a more menacing tone, and he threatened to move back into her apartment. Panicked, Shele called Meyer, her divorce lawyer, for advice. When he didn't answer her call, Shele frantically texted him.

"It's hitting the fan," she wrote. "Said he's going to move back into my apartment and kick me out. Am at botanical gardens. Ready to proceed." A half-hour passed with no response. Shele's alarm and confusion swelled. "What should I do??? He's moving his stuff back—he's moving his stuff back—he's irate."

She then sought counsel from Eve. "I may have to call the police," she wrote. "I may need you to help with my kids if ur around—it may be an emergency."

Shele told her sister over the phone that evening that she now feared for her life.

"I've got to get out," she said.

To Shele's horror, Rod followed through on his threat. He entered that same night and began moving his possessions back in, crossing back and forth across the hall as she and the children looked on helplessly. "I have to protect my interests," Rod told her with cold formality. Shele meekly tried to halt the invasion, telling him that he was not welcome. But Rod ignored her and again called her a "bitch" and a "cunt." Anna, at one point, quizzically looked up at her mother. "What does 'cunt' mean?" the little girl inquired. "Why does Daddy have to move back in?"

After transferring most of his belongings, Rod returned to the privacy of his now half-empty studio and settled in for an online chat with a member of his cyber harem. Threatened with divorce, Rod presented himself as the persecuted party. "Shele just feels that nothing she ever did or could do would be bad enough to warrant my sleeping with anyone else," he said to an online girlfriend. "She doesn't understand that all of the things she has done are the things that grate on someone and little by little chip away at the fabric of a marriage . . . drip, drip, drip . . . like Chinese water torture."

Desperate for support, Shele met Eve at Lord & Taylor in Manhattan the next day. The siblings found a quiet corner of the shoe department to talk when Shele broke down weeping. As the tears dripped, she rifled through her purse and pulled out a letter she'd written to her husband demanding a divorce. "In this letter she was telling Rod that it's time for them to end their marriage," Eve recalled. "It's no good for anybody. She said she was terrified to send it and she was terrified not to send it."

Galvanized by Eve's support, Shele resolved to wrench free of Rod's grip. On the advice of her attorney, she signed affidavits seeking temporary custody of the children, exclusive rights to the apartment and, perhaps most importantly, an order of protection against Rod. "My situation is urgent and desperate," she wrote in the document. "Without the intervention of this court, the defendant intends to continue his abusive ways that place both myself and our children in harm's way. This situation is unnecessary and has come about solely because I have decided to stand up for myself and put an end to the defendant's dominating ways."

Shele enumerated Rod's offenses, telling the court of his request for an open marriage and his erratic and violent behavior. The decision to place him across the hall, she said, had been a grave error. "While I felt it would be beneficial for the children to have their father close by, the defendant is now entertaining his girlfriends at this apartment, which is only steps from the apartment I am living in with our children," she wrote. "This situation is clearly not in the best interest of our children."

"The defendant has made numerous threats of the harm that would come to me if I ever filed for divorce from him and sought custody of the children," she added.

A few days later, on May 12, 2009, Shele opened up to Rose about the severity of her predicament. She told the nanny that Rod had threatened to kill her if she ever sought custody of Anna and Myles. While Rose was intimately familiar with the rancor that marked their relationship, Shele's account disturbed her deeply.

Shele went on to describe the bleak panorama of her despair. Rod had become frighteningly unpredictable. Once able to contain his behavior in front of the kids, he was now discussing his new girlfriends with them, Shele told Rose. She complained that Rod routinely smoked marijuana and abused Adderall and Vicodin—and made no effort to hide it. Rose could do little but offer a sympathetic ear. But she knew better than to dismiss Rod's threats as mere bluster and jotted down a note memorializing her conversation with Shele that same day. "May-12-09," the nanny scribbled. "Came to work, Shele told me what he said, that if she try to get custody of the children he will get rid of her permanently."

Three days later, on May 15, 2009, Shele appeared in front of Judge Deborah Kaplan to plead for protection against Rod. Without her husband being notified or present, Shele summarized her mounting terror in detail. Eve and her father, Joel, accompanied her to the courthouse but could not enter the courtroom.

The judge granted Shele temporary custody of the children, exclusive occupancy of the apartment and an order of protection. While pleased with the outcome, Shele knew that Rod would react with immense rage once he learned of her secret courtroom coup. Winning sole occupancy of the apartment was a crucial legal victory because it allowed Shele to change her locks. Doing so would provide some measure of safety should Rod once again seek to enter the residence. That same day, with Joel and Eve along for support, Shele called a locksmith to complete the job.

Knowing that Rod would likely try to cajole building staffers to give him access to the apartment, the Danishefskys directed the doormen to refuse him. Meyer told Shele to keep a copy of the order of protection on her at all times, which she did. "She was methodical about getting all her ducks in a row as much as possible before she actually made the move," Meyer recalled.

With those preemptive measures now in place, Shele was

prepared to finally serve Rod with the trio of documents that would launch him into a frenzy.

While enraged by Shele's divorce threat, Rod never believed she would have the courage to carry it out. But those assumptions imploded as he sat in a routine meeting at the Herald Square offices of Pragma Securities. An office assistant interrupted the group and said that there was someone at the front desk asking to see him. Puzzled, Rod got up and approached the visitor. Meyer silently thrust legal papers into Rod's hand and departed.

Rod glanced down at the packet and blanched. The stack included divorce papers and the order of protection. Rattled, he returned to the meeting with a ghostly pallor. "I was just served with divorce papers," he announced before slumping into an office chair. Jodi Johnston, a marketing manager at Pragma, did her best to reassure Rod as their colleagues looked on awkwardly.

"He was very upset," she recalled. "This just seemed like a devastating blow to him." With Rod's mood blackening, Johnston suggested that they grab dinner and drinks. Rod confided his fears during the meal and was especially concerned about restricted access to Anna and Myles. The alcohol loosened his emotions and he began to weep, Johnston recalled.

"He was crying. He was saying he didn't see this coming," she said. Rod ruefully mentioned that Shele had once had breast implants during their relationship but later had them removed. Now, with the prospect of a severance from Rod quickly approaching, she had had them put back in, he said. His wife was moving on.

Meanwhile, he began to fully absorb the financial decimation he would suffer in a divorce. The decadence that had come to define his existence would no longer be subsidized.

The entrees, the cocktails, the backgammon junkets—they were suddenly imperiled.

"Shele bought me most of my clothing," he emailed a friend shortly after taking inventory of his finances. "[She] has paid for all major trips and vacations." In another message, he calculated that he earned only one-sixth of the income Shele was making at the time.

At Pragma, where his job was teetering, Rod made $93,000 in 2008 working just two-thirds of the year and an additional $125,000 in the first seven months of 2009. Shele, meanwhile, earned a far more robust $419,000 plus bonuses during her final year at Merrill Lynch.

But it didn't take long for Rod to steady his mind and marshal for war. On May 18, he fired his first salvo. In an affidavit, Rod demonized Shele, calling her pursuit of a divorce "scurrilous" and contending that he was "shocked and appalled by the horrific lies riddling Shele's motion papers."

In breathless language, Rod presented himself as the true victim and sought to convince the court that it was being duped by a domineering and deceitful shrew. "It seems that my wife—a calculating and controlling woman—has manipulated this court to believe that she is a victim, when the facts reveal that it is I who is the victim of Shele's domination, manipulation and belittling of me because I earned less money during our marriage and couldn't keep up with her financial demands."

Rod depicted Shele as a profligate spender who detested her husband's financial impotence and longed for luxuries he couldn't provide. As proof of these lavish tastes, Rod noted that she purchased a pair of $6,500 earrings to celebrate their 10th wedding anniversary.

He argued that the court system had snatched away his children with little redress. In a further humiliation, Rod complained that he was unable to retrieve any of his belongings from the apartment he once lived in without an NYPD chaperone. "Shele has deceitfully turned the system on its ear and is now using our children as pawns to continue what appears to be her calculated strategy to break me," he said.

Rod systematically denied each of Shele's assertions in her divorce papers. Aware that the charge would cripple him in court, Rod forcefully denied ever having physically abused Shele, calling those claims "pure fiction" and underlining the phrase for emphasis. "I never struck Shele in my life," he reiterated.

Rod fought to discredit Shele's claims that she feared for her safety in his presence. A day after the Mother's Day fiasco, on May 11, Rod said, Shele had texted him and asked that he go to their apartment and watch the kids while she conducted a client meeting. He agreed.

Far from being a rampaging menace, Rod said he read to both of his children before giving Myles, then 2, a bottle, and later playing a few rounds of backgammon with Anna, then 8.

"My wife returned home at 9 P.M. and we slept together in the same bed," Rod wrote. "A woman living in fear of her husband for what he may do to him or the children would not 'text message' him to care for the children and relieve their nanny."

Rod said he watched the kids again the following night until Shele returned home and that they slept together again the following night. Those instances, he argued, contradicted Shele's dire portrayals. He called her allegations "the product of what I now finally see is an incredibly dishonest and manipulative, mean-spirited person, who is resentful that I admittedly had an extramarital affair."

Hoping to rebrand his fling, Rod claimed that he had nobly told Shele about his affair to help repair their flagging relationship. He turned Shele's claims that he had sunk into addiction against her, telling the court that he engaged in only an occasional puff of marijuana while she struggled with a serious pill problem. He admitted taking Vicodin and Adderall, but said he took the former for a legitimate back condition and the latter for clinically diagnosed ADHD.

Shele, he charged, gobbled down prescription drugs recreationally, both to suppress her appetite and to enjoy their narcotic effects.

"The fact that she is insisting on drug testing, when I know she failed two tests from her new employer, UBS, is astounding," he wrote. "In fact, I am concerned that my wife overmedicates with legal prescriptions, procures illicit drugs and has an eating disorder."

In the midst of this evisceration, Rod noted that he had been trying to reconcile with Shele in the weeks leading up to her divorce filing. Referencing their abortive Passover trip, Rod claimed Shele came to his room and that they were intimate. Rather than shrink in fear from Rod, Shele still gravitated to him, the filing asserted.

Wanting to establish a clean slate before a renewed push to save the marriage, Rod said he even got tested for sexually transmitted diseases and attached his results.

Rod asked the judge to revoke the order of protection against him and to restore his visitation rights to the kids.

Whatever faint trace of civility that remained after a decade of marriage was now completely effaced.

CHAPTER SEVEN

Warfare

With their competing narratives submitted to the court, Rod and Shele scheduled a joint appearance in front of Judge Ellen Gesmer on the morning of Wednesday, May 20, in Manhattan. Girding for what promised to be a tense confrontation, Rod arrived to the courthouse flanked by his parents, while Joel and Jaelene accompanied Shele.

The parties idled in a hallway while waiting for the case to be called. Rod found a quiet corner and pulled out his cell phone. He dialed UBS Financial Services, Shele's employer, and asked for the human resources department.

Once connected, he told a staffer that Shele was a drug addict who had systematically raided their joint bank accounts. He listed her alleged vices in minute detail, warning UBS that it was employing a dangerous and dissolute woman.

The message transmitted, Rod calmly turned his attention back to the day's court appearance. The order of protection was set to expire on May 20, and it was up to Gesmer whether to extend it. In the courtroom, Rod repeated the arguments he made in his affidavit. In an effort to placate him, Shele, in consultation with her lawyer, offered to remove the kids from the order of protection.

Gesmer agreed to that arrangement and sternly warned

Rod to keep his distance from both Shele and the apartment.

She also mandated that Rod provide a separate document to Shele that would formalize their divorce under Jewish law. Called a *get,* the document is worded in Aramaic and written in Hebrew script. The religious agreement—which must be presented by the husband or his representatives to his wife in a Jewish court—establishes that the bonds of marriage are dissolved and that the woman is now "permitted to every man."

Even if divorced under domestic law, a Jewish couple is still considered rabbinically married until the wife obtains a *get* from her husband. If she pursues romantic relationships without it, she is rendered an adulterer in the eyes of God. Since the husband can withhold the *get,* it is not uncommon in Orthodox Jewish communities for men to purposefully stall in order to gain the upper hand in a divorce or simply to torment their partners. In exchange for Rod's promise to provide the document to Shele, she agreed not to press any criminal charges against him for past misconduct.

The parties also agreed to a custody schedule for the next few months. Rod was granted several hours with the kids on most weekdays and full custody every other weekend. Gesmer permitted Rod access to the apartment the following afternoon at 1 P.M. to retrieve his belongings. The judge granted Rod and Shele exclusive rights to their respective apartments.

Hoping to avoid any additional hostility in those early stages, Shele treaded lightly. She made several concessions with the hope that it would ease and expedite their split. But she had miscalculated, and Rod's vindictive call to her employer just minutes before the court proceeding began was only the beginning.

UBS branch manager John Alex, who had recruited the Danishefskys, was assigned to investigate the allegations.

Shele had been with the firm for only four months and had already established a sparkling reputation. Alex called Rod to get more details.

"Shele's trying to financially hurt me by draining our account, and she's on drugs," Rod told the startled supervisor. Unable to curb her spending, Shele was single-handedly bankrupting their young family, he said.

Suspicious of Rod's tale, Alex soon realized that the plundered account Rod referenced was with UBS. He had an assistant pull up the ledger and vetted each purchase. Rod, it turned out, was burning through $8 for each dollar Shele spent. When Alex called Rod back to review his findings, the aggrieved husband said he was no longer at liberty to discuss the matter due to pending legal concerns.

Rod's depiction of Shele as a functional junkie rang hollow to Alex. All new UBS employees are subject to drug tests, and Shele had passed hers. But despite these reservations, corporate protocol mandated that he discuss the accusations with Shele. On May 22, he called her into his office. "I received a call from your husband," he began ominously before telling her of Rod's charges.

Unable to suppress her shock, she dissolved into tears in front of her boss.

"Shele was a very poised, professional woman, and she basically collapsed emotionally in the office," Alex recalled. "She had a lot of tears coming down her face. She was trying to stay poised but she let it go and blurted a couple of things out."

Shele detailed the deterioration of her marriage and Rod's menacing behavior.

"He's going to kill me," she stammered.

Days after Rod's vengeful phone call to Shele's employer, he mounted a surprising reconciliation campaign. Oozing contrition and self-awareness, a weeping Rod implored Shele to pause the divorce and give their relationship another shot.

He proposed a rehabilitation plan, assuring her that he still loved her and was willing to take any measure necessary to keep their family intact. He would attend anger-management classes. He would accompany her to synagogue to help stamp out his propensity for vice. Rod even encouraged Shele to contact a close friend who would vouch for his desire to change and win back her trust.

The communication was a violation of the protective order and ended without Shele making any commitments. But Rod had once again managed to weaken her conviction. Using her UBS email account, because she suspected that Rod had been accessing her personal email, Shele reached out to Eve.

"Rod wants to get back together," she wrote, just five days after the breakdown in her boss's office. "What should I do?"

The mere suggestion incensed her sister. "I cannot believe you're asking that question!" she shot back on May 27. "First of all, how in the world did you get to talking about that? Per your lawyers he's not allowed. Secondly, after all of your history w/ him—and now his underhandedness of calling your mgr., you still question whether you should take him back? I know to me it's a clear cut situation and easy for me to say, but you also don't love him anymore, right?"

Shele replied an hour later and acknowledged that her wavering was ill-advised. "I'm a sucker for tears," she wrote. "He was begging for a second chance. . . . I agreed to have a conversation with him tonight."

Deeply alarmed, Eve wrote a long and forceful email that same afternoon.

"A leopard cannot change his spots! Your children are afraid to be w/ him—he has done awful things to you. His backgammon nonsense takes precedence over you and his children. How crazy is that?????? Per your own admission, you do not love him anymore. Don't you yourself want out? Aren't you tired of the drama and walking on eggshells? Your lawyer would be FURIOUS if he knew you agree [sic] to a conversation. He actually told you Rod would try to do this and he told you don't fall for it.

"This is Rod—he cannot change. He'll tell you he will so he can gain control again, but he'll revert back to the same character that he is. It's his make-up, it's his upbringing. You are a role model to your children and you were right when you started this whole procedure. You're showing them that it's not ok to be treated like you've been and you have to get yourself out of the situation. What about the fact that he called your manager last wk and accused you of horrible things? Does that with everything else get forgiven? It's very easy for me to sit here and only see the bad—and not any of the good—but is there any good? I just don't see it. After running around w/ other women, I couldn't do it. There's absolutely no forgiving that and any other of his disgusting acts. He does not deserve you! You're so much better than that!"

By initiating the divorce, Shele had seized the early advantage against Rod in their legal confrontation. Aware of his inferior position, he resorted to guerrilla tactics to level the playing field.

Putting his technical skills to use, he hacked her email accounts. Since he had set up her primary address, shele.covlin@gmail.com, Rod was able to have Google send him her password on June 8, 2009.

During his initial trawl, Rod sent himself 24 messages that included 1,500 pages of attached documents. He also had her future messages automatically forwarded to his email address. Any communication she composed or received—

including drafts—was now being deposited directly into Rod's inbox without her knowledge. To scrub any trace of the pilfered correspondence, Rod occasionally tiptoed into her account to delete the history of forwarded messages.

Rod was particularly interested in Shele's exchanges with Meyer, in which she discussed her strategies for the divorce. Rod also closely monitored messages related to Shele's personal finances and job.

But he was sloppy. He inadvertently alerted Shele to the breach after he viewed an email she sent to the Manhattan Day School, a Jewish private school on the Upper West Side, where Anna was a pupil. The message stated her desire to enroll Myles. Fearing the impact of an additional $12,000 in tuition costs on his own meager reserves, Rod became enraged. He emailed his attorney and demanded that Shele be barred from placing Myles in the school. "I do NOT want my son attending MDS," he fumed.

After her lawyer relayed the request, Shele knew that Rod had burglarized her email account because he had no way of knowing her plans otherwise. Spooked by the intrusion, Shele instructed all of her contacts—including close friends and family—to stop using her Gmail. Instead, she asked that they communicate exclusively by phone or through her work email, which had additional security layers.

In July 2009, Shele received yet another disturbing automated alert. Her cell phone provider, AT&T, sent her a text informing her that her account password had been changed. Deeply unnerved, Shele immediately called AT&T to change her password once again.

But it was too late. In the brief 11-minute window before she regained control, Rod had downloaded her phone records for the prior 17 months. Shele was forced to ask her circle not to use her cell phone for sensitive calls or texts. Only her work landline, she said, was safe from Rod's surveillance.

Now in possession of Shele's call history, Rod obsessively dialed numbers that appeared frequently. The calls—on which he never spoke—lasted anywhere from five to 17 seconds. When people answered, he would nervously hang up and attempt to piece together their identity. On July 12, Rod used his mother's name to create an account on Intelius, a company that provides the people associated with phone numbers. A day later, Rod plugged in a set of digits that appeared frequently and at odd hours on Shele's log. The database revealed that Shele had simply been dialing FreshDirect, the grocery-delivery service.

With his espionage falling flat, Rod tried more sophisticated methods. Later that month, he visited J&R Music and Computer World in downtown Manhattan, a specialty electronics store. He purchased a sensitive microphone used to record phone conversations, along with a separate digital voice recorder. Just a week later, he expanded his rig with an Olympus A-329 AC Adapter for voice recording.

In addition to launching the spy operation, Rod also appeared concerned that his own studio had been bugged with recording devices. In an August email exchange, a representative from Sherlock Investigations reported to Rod that his residence was free of unwanted eyes or ears. "It was nice meeting you today and talking with you," the staffer said. "I'm glad your apartment is free of electronic surveillance equipment. The place I was telling you about was SpyTech Inc. . . . I think they can do what you need."

That firm specialized in covert surveillance, and Rod seemed intent on monitoring someone's communications. Investigators would later theorize that he had set up recording equipment in Shele's apartment.

With close friends, Rod was open about his tactics. He admitted to longtime friend Marshall Baron that he had installed a keystroke logger on Shele's personal computer.

Every letter she typed and website she visited was compiled and emailed to Rod, including her passwords.

"He said he had access to her emails and that he was reading through things, and that he was upset with the number of people she was talking to and he was upset about the way he was being portrayed in her emails," recalled Baron.

Forced to abandon use of her phone and email, Shele had now become fearful that Rod was attempting to track her every movement—both online and in person. In the summer of 2009, Shele met a friend, Melissa Fields, at the Central Park Zoo. Fields had a niece the same age as Anna, and the two girls wanted to get together for a playdate. Shele, who brought Myles along, met Fields at the zoo gates.

"Shele was nervous and was looking around quite a bit," Fields recalled of the strange behavior. "I asked her if something was wrong, and she said she was worried that her ex-husband was following her. She was sure that he was following her. She was sure that he had, as we had previously discussed, hacked into her emails, and she was nervous that he was going to show up."

While they never spotted Rod that day, he might as well have been present. Whether near or far, he maintained a powerful psychological hold over Shele.

On one occasion, while talking to her neighbor Hannah Pennington in the hallway outside of her apartment, Shele suddenly paused mid-sentence. As their kids scampered up and down the corridor, her gaze rested upon what appeared to be a section of moulding near the ceiling. She pointed it out. "I think he installed surveillance equipment so he knows when I am coming and going," she said.

CHAPTER EIGHT

At Any Cost

Ultimately, Rod's dragnet produced little of value in his fight with Shele over money and the children. While the email hacks offered a glimpse into her state of mind, they did not turn up the damaging intelligence he had hoped for. The reality of Rod's position was sinking in. Shele held all the legal cards and would likely be able to dictate the terms of their divorce. He had to take drastic and immediate action.

On July 8, Rod picked up the kids from Shele's apartment for a regularly scheduled visit from 6 P.M. to 9 P.M. As was now customary, Shele descended to the building's lobby around 9 P.M. to receive the children from Rod. But the minutes ticked by and the trio failed to appear. She called and texted Rod repeatedly, but he didn't answer. As minutes became hours, Shele's dread grew. She returned to her apartment, gripping her phone.

At 10:15 P.M., she called Eve, hysterical. "Rod was supposed to return the children over an hour ago!" she told her sister. "He's not responding to any of my calls, he's not responding to emails, he's not getting back to me. I don't know where he is!"

While concerned herself, Eve tried to calm her panicked sister. Shele began calling anyone she could think of in search of Rod and their children. She dialed her lawyer, Rod's parents and even the police in Westchester County, where her in-laws lived. Rod had been sporadically staying with Carol and Dave, and Shele suspected that he might be there. But the Covlins insisted that they had not seen him.

At her wits' end, she repeatedly rang the local NYPD precinct and demanded that someone investigate. Finally, at 1 A.M., Officer Crystallee Vargas knocked on her apartment door.

Shaking with fear, Shele invited Vargas and her partner inside. "My husband didn't bring the children back on time," she told them. "I have an order stating they need to be back at a certain time. I just want to make sure they're okay."

Shele described the acrimony between her and Rod and hinted at his capacity for reckless and even violent behavior. The officers scribbled notes as they interviewed her for over an hour and promised to try to find the children. Vargas was moved by Shele's heartbreaking predicament.

"I felt nervous. I felt worried for her," she recalled later. After they left the apartment, both Vargas and her partner headed for the elevator bank down the hall. But before they descended, Vargas returned to Shele's door to make sure the distraught mother was stable.

"I knocked on the door and she threw herself into my arms," Vargas recalled. "She hugged me and began to weep uncontrollably. And as a person, I just hugged her back and she trembled." If she hadn't held her up, Shele would have crumpled to the ground.

"Oh my God!" Shele wailed in Vargas' arms. "I'm so scared. I'm so scared. I'm afraid Rod is going to kill me!"

Shocked by the depth of her fear, Vargas rubbed Shele's back and reassured her. "It's going to be okay," she said before leaving. "We're going to help you."

After another unbearable hour, Shele's phone rang at

roughly 3 A.M. It was a staffer with New York City's Administration for Children's Services.

Anna and Myles were safe, the voice said, easing Shele's worst fears. But it would be a fleeting relief. Rod had taken the kids to NewYork-Presbyterian Hospital that night and told doctors there that Shele had been sexually abusing their 2-year-old son. Rod tried to lend credibility to the claim by noting that Shele was not his biological mother.

The news clubbed Shele like a hammer and she nearly toppled over. She knew Rod could be vindictive, but had never imagined this. Shele now understood with fearsome clarity that Rod was capable of anything.

The social worker said hospital personnel had vetted Myles and found no physical or mental signs of sexual abuse. Other than some slight bruising on his legs, nothing was amiss. But they were required to open an investigation and alert the NYPD.

After Rod reported the allegation of abuse to an emergency-room doctor, an ACS social worker interviewed him. He told child-protection specialist Angelberth Ezeogu that Shele had been drinking to excess and abusing prescription pills as their marriage dissolved. "My 2-year-old son, Myles, said that she pushed him outside of their apartment and he fell and hurt his legs and forehead," Rod reported. "He also said that she poked his penis and his butt."

After conferring with hospital personnel, Ezeogu told Rod that the children would be returned to their mother pending the probe's outcome.

Incensed, Rod grabbed Myles and grew belligerent. "The police will have to pry him out of my arms and arrest me before I let him go back to Shele!" he screamed.

But hospital workers insisted that he had to relinquish the children and he finally relented. At 5:30 A.M.—eight and a half hours after they were supposed to have been dropped off—ACS workers delivered the groggy and confused siblings to their mother. With tears streaming down her face, Shele drew them in close and rocked them to sleep in her bed as the sun climbed over Manhattan.

But the ordeal had only just begun. Shele would now be forced to fend off accusations that she had committed the most depraved act imaginable against her little boy.

Emotionally battered, Shele sought solace in Eve's company during that week's Sabbath. On Friday evening, before sunset, the sisters ushered in the holiday by each lighting a pair of white candles. They stood over the table as they moved their hands over the snapping flames, then covered their eyes and softly recited a Hebrew prayer in unison.

"Blessed are You, Lord, our God, King of the universe, who has sanctified us with His commandments and commanded us to light Shabbat candles."

Shele began to cry and turned to her sister.

"Rod's hatred of me is stronger than his love for his children," she said, letting the words—and their implications—hover above the candlelight.

Detective Shirley Figueroa, of the NYPD's Special Victims Division, was assigned to investigate the child-abuse allegations against Shele, while ACS social worker Diane Castellanos launched a separate probe on behalf of the agency. Figueroa had difficulty reaching Rod for several days. Finally, on July 12, he agreed to meet her for an interview at the Manhattan Child Advocacy Center in East Harlem. While the officer tried to steer their exchange toward the abuse allegations, Rod was more interested in denouncing his wife.

"He started talking about his relationship with Shele and how she was spending money on nannies and how she was limiting the time he got to spend with the children," she recalled. He went on to complain that Shele was violent—and even claimed that she had scratched him after an argument and left scars. She had a raging drug problem, he alleged.

With Rod's diary of discontent finally complete, Figueroa pressed him about the sex-abuse allegations. Rod said he had picked up Myles from the lobby of their building and gone up to his apartment while waiting for Rose to bring him a bottle.

"Out of the blue, Myles said, 'Daddy, I want to live with you,'" Rod told the detective. "I was happy, because he has never said that before. I asked him if anybody hurt him. He became very shy and put his hand on his lap as if something happened to him. I thought it was strange."

Rod said the pair then left the apartment to retrieve Anna from her therapist; she had been seeing Helen Speransky for several weeks to help her cope with the pending divorce. As the three of them walked home, Myles abruptly spoke up. "Mommy touched my peepee and my tushy and it hurt me," the boy said, according to Rod. Anna then interjected, asking Myles to describe the pain. "Did it hurt a lot or a little?" she allegedly inquired. "A lot," he replied.

Rod said he'd questioned Myles about where the incident took place. "Did it happen in the shower?" he asked. "No," Myles replied. "Did it happen while you were playing?" Rod asked. "Yes," Myles answered.

Prior to speaking with Rod, Figueroa had already interviewed Myles, Anna, Shele, the examining doctor and Rose.

Anna had flatly denied to Figueroa that Shele would ever hurt Myles. "My mother would never do that," she said.

With little evidence to buttress Rod's claims, Figueroa determined that there was no basis for a case. The Manhattan District Attorney's Office arrived at the same conclusion and declined to pursue charges.

As part of the separate ACS investigation, Castellanos

interviewed Rod four times and Shele five times. She also spoke with Anna, Myles and the nanny. Both children were forced to undergo thorough forensic examinations at the Child Advocacy Center, including interviews conducted by medical personnel trained to gather evidence of sexual abuse that can be used in court. Castellanos also concluded that there was "no credible evidence that [the] mother physically or sexually abuse[d] Myles."

The social worker did, however, determine that Shele was a victim of domestic violence.

A few days after making the false allegations, Rod had a scheduled visit with the kids. But given his growing instability, Shele did not show up in the lobby to hand them over. Rod rapped on her apartment door, but no one answered. Shele's attorney informed his lawyers by email that she would no longer abide by the visitation schedule.

Rod immediately called the police and demanded that they take action. Compelled to investigate, cops paid visits to Shele's parents' and brothers' homes in New Jersey looking for Myles and Anna. Rod took to Facebook to publicly shame Shele for "kidnapping" their children.

Shele asked Judge Gesmer to curb Rod's visitation. Most significantly, the affidavit asked that the order of protection against Rod once again be extended to include both Anna and Myles and that an attorney be appointed to represent each of them.

Shele said she had made a grievous mistake in agreeing to the joint-custody arrangement in May. She had hoped the gesture would mollify Rod and shield the children.

Calling Rod's sexual-abuse claims "unthinkable" and "heinous," Shele said the joint-custody agreement ended up placing "our children's well-being in jeopardy."

"That night was the worst night of my life," she wrote. "Only a sick and psychologically unstable person would fabricate such horrific and twisted allegations. The defendant also has a history of acting out in inappropriate and bizarre ways when he feels he is under pressure, in the past threatening suicide."

Shele told the court that Rod routinely promised to "ruin" her life if she ever pursued a divorce or sought to curtail his visitation. "However, I never imagined he would go this far," she wrote.

Her primary concern was Rod's toxic influence on the children. "I believe that in the approximately 30 minutes that the defendant was alone with our son, Myles, before picking up our daughter from her therapist's office, the defendant used that opportunity to coach our son into saying false things that our son would not even comprehend at his young age," she wrote.

After Rod had taken Myles to the hospital, he told the medical staff there that Myles had said his mother "put [her] tongue on [his] penis." "The mere fact that my son would make that statement causes me to be seriously concerned about what the defendant may have said to him, coached him to say, or worst of all did to him. Children who are three years old do not make statements like that unless they are coached," Shele stated in the filing.

She described frantically calling Rod's parents that night. Carol and Dave had insisted that they had no idea where Rod had taken the children. "This I later found out was not true, as the defendant spoke with his parents and they were aware of his whereabouts," she wrote bitterly.

Rod's trumped-up accusations forced the children to endure hours of intrusive questioning and, for Myles, an uncomfortable physical procedure. In the wake of the needless investigation, Myles became attached to his blanket for comfort, a habit he had never exhibited before.

Shele also complained that Rod had ignored Gesmer's directive that the parents not defame each other to the children. "The defendant tells our daughter that I had him thrown out of the only home he had and now he has to move away," she wrote. "The defendant even tells our daughter that he wants to make up with me, but my lawyers and I want to fight with him."

Letters from her attorneys had done nothing to deter Rod from poisoning the children against their mother. Even the lobby handoffs were becoming difficult. "If I come down a few minutes early and he is there, he screams and yells that I have an order of protection in the presence of the children, which on at least one occasion has caused our children to cry," she said. "On another occasion, the defendant would not let me say hello to my children when I saw them in the lobby and tried to go up to them and hug them, yelling and screaming again about the order of protection."

Rod's public outbursts had even prompted doormen and building residents to approach Shele and ask her if she was okay.

His deteriorating state "raises serious concerns about the defendant's mental health," Shele wrote.

The motion demanded that Rod's visits be supervised, and that he undergo a psychiatric evaluation to assess his sanity and fitness as a parent.

"This has gone too far and our children's well-being must come first."

Rod's professional world was becoming as unstable as his personal life. Despite warnings from co-workers that his job was in peril, Rod continued to slack off at the office. "He was fixated on his separation," said Marshall Baron. "There were times when he was playing online backgammon at work and his work wasn't getting done, and that was becoming a problem."

He was assigned a new supervisor, who quickly tired of his delinquency. Citing constant absences and meager output, the manager told Rod that his time at Pragma was over and he was fired on July 21. While the sacking was a foregone conclusion to his colleagues, Rod was floored. "He was extremely angry," Baron recalled. "He felt as if it wasn't warranted. He also felt betrayed."

Rod had now squandered his lone source of income—one that, with bonuses that year, had earned him $136,000 in just six months. Baron, who was also going through a divorce, did his best to help Rod land on his feet and alerted him to job openings. But rather than redouble his search, Rod focused instead on the circle of conspirators he believed were driving him destitute. The primary nemesis, of course, was Shele. Rod blamed her for his job loss, reasoning that her push for divorce had robbed him of the peace of mind necessary to perform at work.

A month later, the estranged couple appeared in court together for the first time since Rod lodged his debunked sexual-abuse allegations. Judge Gesmer was disgusted by Rod's molestation smear. She nixed the children's overnight stays and reduced his weekday visits to just two hours, twice a week.

Gesmer reserved her harshest measure for last—telling Rod that he could no longer spend a moment with Myles and Anna without official supervision. The judge instructed Shele to hire a social worker to monitor the visits. In a final blow, she issued an order of protection barring Rod from any unauthorized contact with Anna and Myles, including phone calls and emails. An unsanctioned text, call or birthday email was now a violation of the law. "It's stuff I would never have believed could happen in the US court system," Rod wrote to a girlfriend soon after Gesmer's ruling. "True insanity."

Rod's plot to wrest complete custody of his children from Shele had backfired in crushing fashion. She was now dictating his relationships with Anna and Myles. Rod obsessively carped about the humiliation to friends, complaining that the court system favored mothers.

"He felt he should have custody of his two children," Baron recalled. "It came up several times. He was indignant when he had supervised visitation put in place. He was angry. He blamed Shele for that." Rod portrayed her as a devious manipulator who was taking advantage of a legal structure systemically arrayed against his interests as a man.

"I've now read, experienced and been informed enough— when women lie and use the court system in divorce the way Shele has, typically these things go on this way until the children are no longer minors," he wrote to a friend. "Basically, I am screwed for the next 15 (minimum) years. Nah. I'm screwed. It's simply unimaginable and deeply disturbing. Shockingly disturbing. Horrifyingly disturbing."

Rod's perception of Shele was becoming increasingly black. In his eyes, she had devolved into a singularly evil actor, hell-bent on his annihilation.

"Shele has done things I never even thought she would ever be capable of," he told a friend. "And it's become clear that she has been planning this for a long time and had been thinking about it for several years, the way she is using the courts and abusing the system. It's simply hideous."

Arming himself for further conflict, he purchased several books on courtroom tactics for persecuted dads, including "The Father's Emergency Guide to Divorce-Custody Battle: A Tour Through the Predatory World of Judges, Lawyers,

Psychologists & Social Workers in the Subculture of Divorce" and "Divorce Poison: Protecting the Parent-Child Bond from a Vindictive Ex."

Rod's rage was turning primal. "I feel like an animal caught in one of those steel traps," he wrote to a friend. "I am ready to gnaw my paw off to escape."

CHAPTER NINE

Bad Bet

While Rod's termination razed his income, it also afforded him time to focus on his true passion—backgammon. He began playing the game regularly and managed to score the occasional payday through tournaments.

"Seems I am now a professional backgammon player," he wrote to a friend on August 4, 2009. "Lost my job 2 weeks ago. Seem to be able to average really good money playing guys on Wall Street."

Rod used his dissipating cash reserves to attend tournaments around the country. He managed to take part in 13 backgammon gatherings between January and August of 2009. After the cost of airfare, hotels, taxis, food and entry fees, the trips were rarely profitable, no matter how he performed. But it seemed to comfort him. Whenever the backgammon box snapped shut and the court gavel banged, Rod was instantly jarred back to the grim reality of his situation.

In an August 13, 2009, family court appearance, Rod clawed back a few inches of ground. Gesmer eased the terms of his visitation, extending the length of his semiweekly visits to four hours. With Shele's consent, Gesmer also agreed to replace the mandatory social worker with Covlin's father.

But Rod's momentum would be short-lived. Gesmer then

stripped him of his most valuable chip—the withholding of the *get*, the Jewish certificate of divorce. Using it as one more mechanism of control over Shele, Rod hadn't provided it. Gesmer gave him one week to sign the document.

Stymied on that front, Rod moved on to his financial woes, telling the judge that he had lost his job and could not pay child support. Gesmer reluctantly absolved him of that burden but told him that if he could not afford to provide for his children, he could not afford to play backgammon. She barred him from participating in his beloved sport.

He was now without his job, his wife, his children—and his only remaining source of contentment in an otherwise desolate life. Again, he blamed Shele. In emails, texts and lengthy phone calls, Rod condemned her to anyone willing to field his fury.

Shele, meanwhile, fully appreciated the implications of the backgammon ban. She texted Eve a few hours after the divorce hearing. "He is not allowed to go to backgammon tournaments anymore," she wrote. "Judge referred to it as gambling, and since he claims he can't afford to pay anything for the kids she felt it necessary to eliminate this vice. He must really hate me now!"

Rod was aware that Shele continued to dominate in court. "Unfortunately the divorce is not going all that well and I won't be able to attend any tournaments for a little while," he emailed a friend. "Having lost my job recently, my attorney feels that 'gambling' won't look good to the judge. So sorry."

Growing desperate, Rod filed an affidavit in August asking Gesmer for spousal support. He had already burned through his severance and his minimal savings. "My parents have lent me money for my living expenses, but they can no longer afford to lend me more," he wrote. "I am now unemployed and have no resources."

In a financial disclosure to the court, Rod reported that he had a retirement account containing $78,469 and total credit card and student loan debt of $109,371. The interest rates on some of his cards were spiraling to 33 percent, tightening the financial noose. Rod also complained to the court that Shele had contacted his landlord to inquire about the status of his lease. As a cosigner on the apartment, she was concerned that she would be responsible for unpaid rent now that he was nearly insolvent.

Shele told the building manager that Rod had lost his job and asked if they could be removed from the lease if a new renter took it over. The maneuver further infuriated Rod, who felt that he was entitled to remain in the apartment to be close to the children—with Shele picking up the tab.

Rod told the court that his monthly expenses totaled $7,730.47—with more than a quarter of that sum stemming from stifling student debt and credit-card payments. He tepidly assured Gesmer that he was making every effort to find a new job, telling her that he was "revising [his] résumé" and "networking with colleagues."

But Rod argued that his joblessness came in the midst of a crippling recession spurred by the collapse of the subprime mortgage market. Strapped companies were shedding employees to cut down on losses, making Rod's predicament particularly difficult. He leaned on these grim economic headlines to coax sympathy from Gesmer, arguing that he was being thwarted by forces beyond his control.

He even put a generous timetable on his unemployment. "It is reasonable to presume that this time frame may be protracted beyond a nine-to-12 month period," he told the court.

Rod unabashedly told Gesmer that he had been financially dependent on Shele throughout their time together. "In fact, over the course of our marriage, Plaintiff earned about four to five times more than I did," he wrote. "There is no doubt that Plaintiff is the moneyed spouse in this marriage."

He backed up the claim with a meticulous accounting of her assets, noting that she had $890,000 in a UBS money market account—a forgivable loan that the company had given her as an incentive when it hired her. Rod also inventoried another $383,000 in a UBS brokerage account, $266,197 in a Merrill Lynch 401(k) retirement account and another TD Bank account containing $100,000. In addition, he told the court that she had $1,273,000 in other assets accrued during their marriage. He, on the other hand, had a pitiable total of $4,125 in his savings and checking accounts combined.

Rod asked the judge to direct Shele to pay him $50,000 in maintenance and assured her that he would abide by her ban and not squander the money on tournaments. "I have not been engaging in backgammon because I am unemployed and I need every cent that I have to pay bills," he stated.

In reality, he had tumbled dice at a tournament on August 12. Rod had quickly found ways to run afoul of Gesmer's backgammon ban as he awaited her decision. He had friends pay for tournament expenses with their credit cards and he repaid them in cash to avoid any paper trail.

Just two days before the critical court date when Gesmer would rule on his motion, Rod played in a high-profile tournament. He wrote a woman at the time that his life had been reduced to three basic elements—"divorce, kids and backgammon."

On September 19, Shele and her attorney filed a scathing response to Rod's legal panhandling. Not only did she wholly reject his demands—but in turn argued that he should provide her $2,000 a month in child support. She scoffed at

Rod's claims of blameless privation, arguing that he alone was responsible for his financial straits.

"The defendant's claims of poverty, if true, are his own doing, and result primarily from his backgammon obsession and loss of yet another job, which I am certain was not due to cutbacks or layoffs as the defendant wants this court to believe," Shele said in her motion.

She ripped Rod's listed expenses as "overstated and ridiculous" and questioned his claim that he spent $400 a month on charity, $3,000 on loan repayments and $1,100 on food. She noted that he didn't list a single expense related to Anna and Myles.

"I pay all of our children's expenses with no contribution from the defendant," she wrote. The extent of Rod's largesse during their marriage, Shele argued, was covering a few utility bills. His own earnings were funneled directly to his personal interests, most of them centered around backgammon.

"I paid for the defendant to attend graduate school and obtain a master's degree so he could pursue a career in finance and provide for our family," she wrote. "However, he apparently had other ideas."

Shele insisted that much of his spending stemmed from Rod's rampant infidelity. "The defendant had extramarital affairs and undoubtedly spent considerable amounts of money on his paramours that contributed to a large amount of this debt, along with his costly backgammon excursions," she wrote.

But Shele reserved her most biting prose for Rod's insistence on maintaining the Manhattan apartment at her expense. Shele told the court that Rod had moved back in with his parents in New Rochelle and only used the apartment for a few hours a week, during visitations with the kids. She said she had agreed to finance his studio only after Rod's suggestion of an open marriage. "I had absolutely no interest in such a sick and twisted concept, and no longer wanted to share a bed with the defendant," she wrote. "The defendant insisted that he would only move out if I cosigned a lease." Making matters worse, she said, the front door to Rod's studio became a turnstile for a procession of love interests.

She argued that her own finances were also in turmoil. Shele said the ongoing financial crisis at the time—which was battering Wall Street and destroying former powerhouses like Bear Stearns and Lehman Brothers—had drastically reduced her income. Over the first seven months of 2009, with a recession then at full boil, she earned only $48,066. The $890,000 forgivable loan that UBS used to recruit her away from Merrill Lynch helped to ease some of the strain, paying out $100,000 annually as long as she remained with the firm. She told the court that she would likely clear roughly $200,000 that year overall.

While she did not have to pay rent for her apartment because of her parents' ownership, Shele said her other domestic expenses were considerable. Tuition and nanny costs, she said, piled up quickly each month. Rod, she argued, should be the party providing child support. "I am not seeking an excessive amount of support, I am only asking that the defendant contribute some money towards our children's expenses," she wrote.

Gesmer rendered her decision on November 24, 2009, with both sides present. She called several of Rod's expenses "questionable" given his indefinite unemployment—especially $900 on dining out and $200 on clothing each month.

But Gesmer applied equal scrutiny to Shele's spending. She critiqued several elements of her listed monthly expenses of $30,692. Although most were related to nannies and private school, she noted that Shele spent $1,000 a month on clothing for herself and another $1,000 a month to outfit the kids. However, Gesmer ultimately sided with Shele. "The husband has not shown that he is entitled to maintenance," she ruled. "Moreover, he has not provided any explanation of why he cannot earn income as a consultant, as he has done in the past."

Rod's legal gamble had failed spectacularly. Gesmer ordered him to pay $425 a month in child support indefinitely, retroactive to September 18, when Shele filed the support request.

Avalanched by debt and with few tools to dig himself out, Rod began to suffocate.

Gesmer formalized Rod's visitation schedule through early 2010, giving him supervised access to the kids for "four hours twice a week and a full day every two weeks under the supervision of his father, sister, nanny or babysitter."

After the court ruling, the malice between Rod and Shele worsened. Rod became livid after claiming that Shele excluded him from their son's *upsherin,* a Yiddish word meaning "hair-cutting." In some Jewish communities, a child does not cut his locks until the age of three. When the time comes, friends and family gather for a celebratory snip to mark the transition from baby to boy.

Shele emailed Rod an invitation to the *upsherin* on September 18, but he and his family did not attend. Rod would later argue that Shele purposefully held the event on a date when she knew he and his parents would be unavailable. She denied the accusation, noting that she had no knowledge of their calendar.

Nonetheless, Rod shoveled the perceived injustice atop his smoldering pyre of resentment and rage. He emailed a girlfriend at the time to complain that Shele was using money to curry favor with the kids. "Shele was trying to buy the children, and he didn't have the money to spend on them," the woman recalled him saying.

Now all but penniless, Rod found himself unable to pay yet another debt—money owed to his irritated lawyers. With no sign of payment forthcoming, they filed an application to withdraw from the case. Gesmer called for a hearing to determine if Shele would be ordered to pay Rod's legal fees since she was the breadwinner. On December 22, in a rare courtroom victory for Rod, Gesmer saddled Shele with his $50,000 legal bill. But he had his eye on a far larger prize.

CHAPTER TEN

Liberation

On December 11, 2009, Shele invited her neighbor, Hannah Pennington, and her daughters to the apartment, along with another close girlfriend. It was the first night of Hanukkah, and Shele found some desperately needed comfort in their company.

In the midst of their conversation, the phone rang. Anna answered, and Shele immediately knew by her tone that it was Rod. He wanted to speak to Myles, but the boy said he didn't feel like talking. Rod pressed Anna, and eventually told her to put Shele on the phone. No longer willing to endure his harangues, she refused.

"If I get on the phone, I will just get in a situation where he yells at me for not complying with what he wants, and I'm not doing that," she told her friends. Anna was growing distraught by her father's aggression before the call finally ended. "My stomach hurts," she groaned, telling her mother that she was going to the bathroom for the third time that evening. The immense trauma of her parents' warfare was taking a severe toll.

The anguished mother seemed at a loss, deeply worried about the children and their ability to absorb the dysfunction, her friends recalled. On December 18, the day before yet another court date, Shele's attorneys sent Rod's lawyers a letter expressing concern over his treatment of the kids during visits. Shele accused him of hitting the children and yelling angrily with minimal provocation. Rod's legal proxies sent back a scorching rebuttal, charging Shele with equally deplorable behavior. With the divorce trial imminent, both sides were rolling out their legal artillery.

"Indeed, I have also received numerous emails from Mr. Covlin in which he reported such incidents as your client withholding and/or destroying pictures that Anna made him; your client taking all the friendship bracelets he made for Anna away, Anna telling him that she and Miles [sic] have not had baths in three days, as well as the children telling him that Ms. Covlin yells and screams at them, and so on," wrote attorney Jeanna Alberga, who misspelled Myles' name.

Rod's father, Dave, who was the primary supervisor during Rod's custody visits, also submitted a letter to Shele's attorneys casting Rod as a doting and attentive dad who had rightly earned the love of his two children. He often took the kids to Central Park and the American Museum of Natural History, Dave reported. Hoping to cultivate a love of books, he read to them nightly.

"He has not screamed at the children and he has never physically harmed or struck the children in any fashion during this time," Dave wrote. What Shele deemed excessive discipline, Dave countered, was simply responsible parenting.

The missive then went on the offensive against Shele, asserting that she was prone to unhinged bouts of screaming. "I must say that Myles has complained several times that Mommy yells at him and makes him cry," Dave wrote. "Anna has confirmed that this has been happening more frequently."

Shele, Dave said, was undercutting the children's affection

for their father. "I also heard Myles say to Roderick that he liked him," Dave reported. "Roderick asked him, doesn't he love him? Myles told Roderick that Mommy told him to say he liked Daddy. Anna again confirmed this." The letter concluded with a feeble insinuation that Shele abused the kids. "The only evidence I have seen of any physical distress was one bruise on Myles' head when he came over one day," he wrote. "Apparently Mommy had accidentally banged his head into something. Again this was confirmed by Anna."

The acrimony between the two camps was reaching a crescendo. Every syllable of correspondence dripped with contempt and mistrust.

"She thought he would do whatever it took to get the kids," Shele's lawyer, Meyer, recalled. "She was definitely concerned that he was going to hurt her."

As the divorce proceedings trudged on, Rod maintained his ceaseless pursuit of fresh female company. He manically propositioned hundreds of women on Facebook from 2008 to 2009, once managing to introduce himself to 47 women on a single day.

There was a desperate fervor to Rod's solicitations. On a Thursday night in November, around 6 P.M., Rod sidled into the seedy anonymity of the Craigslist personals section. "Drinks anyone? Tonight, Friday, Saturday or Sunday?" The enticement failed to produce a single lead.

But while Rod's seductive skills were uneven, he was still a tall, educated and occasionally charming man. Those attributes had managed to catch the attentions of Jeanne Robin, a comely brunette with short brown hair, a lofty title and an appetite for spontaneity. An administrator at Johns Hopkins University in Baltimore, she first encountered Rod online while playing Castle Age, a medieval fantasy game hosted on Facebook.

After weeks of heavy-handed flirtation, they finally arranged to meet in the flesh on October 21 in Manhattan. Robin, who was married but enjoyed the liberties of an open relationship, agreed to meet Rod at a comic-book store. She arrived first and was thumbing through titles when Rod sauntered over.

With characteristic terseness, he muttered a greeting and smiled. She recalled that another brave suitor attempted to strike up a conversation with her inside the shop, but Rod chased him off with a few pointed warnings.

"We had a nice lunch," Robin said. "He was charming, witty and fun." With one appetite sated and another inflamed, they agreed to head to a nearby hotel. Aware of his brittle finances, Rod nervously handed his card over to a receptionist, but it was declined.

"It was embarrassing," Robin recalled. "But I knew he was in the middle of a divorce, and finances go to hell in a divorce." She offered to pay for the hotel room herself, but Rod cobbled enough cash together to cover the expense.

With funding secured, Rod and Robin ascended to the room in an elevator and remained there for hours. After a few postcoital pleasantries, Robin headed back to Baltimore.

Rod continued to court other women online, but maintained contact with Robin on Facebook and through an occasional phone call. On December 11, they arranged for a second date. Robin agreed to take the train to Manhattan once again, only this time Rod entertained her at his apartment.

After meeting her in the lobby of the Dorchester, Rod escorted her to the fifth floor, passing apartment 515 on the way to his studio. "That's my wife's apartment," he announced. She found his residence sparsely furnished but clean.

"He showed me a book that he had illustrated and written for his children," she recalled. "He seemed very involved with his children and loved his kids."

Rod and Robin went out to get pizza before coming back and resuming their physical agenda. His hungers satisfied, Rod's mind was able to pivot to other pressing matters in his life. He began recounting his marital mess and veering into embellishment.

"He had told me that his wife had cheated on him so he had to get tested," Robin said. "He told me that it was difficult for him sometimes to get time with his kids. He told me she was a bad Jew and had sort of turned him off of Judaism as she kept the letter and not the spirit of Jewish law."

Robin returned to Baltimore, having enjoyed Rod's company both sexually and conversationally, and hoped to see him again. They continued to chat online during games of Castle Age and occasionally texted each other.

On December 30, 2009, he posted a request for help with a particular aspect of the game and was flooded with offers of aid by a bevy of women. The stampede was visible to Robin online.

"Aren't you a ladies man?" she jested on Facebook. The seemingly benign jab was met with an immediate text to her phone. "You can't say stuff like that in my social media," he scolded. "I'm in the middle of a divorce." Robin immediately acknowledged her flub, saying, "[I] didn't mean to get you in any kind of trouble." She watched her phone for a reply, but it never came. Robin reached out the following day. "I was concerned I had really affected something in the proceedings," she recalled.

But again, her messages went unanswered. They would eventually speak—but under far different circumstances.

While most of Rod's interactions with women amounted to sexual adventurism, one target would eventually entrench herself—and ultimately determine the course of his life more than he could ever have known.

Debra Oles had first noted Rod's imposing physique at a

backgammon tournament in January 2009. From a distance, she watched him swagger around the premises with an arrogant and abrasive manner she found intriguing. "I had never seen him at a tournament before," the fellow backgammon enthusiast said. "I took notice of him because he was rude to a couple of people. I watched him play a match against a backgammon great."

They chatted briefly at the event and connected on Facebook. In July, they crossed paths again at another tournament in Michigan. After the day's play finished, Debra and Rod headed to a local TGI Fridays for dinner and drinks. With both parties emboldened by alcohol, Rod asked Debra if she wanted to retreat to his hotel room for a few additional rounds. She accepted the offer.

Upon arrival, Debra went to the bathroom to freshen up. When she reemerged, Rod was standing in front of her, naked from the waist down. "He grabbed me and maneuvered me over to the bed," she recalled. "I was attracted to him, I didn't say no."

Debra, who lived in North Carolina, succumbed to Rod's allure, despite being married with three children. She was 14 years his elder, and his interest took her by surprise. Rod said he had been separated from his wife for a year and a half and was in the midst of a grueling divorce. It was a lie. At the time, he and Shele were still together.

The unlikely pair continued to see each other regularly at tournaments. Once Rod and Shele officially separated, Debra would occasionally trek to New York to visit him at his studio apartment or at his parents' home in New Rochelle. The couple also frequented his family's vacation house in Massachusetts, where they could cavort undisturbed. Painted a whimsical yellow, the 902-square-foot bungalow is nestled in the town of Hancock amid the Berkshire Mountains.

Surrounded by woods with a sprawling green lawn and a firepit, Rod cherished the home as a rustic escape.

During a September 2009 visit, Debra recalled awaking from a deep sleep and seeing Rod next to her in bed, his face illuminated by the glow of his computer screen. Debra peered over and saw that he was logged into Shele's email, perusing her messages, including several from her attorneys. "I thought it was odd," she said. "It was clear [Shele] didn't know he had access to her account."

Later that weekend, Rod made an offhand comment that lodged in her mind. "Give me a year and I'll have anyone brainwashed," he told her.

"You couldn't brainwash me," Debra replied. "I am too strong-minded."

Due mostly to their common passion for backgammon, Rod grew increasingly fond of Debra, and their bond tightened. In November, the couple spent time in the Massachusetts home before returning to Manhattan to play in the Mayor's Cup, a prestigious tournament held at the New York Athletic Club.

In a photograph taken at the event, just a month before Shele's death, Rod appears in his beloved Burton snowboarding jacket. He had developed an almost childlike attachment to the garish green garment, emblazoned with peculiar anime illustrations.

The photo depicts a gaggle of backgammon enthusiasts seated at a long table in a dimly lit restaurant. A young blonde in a red dress is standing between Rod and another man, her hands on each of their shoulders. In keeping with the spirit of his jacket, Rod mugs absurdly for the camera, arching a single eyebrow while staring up at the ceiling. Debra also appears in the image with her back turned, tapping away on a BlackBerry.

She returned to New York City once again on December 10, 2009, and stayed with Rod in his apartment. After another game of backgammon, the pair took a break for dinner, and Rod made an unsettling comment Debra never forgot.

"He was leaning up against the door next to the kitchen," she said. "He said, 'I can cry on demand and make it look absolutely genuine.' I'm like, 'No you can't.' And right then and there he began to weep."

Rod, Debra began to realize, considered himself a master of deceit—and took pride in the skill.

But despite Rod's eccentricities, Debra found herself attracted to him. Much of his appeal, she said, was rooted in his size and masculinity. Rod boasted that he was a black belt in tae kwon do and was capable of annihilating a lesser man with ease. Despite this macho affect, Rod always observed the basic tenets of chivalry, opening doors for Debra and carrying her bags.

This tenderness vanished when they shed their clothes. Debra recalled Rod's sexual ferocity—especially during their many trips to Massachusetts. Intimacy would quickly give way to bestial aggression that would border on battery. "Sometimes he was so rough," she said. "It hurt me so bad that it took me two months to heal once. He wasn't always like that. I don't know if he was getting his anger out. I just really think he has a hatred of women."

On one occasion, Rod gingerly expressed an interest in anal intercourse with Debra. "I've never done that before," she told him. "I don't like it. Don't do it to me." Rod retreated, but renewed his effort later that evening, after they'd downed several drinks.

They became amorous and Rod forced himself into her anally. "He was really rough," she recalled later. "It almost felt like being raped. It was awful and it hurt so badly that I didn't think he was ever going to finish. It embarrassed me.

I know people do that kind of stuff, but I felt it was just so humiliating."

Rod strategically alternated between brute and butterfly. He once took Debra to a Manhattan sex shop and walked over to the strap-on section. "He wanted me to put it on and use it on him," Debra recalled. Under unrelenting pressure, Debra tried to indulge Rod but couldn't stomach the act. "I just thought it was weird," she said. "I just couldn't do it."

Debra's forays into big-city debauchery were a stark departure from her staid origins. Born and raised in Iowa, she was still married to a high-ranking officer with the U.S. Marine Corps Forces Special Operations Command and had three children with him.

While Rod's dating carousel continued to spin, Debra was the only partner who remained on board. She said that Rod often talked about Shele, always with anger and resentment. "It almost seemed like he was jealous because she had accomplished so much," she said.

As Rod sought novelty and titillation in his dating life, Shele set out to discover love and commitment. Rod finally provided the *get* on September 12—three weeks after it was due.

Shele crafted a profile on Jdate and was taken aback by the barrage of responses. There was no shortage of suitors, and the interest lifted her hopes for her future. She had blossomed into an elegant and successful beauty late in life and was only beginning to realize it. After years of Rod's disparagement, Shele's wounds stood a chance to heal.

While Rod foraged on Craigslist, Shele's dating pool was far more distinguished. Former hotelier and real-estate developer Neal Rothenberg had first met Shele at a charity event in Manhattan in May 2009. He was immediately struck by her refinement and intellect, but was legally married at the time.

Six months later, he was single, and found Shele's profile on Jdate. They agreed to meet a few days later at Abigail's on Broadway, an upscale kosher restaurant in Midtown Manhattan. "We spoke about the stock market," said Rothenberg, who wears a yarmulke and glasses. "The conversation quickly evolved to her personal issues and problems." Shele told Rothenberg that she had a Jewish bill of divorce but that the civil proceeding was proving to be far more complex.

The lanky Jewish businessman, 11 years her senior with a graying beard and mane, struggled to gauge her romantic interest. While she made every effort to project engagement, Rod's shadow crept over the table.

"She was uptight," Rothenberg said. "She was checking her BlackBerry and constantly looking at her watch and very concerned about time." It turned out that Shele had good reason for her preoccupation. Rod had a scheduled visit with the children and was supposed to hand them off to Rose before the nanny left at 8 P.M. If Shele didn't return before then, Rod would have an excuse to enter the apartment with the children and wait for her return. It was a harrowing thought.

Rothenberg drove Shele home that night and told her that he would be traveling to Europe and Israel in a few days for Hanukkah, which began on December 11.

They exchanged several emails during his absence, further bolstering his romantic hopes. "I had a very good time," Shele wrote to him of their evening together. "Please call me again."

But a few days before his return, Rothenberg got a message from Shele on Jdate. It wasn't what he expected. "It was very disjointed and didn't make a lot of sense," he recalled. "The message could have been suggesting that she didn't want to go out a second time."

The abrupt reversal—conveyed in such bizarre language—made little sense to Rothenberg.

He called Shele soon after touching back down in New York. "I just want to be clear that you want to go out a second time," he said.

"I definitely want to go out," she replied. "That message was not from me." Rod, Shele explained with embarrassment, must have hacked her Jdate account and sent the message. Their correspondence, Shele said, should be restricted to her cell phone and work email.

Rothenberg was so smitten with Shele that he was willing to overlook her domestic mayhem. They agreed to a second date on Monday, December 28, 2009, at Mike's Bistro. The busy haunt, then situated on bustling 72nd Street in Manhattan, was another chic kosher destination.

Rothenberg had hoped that Shele would be a bit more at ease this time, but she was distracted and jumpy—even more so than on their first date.

Overwhelmed by her marital strife, Shele buried Rothenberg in the details of her collapsing union. She told him that Rod was younger than her and athletic. It was a curious topic to introduce, considering her companion's physique, but Rothenberg slowly began to understand her reasoning. "He's a martial-arts expert," she said. "He's very strong. I'm afraid of him."

She told Rothenberg that Rod wanted $250,000 from her to simply vanish. "It was, kind of, to make him go away," he said. "She told me that he was demanding that. She made it sound like an extortion attempt."

No stranger to high-stakes negotiations, Rothenberg didn't hesitate in offering his advice.

"Get lawyers at the table, bring the money and do the deal before he changes his mind or the price goes up," he advised.

Increasingly comfortable with Rothenberg, Shele continued to open up. She explained that Rod lived across the hall and had bullied her into cosigning his lease and paying the deposit. Rothenberg said he was surprised by the gush of deeply personal information.

She told him that, in spite of a protective order against Rod, she gave him a set of keys to her apartment—even after changing the locks.

"Why on earth would you give him a key if you have a protective order?" he asked her.

"It's complicated," Shele replied.

Hoping to lighten the evening's tenor, Rothenberg mentioned that he would be attending the governor's State of the State address in Albany, an esteemed annual gathering of New York's rich and influential. There would be a glittering party afterward.

"If I'm available, can I come along?" she asked.

"Sure," he answered. "I'll get you a ticket."

The uplift was fleeting. As had happened on their first date, Shele nervously and repeatedly monitored her watch and fumbled with her BlackBerry. She had to return home before 8 P.M. in order to avoid a confrontation with Rod. While most couples were being seated for dinner, Rothenberg and Shele were concluding theirs.

He drove her home. "She couldn't even wait for me to go around and open the door for her," he recalled. "She was in a big hurry."

But despite their jarring dates, Rothenberg was enthralled with Shele. When untethered to Rod, their conversations were brisk and engaging. They shared a passion for finance and enjoyed exchanging observations and insights about the field.

Eager to secure a third date, Rothenberg emailed Shele in early January to tell her that they were all set with tickets for the event in Albany and that he couldn't wait to make the trip together.

He kept refreshing his email account, hoping to see an excited confirmation from her. It never came. A second email also went unanswered. His concern brewing, Rothenberg called her cell phone. It went straight to voicemail. Finally, he dialed her office. A receptionist told Rothenberg that she was not in.

"Can you ask her to get back to me?" he asked.

"No," came the reply. "Because she's dead."

CHAPTER ELEVEN

Endgame

The day after Christmas, Shele headed to Sabbath services at the Lincoln Square Synagogue in Manhattan with the children. The city's normally busy streets were frigid and unusually desolate. Outside the synagogue, Shele spotted Jonathan Herlands, a real-estate and trust lawyer, whom she knew in passing. As Anna and Myles played on the steps nearby, she approached him with an abrupt question. "I understand you're an estate attorney," she said, with a note of urgency. "I need to change my will. I want to make sure Rod doesn't get any part of the estate."

Herlands, who knew of the couple's divorce, was nonetheless taken aback by the inquiry, especially on the Sabbath. The discussion of business matters is strictly forbidden, and Shele's breach of Jewish practice spoke to her cresting anxiety.

He politely told her to contact him during the week and brought the discussion to a hasty close. Shele relayed her email address and requested that he reach out to her as soon as possible. Herlands sent her a message the next day at scovlin@gmail.com, but Shele declined to retain him after he said that her case was unusually complex and time-consuming. She texted another friend, "I need trust/estate attorney asap."

In 2001, Shele had established the Shele D. Covlin Trust. She named her brother Philip as trustee and her husband and children as equal-share beneficiaries. That same year she took out a $1 million life-insurance policy with American General Life Insurance and a $1 million policy with Hartford Life Insurance and designated the trust as beneficiary. In 2004, she drafted her will and named Philip as executor and Rod as beneficiary and guardian of their children. On January 29, 2009, Shele had acquired a new life-insurance policy with Aetna through her employer, UBS Financial Services, for $1,625,000, which also named Rod as beneficiary. Without his knowledge, she later changed the beneficiary of the UBS policy from Rod to the kids. Shele also had $1.6 million in assets. All told, she was worth more than $5 million in the event of her death, and she wanted to ensure that Rod wouldn't receive a penny.

On December 30, Shele arranged to have her longtime hairdresser, Adam Aminov, come to her apartment at 8 A.M. to cut her son's hair and refresh her own. Anna had her hair blown out while Shele had a keratin straightening treatment.

Rose arrived at the apartment at 8:45 A.M. to take the children to school. Coiffed and chatty, Shele stopped to banter a bit with a longtime building staffer before heading off for work. She confided in the employee—who was familiar with Rod's antics—that she planned to dislodge him from her will in the next day or two. With that, she departed. Rose returned to the Dorchester with the children at 4:38 P.M.— more than half an hour late for the scheduled start of Rod's 4 P.M. visitation.

Rod's father was supposed to supervise but didn't arrive

until 5 P.M. Unwilling to leave the children with their dad without the court-mandated monitor, Rose was forced to sit in the studio apartment with Rod and the children in icy silence until Dave's arrival.

As the relieved nanny got up to leave, Rod asked her a question. "Do you know when Shele is going to be home?"

"She'll be home by 9 P.M.," she replied. Rose was actually scheduled to babysit Anna and Myles after Rod dropped them back off at Shele's apartment until 10 P.M., but Rose inched up the time so Rod wouldn't chafe at his wife being out late.

Rod had another question before Rose stepped out. "Are you going to sleep over?" he asked.

She found the question odd. It had been years since she had stayed the night. "No," she replied, and left.

Meanwhile, Shele decided to drop by the Friars Club, her preferred after-work haven, a little after 7 P.M. The private venue in an English Renaissance mansion on East 55th Street at Fifth Avenue is famous for its celebrity roasts and notable members, including Jerry Seinfeld and Whoopi Goldberg. During its heyday, icons from Frank Sinatra to Liza Minnelli were mainstays at the restaurant's bar. Shele wasn't a member of the exclusive club but had enough connections to secure regular invitations. Rod, on the other hand, did not. It had long been a point of envy and contention in their relationship. He also complained to his parents that Shele's attendance at the club increased from once to several times a week at the expense of their children.

Shele spotted a friend, Melissa Fields, and the two began chatting. Shele quickly guided the topic to her marital upheaval and told Fields that she had a meeting with an estate attorney the next morning. Shele, Fields recalled, was agitated, and repeated her discomfort with Rod's presence in her will. Fields was the second person she told about her intention that day. Fixated on the task, she was unable to keep it a secret.

As always, Shele's eyes kept darting to her watch and phone. She had forgotten that she had asked Rose to stay late and thought she had to be home by 8 P.M. Shele urgently hailed a cab and rushed home, stepping inside the service entrance to her building with just nine minutes to spare. When she opened the door to her apartment, Rose looked surprised. The nanny reminded her that she was supposed to watch the children until 10 P.M. so Shele could stay out.

"Oh my gosh, I forgot all about it," Shele said breathlessly.

The sitter encouraged her to head back to the club.

"No, Rose, now that I'm here, there is no way I'm going to leave," Shele said.

Their visitation complete across the hall, Anna and Myles cheerfully bounded into the apartment. "Do you want anything to eat?" Shele asked her kids. Myles said he was hungry and Shele gave them sliced apples and biscuits. She walked over to Anna and embraced her, congratulating her for a school achievement. After lingering for a few minutes to chat, Rose left the apartment at 8:11 P.M.

They would never see each other again.

At 9:31 P.M., Shele turned on her laptop and typed a Google search for "long division" to help Anna with homework. Less than an hour later, she logged on to her Jdate profile. After that, all electronic activity ceased on her devices, including her phone.

Rod, meanwhile, had reattached himself to his computer screen once the kids returned to their mother's. He was constantly logged in to Facebook, monitoring his female prospects. There was always a backgammon contest in progress, along with the occasional Castle Age adventure. Sometimes he would juggle all three of his cyber obsessions at once.

Rod could immerse himself in this pixelated playpen for hours and hours at a time, only winding down as birds began to chirp outside. This night, however, was different. The activity paused at 1:03 A.M. for more than three hours.

Building surveillance showed Rod walking out the front door of the Dorchester Towers at 4:13 A.M. Before exiting, he asked the 24-hour concierge if he wanted anything from the local all-night market.

"A Snickers," the man said. Rod purchased two bottles of Pepsi and the candy bar. He walked back in at 4:24 A.M., handed the doorman his snack and went up the elevator back to his apartment. He would reemerge at 5:02 A.M., this time exiting the building through a back door. He headed to a convenience store to buy two bottles of seltzer and reentered through the front door at 5:07 A.M. Once upstairs, he went back online for nearly an hour. He emailed the landlord about minor repairs and sent messages to some friends about an upcoming tournament. On Facebook, he messaged a girlfriend about a Castle Age tactic that called for building an army of monsters.

At 7:04 A.M., Anna called Rod's cell phone from apartment 515's landline and screamed, "Something is wrong with Mommy!"

Rod said he bolted across the hall and commanded his daughter to open the locked door. Once inside, he said he raced to the master bathroom and lifted Shele's dripping body out of the water. He told Anna to use the apartment's intercom to call down to the building's lobby. Doorman Louis Melendez answered.

"An ambulance is coming for Mommy," Anna stammered. "She got hurt."

Melendez said he would direct emergency workers straight upstairs.

With Shele still motionless at his feet, Rod's first phone call was a decidedly curious one. At 7:12 A.M., phone records show that he dialed the pager of his divorce attorney, Luis Penichet. The call lasted only six seconds, and it's unclear if it connected. Two minutes later, Rod called 911. An operator guided him through basic CPR while a dispatcher sent first responders to the address.

Officers Joseph Pagano and William Irwin were working the midnight shift for the 20th Precinct and were on a routine patrol in Manhattan when the assignment crackled over their radio at 7:15 A.M.

The call was categorized as a 1056, police code for someone in need of urgent CPR. Pagano told his dispatcher that he and his partner would take the assignment and they sped to the Dorchester with lights flashing and sirens blaring.

Firefighters and emergency medical workers were the first to enter the front door, arriving at roughly 7:19 A.M. NYPD officers Sean Noce, James O'Connor, Irwin and Pagano followed them soon after. Noce and O'Connor were considered the backup unit that morning and left the scene about half an hour later, leaving Pagano and Irwin to handle the call.

Rod and Anna were seated on the living-room sofa, sniffling and stupefied. Irwin poked his head into the harshly lit bathroom and saw Shele splayed on the tiled floor, stiffened with rigor mortis and partially shrouded by a blanket. The tub was still filled with bright red bathwater and a plastic training potty bobbed atop it.

Irwin quickly scanned the room and saw that a cabinet above the bathtub faucet had been partially ripped from its upper hinges. It dangled precariously.

"What's the time of death?" Pagano asked an EMS worker in his police monotone.

"7:25 A.M.," came the reply.

With that declaration, FDNY and EMS personnel, no longer needed, left the scene.

The officer cursorily assessed Rod's appearance. He was wearing a spotless white T-shirt and dark sweatpants.

"What happened?" Irwin asked delicately.

Rod drew a deep breath before speaking.

"My daughter came and got me from my apartment across the hall," he began, slightly altering his initial narrative that Anna had called him. "She told me, 'Mommy isn't moving.'"

Rod said he rushed to the bathroom, pulled Shele from the tub and covered her with a blanket. He said he knew she was dead before calling 911 and administering CPR.

Irwin recalled Rod's eyes flitting about the room as he spoke. His answers were clipped and cautious. "[He] would only answer very shortly each question and just would face the floor," he said.

The officers classified the call as a DOA, meaning dead on arrival. That designation required a series of notifications to their superiors and other officials. They called their supervisor, Sergeant Mary O'Donnell, at 7:55 A.M. Next, they dialed the medical examiner's office to convey a brief summary of their findings.

The officers quietly made their calls in the living room with Rod and Anna sitting nearby. Irwin attempted to ease the suffocating gloom with some gentle banter. It turned out that both he and Rod had grown up in suburban Westchester. Rod was raised in New Rochelle, and Irwin knew the town well.

Irwin encouraged the father and daughter to stay strong. Having done his best to soothe them, he warned Rod that there would be several more rounds of inquiry from detectives and other officials.

"I know it's hard," Irwin told him. "I apologize. It is going to be verbatim over and over again."

O'Donnell and Officer Yadelin Sanchez arrived at the apartment after 8 A.M. and were briefed by Irwin and Pagano. Rod then walked O'Donnell and Sanchez to the bathroom, where Shele's body still lay, and repeated his narrative. As they turned back down the long hallway toward the living room, Rod introduced his theory to them.

"I don't know what happened," he said, his voice breaking. "She probably just tried to, you know, grab the cabinet, and then the cabinet broke and she just fell and probably hit her head."

Rod was trembling with emotion and the two female officers offered some comforting words. He suddenly turned to O'Donnell and hugged her.

"He kept saying, 'I can't believe this is happening. I can't believe this is happening,'" Sanchez later recalled. But the veteran cop had seen all manner of crime-scene theatrics in her day. "He was acting like he was crying, but I didn't see no tearing," she said.

The officers escorted Myles, who had awoken earlier, and his sister to Rod's apartment. Rod remained in Shele's living room. Rose arrived shortly after 8 A.M. with her grandson in tow to report for her morning duties.

After hearing the news, Rose collapsed, shrieking. Police helped to gather her from the floor. Once she had composed herself, the nanny immediately called Eve.

"There's been an accident. Can you please come?" she told Shele's sister. "And call your brothers."

"Rose, what do you mean?" Eve asked.

"There's been an accident. Shele fell in the tub."

"Rose, you've got to call an ambulance," Eve urged.

"No, Eve, please just call your brothers and come here," Rose said. "The police are here."

That final detail turned Eve's stomach. "Rose, is Shele alive?" she asked.

There was a long pause.

"No," Rose replied.

Eve dropped the mug of coffee she was holding onto her dining-room table and it shattered.

"Rose, just tell me, did he have anything to do with it?" Rose said no.

"He's right in front of you, isn't he?" Eve asked.

"Yes," she replied.

Barely functional from the shock, Eve called her brothers and husband in quick succession and told them to head to Shele's apartment. Marc worked in a building directly across from Fred Danishefsky and could see into his office window. Fred was at his desk when Marc received Eve's call. When he hung up the phone, he could see that Fred was already gone.

As Marc arrived that morning, he was stunned to find Rod sitting on Shele's sofa. "In my mind, what's Rod doing in Shele's apartment?" he later said.

Rod looked up at Marc. He was the only member of Shele's family whom Rod was passably close to. "This is the brother-in-law that used to sit and shoot the breeze with me at all these different family functions, and he had no problem telling me some of the most confidential issues, but he didn't tell me what happened to Shele," Marc recalled. "He looked up at me. He put his head down, his eyes lowered, he looked down at the ground and never engaged me again the entire day."

Eve arrived at the apartment after Marc and her brothers. Her husband met her in the hallway as she walked toward the door, her face an ashen mask. Marc gripped her in an extended hug, his wife's heart thudding against his own.

Police asked the family to leave the apartment and they

gathered in the hallway outside. At roughly 9 A.M., Detective Carl Roadarmel arrived on the scene. Wearing a rumpled suit and tie, the nearly 30-year NYPD veteran was partnered that day with Detective James Martin. The junior officers briefed the detectives before they entered the bathroom.

Roadarmel stoically observed the form beneath him, lifting the sheet that covered Shele's face. Roughly half an hour after his arrival, he asked an officer to summon Rod from his apartment across the hall and asked him what had happened. Rod repeated his version of events before returning to his studio.

The detective then told Eve, who was in the hallway, that he wanted to talk to Anna. Eve shepherded the young girl into Shele's living room. Roadarmel gingerly asked the little girl what she had seen. As she organized her thoughts, Rod suddenly burst through the door.

"You're not going to interview my daughter!" he bellowed.

Roadarmel assured him that it was standard police procedure.

But rather than concede, Rod grew louder. Not wanting to further distress Anna, the detective asked him to step into the hallway.

"We need to calm down," he told Rod, explaining that witnesses are interviewed separately so that their accounts don't influence each other. Hoping to salve Rod's concern, he suggested that Dave Covlin, who had since arrived at the apartment, supervise the interview. Rod reluctantly agreed.

Roadarmel pulled Dave and Anna aside in the hallway and briefly spoke with the 9-year-old, whose narrative mirrored her father's. In a departure from typical police practice, Roadarmel did not take any notes on his interviews that day. But Martin, his partner, jotted down some general observations.

"I did not observe any bruises or marks to the decedent's

upper body," he wrote. "I did observe a small bruise to the decedent's right hand. I observed that the bathtub was about three quarters full with water. I did observe that the left door of the cabinet against the wall over the tub was hanging on one hinge. At this time I observed that the apartment was in good order and that there were no signs of foul play."

In addition to Roadarmel and Martin, another detective, Robert Mooney of the Manhattan North Homicide Squad, had arrived at the scene around 11:30 A.M. Mooney's job was to vet any unnatural death above 59th Street. Roadarmel briefed him on the investigation and indicated that Shele's death appeared to be an accident.

Mooney canvassed the apartment before entering the bathroom, where he kneeled down beside Shele's body and peered closely at her face. He then asked to speak to Rod and Anna and was directed to the studio apartment across the hall. Rod led his daughter to the sofa, where he sat on one side of her with Dave on the other. The detective pulled up a chair in front of them and asked Anna what happened.

"Anna states that last night she and her three-year-old brother, Myles, had been at their father's apartment across the hall from their mother's apartment where they live until about 8 P.M.," Mooney wrote in his notes. "After returning to their mother's apartment she and her brother were hungry. They both ate apples and some tea biscuits and then got ready for bed. Both children got into their mother's bed and Anna read a story to Myles. The children then began to go to sleep. Anna said that while she and her brother were going to sleep she heard her mother in the bathroom running the water into the tub for a bath. She was sure, she said, because when the tub is filling the water sounds different from when the shower is running.

"While their mother is in the tub the children go to sleep. Both children wake up at about 2 or 3 in the morning and realized that their mom was not in bed with them. They both get out of bed and Anna goes to the bathroom door and looks in. She sees her mother still in the tub and her mom is sort of kneeling but her face is in the water. Anna thought that her mother was washing her hair and pushed her brother back into bed. The children both get back into bed and go back to sleep.

"Anna woke up at approximately 7:00 A.M. Again she realizes that her mother is not in bed with her and her brother. She gets up and goes to the bathroom door and looks in. She sees that her mother is still in the bathtub and her face is still underwater. She gets very afraid realizing that something is wrong with her mother and so she got to the phone and calls her father who lives across the hall. Her father instructs her to go and open the front door to the apartment and let him in. Anna does this. Her father goes to the bathroom and sees Shele and then ushers the kids into Anna's room instructing them to stay there. He then called the police.

"In response to questions Anna stated that she did not hear any loud noises coming from anywhere in the apartment during the night. She added that both she and her brother are very sound sleepers."

After questioning Anna, Mooney said he wanted to speak to Rod alone. "Just tell me what happened," he said.

By now, morning had bled into afternoon. It was roughly 12:30 P.M. For the fifth time, Rod was compelled to repeat his story.

Completing his rounds, Mooney then spoke to Rose and Shele's family members for additional background.

He was soon joined inside the apartment by Detective William Brown from the NYPD's Forensic Investigations Division. Brown's task was to photograph the scene and collect evidence.

Brown first trained his lens on the exterior of the apartment, snapping shots of the locks, doorjamb and sterling-silver Jewish mezuzah. Orthodox Jews attach the narrow box, at a slight angle, to the right top third of all doorways—except for bathrooms and closets. The box contains a rolled-up parchment on which is printed a Jewish prayer called the *"Shema."* Recited three times a day by observant Jews, the holy verses affirm that there is only one God, who must be shown the highest measure of devotion.

The placement of the mezuzah—a common sight throughout New York City—formally sanctifies a Jewish home and protects those who reside within it.

Brown's photos of the entry show no signs of damage to the locks or door, which opened into a small foyer with a closet to the left and a galley kitchen on the right. The foyer led into a spacious living room with a dining-room table at the far end and a beige sofa against the wall to the right. The room was packed with children's toys, strollers and books.

The divisive wedding painting that Rod's parents had bought for the couple hung above the sofa.

Just beyond the kitchen, but running parallel to it, was a long hallway. The first door on the right led to the kids' bathroom and the second door on the same side opened to Myles' room. Anna's room, painted bright pink, was directly across the hall. The images depict a to-do list she tacked to the wall. "Play with Myles," she had written.

The hallway ended at Shele's master-bedroom door. Her bed and furniture were to the left of the space and her *en suite* bathroom to the right, and beyond that a walk-in closet. Perhaps reflecting her emotional state, the room appeared disorderly and simply furnished, hosting a rocking chair, a small nightstand and the bed. The mattress sat atop an exposed box spring on a basic metal stand. A book titled "How to Talk So Kids Will Listen & Listen So Kids Will Talk" rested on the cluttered nightstand.

Brown's photos of the master bathroom showed a glass-enclosed shower to the left and a pedestal sink just beyond it. The toilet was at the right and Shele's deep soaking tub was on the bathroom's far wall straight ahead. On the right side of the tub, above the spout, was a wall of cabinets.

In one photo, Shele was sprawled out in front of the tub, her head near the base of the toilet to the right and her feet at the base of the pedestal sink to the left. A bunched-up beige comforter, tangled with a pink blanket, partially covered her legs and pelvic area. Her eyes were closed and several bright red marks that looked like deep scratches covered the bottom half of her face. On her upper left lip was a deep red contusion. Brown also snapped photos of bruises on her elbow and hands. He placed Shele's hands in brown paper bags to preserve any evidence that might be under her fingernails.

Brown did not dust for fingerprints or collect any evidence from the scene. He planned to return the next day after an autopsy was performed—but he never got the call.

"It seemed suspicious," Brown later said. "Given the injuries to the victim's face, hands and elbow, to me it appeared to be more than just a slip and fall."

Brown included his photos in his official report but did not mention or highlight Shele's obvious injuries in the written paperwork. At no point that day were Eve and Marc ever told that Shele had scratches on her face or bruises. Roadarmel also did not note the injuries in his reports, and it wasn't clear if he had even noticed them.

The medical examiner's investigator, Tami Natale, arrived at the scene at about 3:30 P.M. She catalogued the prescriptions in Shele's medicine cabinet, including Vicodin. She also had prescriptions, from as far back as 2004, for phentermine, a weight-loss drug, diazepam, used to treat anxiety, and Dilaudid, a narcotic painkiller.

Fred Danishefsky officially identified Shele and signed an autopsy waiver at 4:55 P.M. without discussing the decision with the rest of his family. In the paperwork, the investigator wrote, "Objection to autopsy—Jewish including toxicology." Shele was then put in a white body bag and transported to the Office of Chief Medical Examiner.

CHAPTER TWELVE

Holy Men

The interaction at the scene between the Karstaedts and Covlins, both still in the throes of shock, was deeply strained.

Eve and Marc quickly sensed that the Covlins had drawn familial battle lines and sought to keep Myles and Anna in their territory. "It was really intense, instantly," Eve recalled. "I didn't feel comfortable talking to Anna. I certainly didn't feel comfortable talking to Rod."

When Eve first arrived, she said to Anna, "Sweetheart, are you okay? Is everything okay?"

"I'm fine," Anna had replied tersely.

Myles was oblivious, ignorant of the catastrophe that had befallen him and his sister. He frolicked happily with Dave in Rod's apartment, where Shele's siblings had briefly joined them.

Myles became hungry and started pulling on Rose's arm. Hoping to comfort him, Marc began to gently rub his back and offered to read to him. He selected a book on trucks. Marc knew it well, as Eve had given it to Shele once their own son outgrew it.

But the oppressive discomfort in Rod's crowded studio soon became unbearable. Shele's faction sought relief out in the hallway. The Covlins, Eve recalled, wouldn't let the kids out of their sight—particularly Anna. "[Rod] was holding on to her," Marc said. "They were lying on his bed together. They were whispering."

Rod then suggested that Shele's body be hurriedly flown to Israel for burial. The request struck Eve and Marc as supremely odd, as Shele had never mentioned this desire. Her family had assumed that she wanted to be buried at Mount Pleasant Cemetery in Hawthorne, New York, alongside the twins she had lost.

But there was an even more pressing question that night. With their mother suddenly removed from their lives, where were the children going to go?

The police knew that there was an order of protection against Rod and that Myles and Anna couldn't be left with him. Eve and Marc were their closest relatives, and Shele had told them to care for the children if anything ever happened to her.

The Karstaedts discussed the situation with the police, who quickly agreed. "We both lived in Manhattan, our children [went] to the same school," Marc said. "They knew that Eve was the closest person on this earth to Shele. It made perfect sense."

But despite what seemed like an obvious choice, the Covlins—especially Rod—loudly protested.

Eager for an accord, Marc floated several possible solutions. He proposed letting the kids stay with Rod in the studio as long as he remained with them as a court-mandated supervisor. But Rod rejected the idea. Marc then suggested that Rod and the kids stay with them in their apartment. "If he [wanted] to stay in our apartment, as much as we would hate it, we would supervise," Marc said. "We were trying to be extraordinarily accommodating."

But the Covlins flatly rejected these remedies and Dave

started yelling at Eve. "It's not right that the children are going to you! They should come to us!"

A pair of young social workers from Child Protective Services unexpectedly showed up at 4:40 P.M. to assess the situation. A police lieutenant from the 20th Precinct had called CPS as a matter of protocol. "We didn't even see them come in," Marc said. "They go into Rod's apartment and they're having a private meeting with Rod, his parents, Anna and Myles."

One of the social workers turned to Anna and asked, "So where do you want to go?"

"I want to stay with my daddy," she said.

"Well, you can't stay with your dad because there's an order of protection, so who would be your second choice?" asked the worker.

"I want to go to my grandparents," she said.

Marc only noticed the social workers as they exited the apartment. "Wait a second, what's going on?" he asked.

"Well, the children are going to go to their grandparents," the woman told him.

He was staggered. "Why?" he asked. "Who arranged this?"

The worker curtly told him to take up the issue in family court.

Powerless to challenge the ruling, Marc suspected that the senior Covlins had coached Anna. "The grandparents certainly loved the children, but it wouldn't have been their choice," Marc said. "We were the closest to them."

Overcome with grief, Eve and Marc were at a loss. They had never dealt with CPS before and were ignorant of its byzantine processes. "We just figured it was for the weekend. It was just going to be a weekend," Eve said. "Our heads were spinning."

The couple later realized that they should have been far

more vocal in opposing the initial decision to place the kids with Rod's parents. They would look back on it as a critical mistake with long-term consequences.

That Monday, Eve and Marc looked on as a judge declined to adjust the temporary custody arrangement. The judge argued that she did not want to create any more upheaval for Anna and Myles. Marc said that Rod was already familiar with CPS because of his child-abuse accusations against Shele and understood how the organization functioned.

"He played us like a Stradivarius," Marc said.

On New Year's Day, 2010, Senior Medical Examiner Jonathan Hayes received Shele's body at the agency's Manhattan facility in Kips Bay. Hayes had performed more than 4,000 autopsies and supervised another 20,000, making him one of the office's keenest appraisers of human death.

Shrouded in a white body bag, Shele was wheeled into the morgue's basement autopsy room, where eight examination tables sat side by side. Hayes was already aware that her family had lodged a religious objection to the procedure. Having spent most of his career in New York City, he was familiar with a wide array of cultural attitudes toward autopsies and knew that observant Jews often balked at them.

Unless medical examiners suspect foul play or a larger public-health crisis, such as a contagious disease, they are required to honor religious objections. Autopsy opponents did not always exercise such influence over the process. In 1983, former New York state politician Sheldon Silver introduced a new law that allowed families to block autopsies on religious grounds, still informally known as the Silver Law. If medical examiners seek to overrule a religious objection, the law requires them to put down the scalpel until the family has adequate time to challenge the action in civil court.

The legislation was put to the test just two years after its passage. In 1985, the family of a New York Orthodox Jewish man who died after falling from a building sued the prestigious Riverside Memorial Chapel funeral home for sending his body to the medical examiner for an autopsy without their permission. The outraged family also named city officials as defendants for allowing the procedure. After learning that the autopsy was underway, the man's relatives had frantically called local rabbis to have them demand that it cease. But it was too late. The dead man's son-in-law went to identify his body at the Office of Chief Medical Examiner and said it had been mutilated.

After a nearly decade-long legal war, a jury awarded the decedent's daughter, Susan Liberman, $1,350,000 in punitive damages. The law established a clear precedent for those objecting to autopsies.

Police and investigators had provided Hayes with scant details of Shele's death. He knew only that she was initially found in her bathtub by her child and was later removed from the water by her estranged husband. The police indicated that it was likely an accident.

Hayes unzipped the bag and gazed down at Shele's face. "I was struck by injuries she had on her face. She had scratches on her face, which I considered suspicious," Hayes recalled. "I immediately said, 'We need an autopsy.'" The narrative he had received from the police never mentioned the alarming red marks.

Hayes, however, did not have the authority to overrule the autopsy waiver. That level of executive decision-making was reserved for Chief Medical Examiner Charles Hirsch. Hayes called his superior at his home in New Jersey.

"I told him the story that had been given to me," Hayes recalled. "I told him I had opened the bag and examined her initially and she had some scratches on her face that we found to be really worrying."

But Hirsch declined to authorize the autopsy, arguing that foul play was unlikely because there were no other people present in the apartment save for Shele's kids. He also noted the lack of police suspicion.

Convinced that Shele's death was far from benign, Hayes was unwilling to let the matter go. He called Shele's father, Joel, at Eve and Marc's apartment. They were all unaware that Fred had hastily waived an autopsy and had coincidentally been discussing the matter when the phone rang.

"I spoke to her father and this was agonizing for him. He had just lost his daughter," Hayes recalled.

Troubled by the nature of Shele's death, Eve and Marc pushed for the procedure. Joel, on the other hand, was torn.

Disturbing the body after death, the Jewish faith maintains, is a needless desecration to be avoided in all but the most extreme circumstances. Orderly transit to the afterlife, according to Jewish law, requires the immersion of the entire body underground without any missing organs or bodily fluids. One's physical form belongs not to himself or to relatives, but to God. Tampering with his divine property is considered a grave religious violation.

In the hours after Shele's death, her dazed brother Fred had offhandedly signed the autopsy waiver. But the official next of kin was actually Shele's father, not her brother, and it was ultimately his decision. Joel, as a rabbi, was well aware of his faith's dictates. But he also knew that declining an autopsy would ensure that Shele's death would be permanently classified as nothing more than a slip and fall, shielding Rod indefinitely. He was haunted by the possibility that his former son-in-law had played a role in his daughter's premature death. On the other hand, the police had given them no indication they suspected foul play.

He bluntly asked Hayes if he thought Shele's death was an accident. While he wanted to provide Joel clarity, Hayes said that only an autopsy could settle the question. The examiner, Marc recalled, did not mention the scratches on Shele's face.

With his daughter's body shelved in the morgue, Joel sought counsel from Rabbi David Cohen, a prominent Brooklyn authority on Jewish law. Seated at the head of Eve and Marc's dining table with his daughter and son-in-law at his side, he put the call on speaker.

Joel outlined his skepticism of the NYPD's assessment. He described Rod's mistreatment of his daughter and her fear that he would one day kill her.

Despite his own misgivings about autopsies, Cohen was ultimately moved by Joel's despair and found his concerns credible. "Go ahead with the autopsy that her soul is crying out for," he said.

The Danishefskys relayed the rabbi's blessing to Hayes, who had been awaiting their call.

Hayes photographed Shele's entire body, including the scratches on her face and the bruising on her hands and arm. He noted a well-healed surgical scar extending from Shele's right ear to her left ear above the thyroid area of the neck—possibly from a recent cosmetic procedure. Hayes documented Shele's childhood scar, calling it "a broad band of rippling, irregular scarring suggestive of an old burn injury." He also logged residual evidence of a breast augmentation.

Under the heading "Evidence of Injury," Hayes noted the scratches and described them as varied and as long as half an inch. The marks were under her eyes and on her cheeks and nose. He also listed the contusion on her left upper lip and bruises on her right arm, elbow and hand.

Hayes was becoming increasingly skeptical of the police account. He arrayed his instruments and prepared to cut.

Across town, the Karstaedts' home phone chimed once again. In a frantic and harried voice, the caller identified himself as Rabbi Meyer Weill of an organization called Misaskim.

Founded in Brooklyn in 2004 by members of a volunteer Jewish ambulance corps, Misaskim, Hebrew for "attendants," began as a 24-hour hotline for bereaved Jews and gradually expanded its reach and range of services. By 2009, the organization had come to play an essential role for New York City's large Orthodox Jewish population.

The group is unapologetic in its staunch opposition to autopsies and cremations on religious grounds. On its website, Misaskim features a running counter of the number of autopsies it has prevented.

To ensure proper burial, Jewish deaths are quickly reported to synagogues. Temples often work with Misaskim to assist families with all phases of grieving and funeral arrangements. The day after Shele's death, the Lincoln Square Synagogue rabbi had contacted Weill to report her passing. Weill's immediate priority was to collect all bodily fluids from her bathroom—including blood—so they could be buried with Shele in accordance with Jewish law. Misaskim had obtained permission from the local NYPD precinct handling the case to enter the apartment.

In New York City, Orthodox Jewish communities cultivate close relationships with their local precincts, and there often exists an elevated level of cooperation with law enforcement. Without any permission from Shele's family, Weill was given total access to the crime scene on January 1, 2010. An officer stationed outside to secure the scene was told that Weill was en route and should be allowed entry.

"I'm here to clean up the bathroom," Weill told the officer, who waved him in. Despite being a civilian, he was exempt from the standard restrictions of a police-secured crime scene and traipsed through the apartment unsupervised.

He proceeded to clean the bathtub, which had already been drained of its bloodied contents.

Weill spent about 45 minutes in the apartment, scouring it for Shele's remains. His mission complete, he then spoke to a detective at the precinct who told him that there was no forced entry and that Shele's death was likely an accident.

Weill had then called the Danishefskys to see if they needed any assistance, and the family revealed their plan to proceed with an autopsy.

"You're making the biggest mistake," he told Joel, abruptly renewing the old man's tortured dilemma.

Weill argued that police had assured him that there were no grounds for suspicion. "They said it was an accident. You can't, you can't, under Jewish law, do this," he pleaded. He scolded Joel for misrepresenting the situation to Cohen and insisted on driving directly to Eve and Marc's home.

With the family gathered at the dining-room table, Weill made his case and leaned on Jewish law to do so. "Let's get Rabbi Cohen on the phone," he suggested. Again, Cohen picked up and the call was put on speaker.

"It was an accident," Weill insisted. "The police say it was an accident. The medical examiner says it was an accident."

Asserting that he had personally spoken to detectives, Weill said all relevant authorities concluded that Shele had—as Rod theorized—simply slipped and fallen.

The family would learn later that Weill had gathered all of his information secondhand, not from detectives on the scene.

Convinced by Weill's arguments, Cohen revoked his permission for an autopsy.

Robbed of religious cover, the Danishefskys were now

obligated to halt the procedure. Joel placed a begrudging call to the ME's office and told an administrator to call off the autopsy. The staffer walked over to Hayes, who had already donned gloves and a mask and was hovering over Shele with scalpel in hand.

"I was just about to make my first incision," Hayes recalled.

"The family changed their mind," the staffer told him. "The family is renewing their objection to an autopsy."

The medical examiner tried in vain to persuade them otherwise, but Joel held firm.

It was a decision they would later regret.

Thwarted by Weill's 11th-hour intervention, Hayes made another call to chief ME Hirsch, urging his boss a second time to overrule the family's objection. "I stressed my concerns," he later recalled. "[My boss] said, 'What are you worried about?' I said, 'I'm worried she may have been killed.'"

Hayes persisted, reminding Hirsch of Shele's wounds and bruises. But his superior again refused to change his position. "We went back and forth several times until he became angry and at that point I caved."

The examiner completed his report, making no mention of his suspicions. Without permission from the family, Hayes was also unable to draw any fluids or fingernail scrapings for toxicology and DNA testing. He listed the cause and manner of death as undetermined.

Unable to delve beneath the surface, Hayes reluctantly zipped up Shele's body bag. The truth of her final moments, it seemed, would be permanently buried along with her.

Shele's corpse was released to the Plaza Jewish Community Chapel on Saturday, January 2, where she was prepared for burial in a ritual known as *taharah,* meaning "purity" in

Hebrew. The process is considered one of the holiest and most vital responsibilities an observant Jew can shoulder because it's a selfless act, which the recipient cannot repay.

A group of congregants called the *chevra kadisha*—an Aramaic phrase meaning "friends of holiness"—volunteer for the service. A series of rituals are carried out to purify the body and to help the soul detach from its earthly longings for transition to the next realm. The procedures also ensure that the body is thoroughly cleansed and presentable for resurrection, according to some teachings.

Rachel Herlands, who heads Lincoln Square Synagogue's *chevra kadisha* gathered several women to perform the somber task. The volunteers placed Shele's body on a special table reserved for washing the dead and covered her with a sheet. "We basically treat them as we would treat them if they were alive," Herlands said.

First, they recited a series of prayers asking for compassion and mercy for Shele's soul. The women gently washed her entire body, section by section, with warm water. To preserve her modesty, she remained covered in the sheet with each area exposed individually for cleaning. One of the volunteers cradled Shele's head during the ritual. The women wiped away the blood that had splattered on her legs and removed the bright red nail polish on her fingers and toes.

They recited Jewish prayers, tending to her as they would to a fragile newborn. "You are all fair, my beloved, and there is no blemish in you," the women whispered in Hebrew, quoting the biblical Song of Songs.

They then slowly poured six gallons of water from her head to her toes in a continuous stream to represent a *mikvah*, a ritual bath used for purification. "Help us prepare this soul to enter the heavenly kingdom and to witness Your Presence," they recited before daubing her body dry with a towel.

Shele's body was then wrapped in simple white shrouds made from linen or muslin known as *tachrichim*.

She was placed in a simple pine casket with a Jewish star emblazoned on the front—the same kind of coffin used for all Orthodox Jews. Soil from Israel is often sprinkled inside.

The group closed with a final prayer: "God, we now ask for assurance from You that this soul will be protected for eternity."

In Jewish tradition, the dead are not left alone until burial. A person known as a *shomer,* which means "watcher" in Hebrew, is tasked with guarding the body. It is a ritual intended to show respect for the deceased.

Shele's funeral was held the next day, January 3, at the Plaza Jewish Community Chapel.

She was buried at the Mount Pleasant Cemetery in Hawthorne, New York, beside the beloved twins she had lost four years prior.

Shele's family then began seven days of mourning, known as sitting *shiva*. In Judaic tradition, only the deceased's immediate family participates. Eve and Marc hosted the ritual in their apartment. The Talmud traces the custom to Genesis when Methuselah, the oldest man in the world, was mourned for seven days prior to the great flood. Later, Joseph observed the same period of official grief for his late father.

The first three days of *shiva* are often marked by periods of weeping and lamentation. Mourners sit on low stools, don torn garments and slippers or socks, refrain from grooming and cover their mirrors. They are not allowed to partake in frivolous or pleasurable activities like listening to music or watching movies.

During the final four days of the seven-day period, the mourners begin to accept visits from friends and neighbors while remaining at home.

The Kaddish, the memorial prayer for the departed, is

recited as part of formal prayer services held three times a day inside the *shiva* home. A memorial candle is left burning as a physical expression of a verse from Proverbs, "Man's soul is the Lord's lamp." Next is the stage of *sheloshim,* the 30 days following burial, when the mourner is encouraged to gradually emerge from grief into the outside world.

The night after the burial, Rod and the kids went to the Karstaedts' apartment and sat the first night of *shiva*. It was a tense reunion. The two families had not seen each other since the day of Shele's death. In what the Danishefskys perceived as a severe breach of protocol, Rod never returned with the children, choosing instead to sit *shiva* separately with his own parents.

A year after Shele's death, he ordered a modest headstone that read BELOVED MOTHER AND WIFE SHELE MINNA COVLIN 7-13-1962—12-31-2009. In a break with tradition and against the wishes of her family, Rod did not include her Hebrew name. The rectangular granite marker was embedded into the ground at Mount Pleasant, flush with the earth.

CHAPTER THIRTEEN

Aboveground

The morning after Shele's death, Rod awoke to seemingly limitless opportunities. The bane of his existence—and sole impediment to his dreams—had been permanently silenced. Rod was well aware of Shele's sizable financial reserves and felt positioned to seize them—either directly or through the children.

Rod was also confident that he would gain outright custody of Anna and Myles, with their mother now relegated to pictures and memories. No more courtroom defeats, no more visitation fights, no more financial pressures.

Whatever tears Rod shed the day of Shele's death had dried completely less than 24 hours later. Josh Pohl, his close friend and the best man at his wedding, rushed to Rod's apartment to fete the New Year and his new prospects. Rod had kept him fully abreast of his wars with Shele.

Toasting to his liberation, Rod and his childhood pal drank and puffed on marijuana. Pohl, an attorney, recalled Rod being near giddy that day, as he "laughed [and] joked about what happened."

Pohl offered a callous assessment of Shele's death. "Problem solved," he said simply.

Rod remarked that Anna preferred him to her mother and

that she would quickly recover from the loss. After two hours of merriment, the celebration shifted to Pohl's apartment, where the pair christened a bottle of Maker's Mark bourbon and tippled deep into the early morning.

The tantalizing potential of a $5 million windfall only sweetened Rod's intoxication. Thanks to his surveillance of Shele's communications, he was fully versed in her finances and the treasure chest he would control after securing custody of the kids.

The day of Shele's death, Rod's girlfriend, Debra, sent him a concerned text message: "Everything ok? You've not answered my texts all day and when I went to send you a Facebook message, your Facebook was gone. What's going on?"

Rod called Debra to explain. With little preamble, he impassively told her that his wife had died in an accident.

"I can't even begin to express the depth of my sorrow for you and the children," she responded.

Two days later, Rod invited Debra to play a backgammon game online. In their chat window, Debra broached Shele's passing.

"It's such a bizarre turn of events. Weird karma," Debra said.

Rod responded flippantly. "I guess," he said. "I ascribe it to . . . shit happens." He routinely used ellipses in his emails and text messages as a substitute for a dash.

While the Danishefskys were still sitting *shiva,* Rod was preoccupied with mapping out his newly flush financial future.

In a January 6, 2010, chat with Debra, Rod could barely contain his excitement. "Even if my wife changed her will . . . insurance money (as long as hers didn't lapse . . . fingers crossed) . . . goes into a trust for me," he wrote. "The rest of the money . . . even if she rewrote the will and gave it to my kids I would still under law get 1/2 and that is if she rewrote it. . . . She might have . . . changed the will . . . but still . . . it would mean that I still ended up with 75% of all of the money."

With Shele's death, Rod assumed that he would eventually secure outright custody of the children. "It's a slam dunk . . . as ahead on the game as my wife had been . . . I'm way way farther ahead than that."

The couple had planned to meet in person at an upcoming backgammon tournament, but Rod eventually bowed out. He later explained to Debra that his custody attorney had advised him not to see her or attend any backgammon events—especially out of state. Shele's relatives, he was told, were refusing to concede defeat in the battle over Anna and Myles.

Debra was but one of many women Rod interacted with in the days after Shele's death. On New Year's Day, he reached out to Jeanne Robin, the married swinger from Baltimore with whom he had carried on a sporadic sexual relationship.

"My wife is dead," Rod blurted over the phone.

"Oh my God! What happened?" Robin replied.

"She must have slipped and fallen in the tub," he said. "I had to take her out of the tub and performed CPR. Did you know that when someone drowns, blood and foam come out of their lungs? It was horrible."

Rod gave a brief summary of the prior night's events, telling Robin that the police insisted on questioning his daughter without him present.

Robin said he shouldn't have been surprised because, she told him, "you're a suspect."

Her frankness startled him. "Why would I be a suspect?" he asked obliviously.

"You're in an acrimonious divorce. They always look at the spouse," she said.

"That's ridiculous!" he replied.

Perhaps blinded by visions of his impending wealth, Rod seemed unable to appreciate the suspicions that would soon engulf him.

While he prioritized expanding his pool of paramours after Shele's erasure, Rod was equally focused on reviving his pursuit of board-game stardom.

In a January 9, 2010, email to his circle of backgammon associates, Rod tersely broke the news of his wife's death before cheerfully turning to his upcoming tournament plans.

"Sadly, my wife passed away last Thursday," he wrote. "I fully expect that I will be able to re-devote myself to the USBGF [U.S. Backgammon Federation] starting after this coming week." A month later he registered for a major tournament in the spring.

Along with a group of other enthusiasts, Rod had helped establish the backgammon federation in 2009 to oversee the sport's growth in America and beyond. "The U.S. Backgammon Federation is very much a reality at this point," he wrote after Shele's death. "Things are moving full steam ahead."

Conventional employment, on the other hand, appeared to be of minimal concern. Weeks after Shele's passing, a well-meaning friend emailed him about opportunities at his company. "I wanted to quickly reach out to let you know about the open positions in financial technology where our firm is actively recruiting," the friend wrote.

Rod replied that he was "not actively looking at the moment."

After watching Shele disappear into the earth, the ruptured Danishefsky family returned to the Karstaedts' home. They sat silently in a despairing and disbelieving daze. Joel had been rendered nearly mute by the horror of his daughter's demise. At one point that evening, he asked Marc to speak to him privately in another room.

"I want you to investigate Shele's death to find out what happened," he told his son-in-law. "I'm very worried. I want you to protect Shele's money for the children, and I want you to protect the children from Rod. I'm unable to do it. I'm too distraught."

The Danishefskys—and Joel in particular—had long held Marc in great esteem. While Shele had married a boorish menace, Eve had in fact found the type of man she and her sister had fantasized about as children. Marc exuded loyalty and solidity in all matters—qualities that would soon be put to the test against the equally committed Covlins.

Marc pledged to honor Joel's request that evening. Shele's father conveyed his willingness to bankroll Rod's decimation. In the end, Joel would spend millions and end up nearly penniless. "He was so convinced that she was murdered that he was willing to give up every single dime that he owned," Marc later said. "He was willing to give up everything to ensure that justice was served."

On January 8, the funeral director who handled Shele's burial made a stunning revelation to Marc. He said that he had noticed numerous scratches on her face. Remarkably, a full week after her death, it was the first time the suspicious injuries had been disclosed to her family.

Marc hired a retired NYPD detective turned private investigator, Michael Swain, to look into his sister-in-law's death. He fortified that effort with his own amateur detective work, taking a month off from his job to do so.

"The goal was to gather enough information to assist the NYPD to keep the investigation open and eventually to have the body exhumed to have an autopsy conducted," said Swain.

On January 17, police escorted Marc, Eve, Fred, a family lawyer and Swain to Shele's apartment to retrieve clothes and other items for the children.

"The children left so abruptly," Eve said, and had left many of their belongings behind. Their legal guardian—a children's advocate appointed by the court—met the group to assist them in gathering essentials.

But the family had an additional motive. Police told them that Shele had been seen holding an iPhone as she entered the Dorchester on the night of her death. But detectives never found the phone in her apartment.

As they stood in a knot in front of Shele's door, the escorting officer tried in vain to open the lock for several minutes. "Can anyone else try?" he asked finally.

Eve, Marc and Fred were equally unsuccessful. "We couldn't get it open—we couldn't do it," Eve recalled. "Right at that moment, Rod kind of popped out of his apartment and stuck his head out."

"Oh, you're having trouble?'" he asked the group, after apparently hearing their struggle from inside his studio across the hall. "Can I help?"

"He came out, took the key, put it in the lock and it opened as easy as pie," recalled Eve.

Without a word, Rod returned to his apartment.

Eve wondered how he was able to effortlessly manipulate the troublesome lock when it had been changed in May to keep him out.

Once inside, Marc took photos while Swain recorded a three-minute video.

The family had not been allowed into Shele's room or bathroom in the days after she was discovered. For the first time, Eve and Marc saw the torn cabinet above the tub, the crux of Rod's defense. "It just looked very violent to me, that it was pulled," she said.

The party searched for Shele's iPhone but came up empty.

Stressing the suspicious circumstances around Shele's death, Marc repeatedly implored the NYPD to revive their probe. But detectives insisted they had no probable cause without an autopsy confirming a homicide. "It was clear we were at an impasse," Marc recalled. Hoping to escalate the matter, he had his lawyer write a letter to the Manhattan District Attorney's Office, outlining Shele's case in detail and asking them to take the reins.

After months of frustration and futility, the Danishefskys were finally given reason for hope. The DA's office responded to their letter on January 25 and agreed to examine Shele's death. On February 9, detectives Frank Brennan and Carl Roadarmel returned to the apartment to search for any surveillance equipment hidden in the HVAC vents. Eve and Marc had told authorities that Shele had long suspected her husband of spying on her. The detective unscrewed the vents in each room but found nothing. He conducted another unsuccessful sweep of Shele's apartment in search of her iPhone.

After receiving Marc's compelling letter, the Manhattan DA's office finally obtained a court order to exhume Shele's body for a belated autopsy. They did not need the family's permission. Still, Marc and Joel felt compelled to once again seek a rabbinical blessing. Marc called Rabbi Cohen and updated him on the new details in Shele's case—stressing the telltale wounds on her face. This time, Cohen signed off.

On March 1, 2010, a backhoe crawled across thick snow toward Shele's gravesite, plunged its mechanical claw into the earth and hoisted her casket back into the light. While the top of the pine box—emblazoned with the Star of David—was largely intact, the bottom of the coffin had separated and mud had leached inside. The crumbling casket was placed in a metal shipping container and transported directly to the ME's office.

At 12:15 P.M., Hayes, the medical examiner, began to unwrap the muddied shroud. Although Shele had been underground for nearly two months, deterioration was minimal.

"This was winter," Hayes said. "The body was remarkably well-preserved."

In some areas, layers of her skin had begun to molt, revealing the dermis beneath. The skin on her hands and beneath her hair was detaching. A quarter-inch area of gray mold had erupted on her right cheek.

Hayes first conducted an external examination, documenting the injuries that were still apparent on the outside of her body. He noted that the scratches on her face and the bruises on her wrist and arm had become far less visible, but were still present. Shele's entire body was mottled with purple from lividity, the settling of blood after death. With the heart no longer propelling it, blood collects in the areas of the body nearest to the ground at death, causing the discoloration. Hayes opened her mouth to expose "a large tearing in the lining of the lip and bruising and bleeding into the soft tissue." It looked as though she had bitten her lip.

For the first time, Hayes noticed two pinpoint hemorrhages in her right eye known in medical parlance as petechiae. These were subtle injuries, and Hayes had missed them during his first examination.

While barely visible, the discovery had major implications. Petechiae, the veteran examiner knew, are often caused by pressure applied to the neck, which disrupts the flow of blood to and from the brain.

"When we see petechiae, it's always a red flag for strangulation," Hayes later said. "You can get it from a cough or vomiting, but we always slow down and become very careful when we see it."

In a case of manual strangulation, which applies pressure unevenly to the neck, the whites of a victim's eyes will often turn red from the bursting of capillaries. The constriction of the neck obstructs the return of blood to the heart while allowing arterial blood to flow to the brain, causing a buildup of blood in the capillaries, which then rupture. These petechiae manifest on the whites of the eyes, the inside of the eyelids, on the tongue and inside the mouth.

An external photo of Shele's neck showed a bruise on the left side and some discoloration under the jaw—but her skin was already breaking down, making it difficult for Hayes to determine if these were injuries or byproducts of decomposition.

But as Hayes peeled back the layers of her neck, he made a shocking discovery: a bone sitting under her chin, above the thyroid gland, was completely broken. The horseshoe-shaped hyoid bone sits above the larynx, with the open legs, known as cornu, facing the back of the neck. The right leg of the horseshoe that curves toward the rear of the neck had been snapped like the tip of a small twig.

Hayes removed the hyoid bone and sent it to forensic anthropologist Dr. Bradley Adams for analysis.

Shele appeared to be in otherwise stellar health with no signs of disease. Her toxicology report tested positive for furosemide, a diuretic, which helps eliminate water from the body, and sibutramine, an amphetamine-like diet pill that suppresses the appetite.

Dr. Adams received the hyoid bone on March 5. It was then processed in Tergazyme detergent and warm water for several days to remove the soft tissue.

He arrived at the same conclusion as Hayes, deeming the break a "complete fracture."

Under the heading "Final Diagnosis," Hayes changed the cause of death from undetermined to homicide by neck compression.

Shele had been murdered.

On April 8, the medical examiner notified the DA's office and Shele's family of the momentous finding. Rod learned of the homicide ruling that same day—and knew he had instantly become the prime suspect in a high-profile killing.

The astonishing plot twist lit up city papers, which ran stories under a series of sensational headlines, including "DIGGING UP SECRET SLAY OF EXEC—GAL'S BODY EXHUMED AFTER 'ACCIDENT'" and "SLAIN FINANCIER FEARED HUSBAND."

The DA's office sprang into action. They arranged for the Child Advocacy Center at the children's hospital of NewYork-Presbyterian to interview Anna once again about the night of her mother's death.

On April 13, the New York Post ran another story on the case under the headline "COPS TO BUST 'STRANGLER' IN WIFE SLAY," citing law enforcement sources. The story stated that Anna would be a "key witness in any criminal case because she was in the apartment during the killing and found her mother's body." The New York Daily News ran a similar piece in December 2011, claiming the DA's office would indict Rod for Shele's murder by the following spring.

But both predictions of an imminent arrest would prove vastly premature.

In the wake of the homicide ruling, on April 13, 2010, social worker Nadiuska Vasquez interviewed 9-year-old Anna, who was accompanied by her legal guardian, Jo Ann Douglas. Prosecutors and detectives watched the interview through a one-way mirror.

Anna began to recount December 30, 2009, telling Vasquez that she had attended art, math and independent reading classes at the Manhattan Day School. For lunch, her school served quesadillas, which she said "were disgusting." After lunch, she attended Hebrew class, where she said she "falls asleep with her eyes open." She told the social worker that her favorite subjects were art, computer class and recess.

"Do you know why you're here?" Vasquez finally asked.

"I've already talked to a lot of people," she replied tersely. The social worker asked what was discussed. "You can ask them," she answered.

Vasquez impressed upon Anna the importance of being honest. The little girl told her she knew the difference between a lie and the truth. She described living with the Covlins and said that she slept alone in her aunt's childhood room. She said that her father had occupied the guest room until the week before—presumably when the ME released the results of the autopsy.

"She noted she did not know the reason her father was no longer living with them," Vasquez wrote.

Anna told her that, prior to living with her grandparents, she lived in an apartment in Manhattan but did not feel comfortable discussing the reason she had moved.

"What makes you feel uncomfortable?" Vasquez asked.

"It's just sad," she answered.

Anna repeatedly told the social worker that she did not want to revisit that period—and that she was now being subjected to cruel playground taunts at school.

She insisted that she had already given two detectives a complete and truthful narrative—but later acknowledged that she "forgot" precisely what she had told them. She said the only reason she had spoken to the detectives in the first place was because she "was really scared about what happened."

Although Anna wouldn't discuss the particulars of her mother's death, she was willing to recount their final hours together. She said she last saw her mom alive on December 30, 2009. Rose had picked her up from school and they walked home together. She and Myles went to their father's studio until 8 P.M., then returned to their apartment. "She was sitting in a chair in the living room, waiting for me to come home," Anna told Vasquez.

An hour later, Anna reported, she and her brother climbed into her mother's bed and drifted off.

"She said she did not want to discuss what she witnessed when she woke up," Vasquez noted in the report. Anna acknowledged that she had awoken at 1 A.M. or 2 A.M. or 3 A.M., but again repeated that she "did not want to have a discussion about what she saw."

After finding her mother, she said, she called her dad on his cell phone and unlocked the door to let him in. "Myles was laughing the whole time because he had no idea what was going on," she recalled.

But Anna refused to "discuss what her father did when he entered the apartment."

The social worker concluded that the traumatized child wasn't being forthright. "Throughout the interview, anytime an attempt was made to obtain more details from Anna about the circumstances surrounding her mother's death, her affect became guarded and constricted," Vasquez wrote. She recommended that Anna be referred to a therapist to address her lingering grief and the trauma of finding her mother's body.

Around this time, unbeknownst to Rod, NYPD detectives had flown to North Carolina and knocked on the door of one of his girlfriends, Debra Oles. She promised not to mention their appearance to Rod and voluntarily gave them her old BlackBerry and the GridGammon messages she had exchanged with him the night before his wife was found dead.

It didn't take Debra long to violate the agreement. Avoiding any electronic trail, Debra wrote a letter alerting Rod to the visit and sent it to his parents' home.

Meanwhile, the NYPD obtained a search warrant on May 28 signed by Justice Charles Solomon to reenter Shele's apartment and canvass for clues once again. By then the scene had been thoroughly adulterated by the ersatz rabbi, Rod, family members, officers and first responders. Rod had already moved out of his studio at the Dorchester in April when his lease was up.

On June 2, Detective Roadarmel and his partner, Frank Brennan, returned to the apartment to execute the warrant and made several sinister discoveries. First, they encountered a hardened glue-like substance jamming the front-door lock. Authorities were forced to use a battering ram to gain entry. Inside Myles' room, the vent cover that Brennan had previously removed and replaced to search for surveillance equipment had been tampered with. The metal plate had been removed from the wall and propped against a bookcase. In Shele's bathroom, the vent cover had also been partially detached.

A mezuzah had been wrenched from the doorjamb and disrespectfully tossed to the floor. Roadarmel also found the ripped remnants of an order of protection against Rod. It had been plucked from Shele's nearby purse.

The partially torn cabinet above the bathtub, which had been hanging by one hinge, had been detached completely and placed on the floor on the opposite side of the bathroom. Inside the tub was a green and blue striped makeup bag that had been sitting on the exposed shelf of the cabinet on a pre-vious visit.

But most unsettling was the sudden appearance of Shele's missing iPhone, in her bedroom near the nightstand. The device was on the floor, partially tucked underneath a pair of suede stilettos and plugged into a white charging cable connected to the wall. Eve told investigators she had looked for it in that very spot, knowing that that's where her sister charged it.

CHAPTER FOURTEEN

Solomon's Sword

Shele's slaying set off a legal maelstrom that would rage for more than a decade. With custody of the children and her millions at stake, Shele's death triggered a dizzying series of civil suits that would pit the Danishefskys against the Covlins and bring them both to the precipice of financial ruin.

On January 4, 2010, while the Danishefskys were still sitting *shiva,* Shele's sister-in-law Peggy Danishefsky, as a representative of the family, had attended a critical Administration for Children's Services conference to challenge the placement of the children with the senior Covlins after Shele's death.

At the courthouse at 110 William Street in Lower Manhattan, Peggy was joined by Rod, the children and Rose.

Soon after the parties gathered in court, Rod suddenly announced that he was firing Rose. The kids, who had depended on the loyal caregiver for the entirety of their short lives, looked down glumly as their father severed the bond. Anna had become particularly attached to Rose and had often called her a "second mommy."

It became clear that Rod was bent on securing absolute control over the children. He knew that Rose held an innate distrust of him and had always sided with Shele during their clashes. She had to be excised.

The tenor of the meeting deteriorated still further after Peggy said she intended to challenge the Covlins for custody. As they entered a hearing room, Rod held open a door for Peggy and leaned in close to her ear, his voice tinged with hate.

"They should be sitting *shiva* for you," he snarled. Peggy shuddered.

Despite her petition, it was ruled that Anna and Myles would remain with their paternal grandparents.

Three days later, Philip and Peggy filed for custody in civil court. The Danishefskys were convinced that the insular Covlins were working to alienate Anna and Myles from their maternal relatives. Each day spent under their spell, Shele's family feared, rendered the children ever more remote.

Hoping to bolster their courtroom prospects, the Danishefskys retained powerhouse Manhattan attorney Marilyn Chinitz, who would represent Tom Cruise in his 2012 divorce from Katie Holmes. In a filing to Judge Ellen Gesmer, Chinitz pressed for Philip and Peggy to receive temporary sole custody of Anna and Myles, as well as a continuation of the order of protection barring Rod from contact with the kids beyond supervised visits.

"The children are in the care of unfit custodians who are a threat to the safety and well-being of the children," Chinitz argued. She said Anna and Myles were being purposefully isolated and denied the psychiatric help that they desperately needed in the wake of their mother's death.

Chinitz wrote that Rod had been alone with the kids, in violation of Gesmer's November 2009 order of protection, and that he was "clearly poisoning the children against their mother and her family, all of whom deeply love Anna and Myles."

In a companion filing, Peggy and Philip reminded the court of Rod's false sex-abuse allegations against Shele and vouched for their own parental fitness.

Philip stressed the importance of Judaism in his life. "I am committed to keeping the religious values and teachings that my sister, Shele, passed on to her children and will continue to keep them in their school so that they can remain in an environment that's comfortable, familiar and secure for them," he wrote. Although Philip and Peggy's own kids attended a local Jewish school in Englewood, New Jersey, the couple felt it was important for Anna and Myles to remain at the Manhattan Day School.

Philip and Peggy, who at the time had two sons and a daughter, lived in a palatial 5,000-square-foot home on 1.5 acres. In the affirmation, Philip told the court that it was ideal for raising children, with a "gated swimming pool, jungle gym, tree swing, basketball court, hills for sledding and playroom with interactive video player system."

The Danishefskys' superior financial resources quickly became another point of contention between the two families.

Philip added that he had no intention of keeping the children from their father or paternal family, believing that Anna and Myles "need to have a continuing appropriate and safe relationship" with them. But he reminded the judge that as much as he wanted to foster that relationship, Rod needed to show he could be a decent father, given his "severe psychological problems" and his "dependency on various controlled substances including marijuana."

Philip bluntly warned the court that keeping the children with Rod would "ultimately destroy Anna and Myles in the same way that he may have destroyed my sister." Peggy wrote that "our children are our life" and promised Gesmer that Myles and Anna would be treated with that same unconditional devotion.

But Rod knew the court was loath to extract the kids from his parents' home and subject them to yet more tumult. He predicted to an online girlfriend that "within the next 2–4 weeks (possibly 8 weeks) I should have [the children] 24/7."

On January 21, 2010, Philip attacked Rod on another front. He filed legal papers to bar him from raiding Shele's estate. The family was aware that she had wanted to completely sever Rod from her will before her death.

Philip filed a petition in New York County Surrogate's Court for probate: the legal proceeding necessary for him to be named executor of Shele's estate, instead of Rod. He also sought permission from the court to act as interim executor of her estate until a final arrangement was formalized.

As an alternative, he suggested that a "neutral party" administer her affairs for the time being instead of Rod. He also argued that Rod should not be given standing in the case since he and Shele had already split under Jewish law. Philip noted Rod had a gambling addiction that could imperil the estate.

Angered by the move, Rod soon filed his own petition for control. On April 6, 2010, the court denied both requests and instead granted letters of temporary administration to the New York County Public Administrator. While Philip failed to secure control of his sister's dangling millions, he had scored a more urgent victory—temporarily denying Rod his jackpot.

But with the exhumation of Shele's body in April, these civil-court setbacks soon paled in comparison to far more serious legal concerns for the reeling widower. Once Hayes peeled back the skin of Shele's neck and spotted the snapped bone, Rod's early triumphalism after his wife's death soon turned to terror.

On April 8, 2010, after learning of the homicide ruling, Rod frantically called Jeanne Robin. "He was very upset," she said of the 50-minute call.

Realizing that Shele's death would come under intense scrutiny once again, Rod was implacable. While Robin outwardly tried to reassure him, she knew that her troubled lover was now at the epicenter of a murder probe. Her suspicions were confirmed roughly a month later when an NYPD detective suddenly appeared at her work.

"We talked for over two hours," she said. "They asked me a lot of questions they already knew the answers to."

That face-to-face meeting was followed by a phone call from another detective—again asking the same questions.

While Robin enjoyed a wide berth as part of an open marriage, her spouse's tolerance did not extend to suspected murderers. "My husband was not comfortable," she said. "I texted Rod and said, 'I'm sorry, I can't talk anymore. My husband is uncomfortable with this.'"

With the death now officially classified as a homicide, Philip and Peggy asked the judge handling the custody case to completely bar Rod from the kids. But despite their pleas, Gesmer allowed him a few hours of weekly visitation under the supervision of a court-appointed monitor pending a final outcome.

All Rod's contact with the children, including by email and phone, was still supposed to be supervised by a social worker. But, while he didn't completely move out of the Dorchester Towers until early April 2010, Rod was spending most of his time at his parents' home with the kids, disregarding the order of protection. He only used the studio apartment as an occasional haven when life with his mother and father became oppressive. Despite his son's age, Dave footed the bill for the Manhattan pied-à-terre after Shele's murder.

In June, Gesmer asserted that she no longer had jurisdiction to extend the visitation restrictions and lifted them. Rod was free to move back into his parents' home and enjoy unrestricted access to his kids. By default, Rod had regained custody of the children, even as investigators bore down on him.

Meanwhile, news of Hayes' homicide determination blared from New York City newspapers—and Rod was once again being hounded by reporters and photographers.

The New York Post's Laura Italiano, the paper's longtime Manhattan Supreme Court maven, cornered Rod at a family-court hearing and posed the only salient questions at the time.

"Did you kill your wife? If you didn't kill your wife, who did?" she asked.

Rod responded with icy silence.

With Anna and Myles now all but quarantined with the Covlins, Joel and Jaelene sued the Covlins and Rod for grandparent visitation in July 2010. They asserted that the Covlins had deviously stolen custody of the kids and disallowed contact.

The filing laid bare the magnitude of their suffering after Shele's death—and their desperate longing to reunite with their grandkids.

"To lose our daughter and not to see our grandchildren is the most heart-wrenching circumstance for not only my wife and me, but for our grandchildren who should not be deprived of their relationship with their grandparents, the connection to their beloved mother," Joel wrote.

"We maintained a rich, full and loving relationship with them; to say we absolutely love and adore our grandchildren would be an understatement. We live for them."

Joel recounted how Anna and Myles cherished playing

games with their cousins, whom they had barely seen since Shele's death.

Anna would take great pride in drawing pictures, which she would present as gifts to her grandparents with great ceremony. They would play along, exuberantly accepting the artwork and making sure to hang it prominently to make her proud.

Joel recalled how Myles was especially affectionate toward him, crawling onto his lap with "a spark in his eye that makes him so precious."

In an abrupt transition, the petition plunged into the grief wrought by Shele's death.

"I miss my Shele terribly. Not only did I have the joy of spending leisurely time with her, but I worked closely with Shele as we were business partners at UBS. She loved to share with me stories about what was happening with Anna and Myles, their milestones and achievements, all of which brought me pure joy and happiness," he wrote. "There is nothing more beautiful for grandparents than to participate in the lives of their grandchildren."

The Covlins, Joel said, were acting as if Shele had been a figment of Anna and Myles' imagination. Contact with their grandparents, he argued, was "a connection to their mother to which they are entitled." The old man called their sudden confiscation "cruel beyond words." He specifically requested a weekly Sunday visit and regular email and telephone communication.

Jaelene's own petition was embroidered with touching details about her relationship with the children. "She loves to make beaded jewelry, and she gave me a beaded necklace and earrings that I treasure," Jaelene wrote of Anna.

She said Myles exulted over simple toy cars and trucks. Jaelene recalled the joyous shrieks and vigorously kissed cheeks that accompanied marathon board-game and ice-cream extravaganzas.

She described the last time she saw Myles at Philip's home a month prior to filing the petition during a rare court-ordered visit. "He told me he loved me," she said simply. "I love both Anna and Myles deeply, and to be cut off from them like this is devastatingly painful for me—unbearable pain."

Once the request was filed, Rod and his parents wasted little time in flooding the court with legal papers in opposition.

Claiming poverty, Rod fired his private attorney and asked for court-appointed counsel. The maneuver delayed the already-plodding proceeding and forced the court to hold a hearing. To qualify for a free civil attorney at the time, he had to earn under $18,530. But the court found that his unemployment checks and Shele's Social Security death benefits pushed him above that sum. The request was denied.

The hearing judge, Emily Goodman, called his claims of penury incredible. "Covlin, who has had an elite private education, had enjoyed a successful career in the financial world, but decided to stop working during the divorce action," Goodman wrote in her August 2011 decision. "He now alleges that even though he was not indicted, no one will hire him due to published reports suggesting his involvement in his wife's violent demise."

She also noted that Rod's parents, who were simultaneously fighting to block Joel and Jaelene's visitation bid, had private attorneys who would assist him.

As the legal wrangling prolonged, Joel and Jaelene's hopes—and strength—began to wilt. Their son-in-law, Marc, pleaded with the court to compel visitation. "Can you speed up access to the children? Can you do anything more for us to see the children?" he wrote.

Losing Shele had turned Joel from a gregarious patriarch to a frail shell of a man. He could no longer summon the will to go to the office he once shared with his daughter. "They were heartbroken," Marc said. "Their health just deteriorated. They took no joy in life." Eve and Marc would take their son to the family home in New Jersey every Sunday to try to lift Joel and Jaelene's spirits, if only for a few hours.

In June 2012, Shele's parents filed another emergency petition in the visitation case, begging to see Anna, then 11, and Myles, then 5. Time, they knew, was running out after Joel suffered a major heart attack earlier that year from which he never fully recovered.

But Rod and his parents refused their plea for even a single 15-minute visit, according to published reports.

"It was like a death blow [for them]," Marc said. "It was hard. It was hard to watch."

By then, it had been two years since they had been able to touch or talk to their grandchildren.

The Covlins doggedly defended their perimeter, continually arguing in court papers that Anna and Myles had no interest in contact with their maternal grandparents.

"In this pursuit—that of preventing his in-laws from having any access to the children—[Rod] succeeded unlike in any other pursuit in a life checkered with failure," Manhattan prosecutor Matthew Bogdanos would later reflect.

The ferocity with which the Covlins kept the Danishefskys at a distance raised suspicions about what they were really protecting.

"You know, Anna was there that night," Marc said. "There was Anna in the apartment. There was Myles in the apartment." He was convinced that Anna was concealing details of what she had seen and heard in the hours surrounding the murder. He remembered the dark circles under her eyes that morning from lack of sleep.

"She either saw him murder her or she saw him, and she certainly saw the aftermath," Marc said. "She was unable to keep the story straight, and what I know of the interviews made no sense at all. It made no sense."

While Rod had succeeded in retaining custody of the children, legal pressures were building elsewhere.

Desperate for money and unable to plumb his parents' dwindling reserves much longer, Rod had applied for guardianship of Anna and Myles' property on April 4, 2011. It was a bid to gain access to Shele's $1.6 million Aetna insurance policy that named the kids as beneficiaries.

Flashing a corrupt ingenuity, Rod purposefully filed the case in Westchester County, in the hopes that the judge there would be unaware of his legal entanglements in Manhattan. Remarkably, the gambit worked. On June 17, 2011, Surrogate's Court Judge Anthony Scarpino granted Rod's petition, unaware he was the prime suspect in his wife's murder. Aetna issued Rod the seven-figure windfall—plus $12,000 in interest.

But it was fool's gold. As part of the application, Rod was supposed to list any pending legal issues. He simply left the section blank, omitting mention of four ongoing cases: the contested will in New York County Surrogate's Court, Philip and Peggy's custody petition, the maternal grandparents' visitation suit and the federal court actions related to Shele's insurance policies.

On December 28, 2011, the New York Post reported that the Manhattan public administrator, on behalf of Shele's estate, had filed a wrongful-death suit against him for murdering his wife. It was the first time that any entity had directly accused Rod of the crime. The Manhattan DA had yet to make any announcement at that point and was still investigating. A lawyer handling the case for the public administrator said that the timing of the suit was simple—to beat a two-year statute of limitations.

The Post's story made its way into Judge Scarpino's chambers. Stunned by Rod's brazen omissions in the Westchester case, he immediately suspended the letters of guardianship that gave him access to the children's funds.

Realizing that his scheme had collapsed, Rod resigned as guardian of the children's property and returned the money to avoid a potentially incriminating court hearing.

With the $1.6 million life-insurance policy now in the hands of the state, Rod was forced to submit applications whenever he needed cash to cover the children's various expenses. Scarpino then would decide whether to approve the expenditures and issue an order to the public administrator to cut the checks.

As it stood, the insurance policies were supposed to be paid to the trust, then ostensibly be split evenly between Rod and the two children. Philip sought to halt this scenario.

On August 22, 2012, Rod, Philip and the public administrator entered into a stipulation in Manhattan federal court. They agreed that the funds be transferred to the Shele D. Covlin Trust, for which Philip would serve as trustee.

Rod agreed that he would not assert his rights as beneficiary of Shele's trust until "(a) there has been a written confirmation by the District Attorney of the New York County that Roderick is not the subject of any criminal investigation concerning the death of Shele, (b) or six years has passed since Shele's death."

Rod was now completely fenced off from the inheritance.

CHAPTER FIFTEEN

Dave and Carol

Already encircled by the NYPD, DA investigators and the Danishefskys, Rod was suddenly confronted by yet another adversary—his own parents.

With Rod's free time devoted to legal chicanery and online philandering, Dave and Carol were forced to handle childcare. From January to June of 2010, the children were still enrolled in the Manhattan Day School, and the senior Covlins took turns driving them there every morning and picking them up. They also ferried them to playdates, after-school activities and Anna's therapy appointments. They cooked their meals at home and put them to bed.

Dave would dutifully read Myles bedtime stories, while Carol sat beside Anna at night and held her hand until she fell asleep.

The children eventually transferred to schools in New Rochelle, George M. Davis Jr. Elementary School and the Albert Leonard Middle School. Dave and Carol purchased all groceries for the home, including for Rod. They frequently bought the kids toys and games. Anna favored Hello Kitty and would brighten whenever Carol brought home a new gift.

Carol bathed Myles twice a week and taught Anna to bake.

Dave took Myles to Sabbath services every Saturday morning, and both kids attended High Holiday services with their grandparents.

"In short, we have taken a great deal of responsibility for the children and done a great deal of nurturing and caretaking of them," the senior Covlins later wrote in court papers.

Although less involved in their daily routines, Rod could still be a loving and involved father. After creating a milk-carton costume for Anna one year for the holiday of Purim, Rod sent Facebook messages to six romantic interests boasting of his parental dedication: "I made a costume for my daughter . . . took me like 25 hours." Purim, sometimes called the Jewish Halloween because celebrants wear costumes, commemorates the saving of the Jewish people from a Persian vizier.

One woman responded, "Better watch out I'm going to think you like me or something ;)"

The onslaught of negative publicity surrounding his wife's slaying had compelled Rod to resign from the U.S. Backgammon Federation—the group he cofounded and treasured. According to the Daily News, a message on the group's website stated that he had stepped down to "devote himself to some personal priorities that he wants to focus on for the near-term future."

Rod and Debra Oles' relationship rekindled again in 2011. She would frequently drive from North Carolina to his parents' home and pick him up for a weekend getaway at the Massachusetts vacation home. The couple almost always brought the children with them during these excursions, and Anna and Debra developed a powerful connection.

"Anna and I had become very close," she explained. "I loved her as a mother would love a daughter. She loved me—she told me she did."

Rod's relationship with his own mother, Debra recalled,

was a tortured one. He would often pin his personal failings on her mistreatment of him as a child. Rod accused Carol of berating him mercilessly as a young boy.

Carol could trigger Rod with a mere glance. "All she would have to do is just change her mannerisms or the way she looked at him, and he would get very upset and say, 'Don't you see what she's doing?'"

As the NYPD investigation inched along, Rod's already-fraught relationship with his parents decayed further. Rod had the same parasitic dynamic with them as he had had with Shele—and resented their setting boundaries on his behavior.

In September 2011, in the midst of another tempest, Carol trailed Rod into his room. "Rod grabbed Carol, lifted her into the air, carried her out of his room and slammed her head-first into a wall," she wrote later in a court filing.

When Carol returned to the room, Rod attempted to throw a computer monitor at her, but was thwarted by the attached cords. "He grabbed the keyboard and threw that at [me] instead," Carol recounted. Whizzing past her, it crashed into a wall with such force that it broke. Myles and Anna both witnessed the outburst.

These confrontations became increasingly frequent—and almost always played out in front of the kids. In a November 2011 fight, "Rod went at Dave very quickly and then shoved Dave with such force that he flew backward a few feet before landing on the floor and hitting his head on the floor of our den," the Covlins reported. "The following morning Dave found that one eye had hemorrhaged."

As he had done with Shele, Rod plotted to slander his parents to their employers in the aftermath of their now-constant altercations.

In March 2012, Rod grew enraged during an argument and announced he was going upstairs to write malicious letters to their employers. Frightened by the threat, Dave followed Rod to his room, where his son was now seated in front of the computer.

"You can't do this!" Dave exclaimed as he reached in front of his son and tried to cover the keyboard. Dave and Carol's court filing explained what happened next: "Rod, who is extraordinarily strong, grabbed Dave with both hands and threw Dave over his shoulder, so that Dave landed on his back on the floor." Myles watched the episode in horror.

When his parents confronted Rod about his conduct, he seemed incapable of remorse and instead blamed them for his rampages.

Carol had had enough. She told Rod sternly that if he ever touched them again, she would call 911 and have him arrested. The threat worked and he kept his hands off his parents.

But Rod's storms could not be contained. Soon, he trained his ire on Myles, physically abusing him in front of his parents. One night in July 2012, Myles began misbehaving during dinner and ignored Rod's commands to stop. "When Myles persisted, Rod, seated, reached out, grabbed Myles by the arm and then stood up, lifting Myles by that one arm, and carried him out of the room in that fashion," the Covlins wrote. "Although Myles was not injured, his arm could easily have been dislocated by Rod's intemperate action."

On September 5, 2012, Rod, his parents and the kids were returning from dinner at a local restaurant. During the ride home, Rod, who was driving, commanded Myles to stop bickering with Anna. Myles continued the quarrel after the family piled out of the car, prompting Rod to pick the boy up by his head. "Rod reached down, grabbed Myles by both sides of the head and carried Myles into the house that way, before setting him down on the floor," his parents reported. "Myles' neck could easily have been injured." Dave yelled at

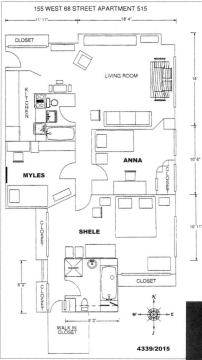

155 WEST 68 STREET APARTMENT 515

CLOSET

KITCHEN

LIVING ROOM

ANNA

CLOSET

MYLES

CLOSET

SHELE

CLOSET

SHOWER

CLOSET

CLOSET

WALK IN CLOSET

4339/2015

A diagram of Shele Covlin's apartment where prosecutors say Rod Covlin murdered her as their children slept nearby. (Source: Manhattan District Attorney's Office)

A studio portrait of Shele Covlin that appeared in the October 2008 issue of *Mann on the Street* magazine. (Source: Manhattan District Attorney's Office)

mann
onthestreet
| WALL STREET & FINANCIAL INDUSTRIES |

MERRILL LYNCH
GLOBAL WEALTH MANAGEMENT

THE DANISHEFSKY GROUP

SHELE D. COVLIN, JOEL E. DANISHEFSKY, AND PHILIP A. DANISHEFSKY

Shele Covlin, her father, Joel Danishefsky, and her brother, Philip Danishefsky, pictured on the cover of *Mann on the Street* magazine for an October 2008 feature. (Source: Manhattan District Attorney's Office)

Detectives watch as Shele Covlin's casket is exhumed, March 1, 2010.
(Source: Manhattan District Attorney's Office)

Shele Covlin's simple pine casket after her exhumation. (Source: Manhattan District Attorney's Office)

(above) Rod Covlin at a dinner during the NYC Open Mayor's Cup Backgammon Championship, which he attended in November 2009, a month before Shele Covlin's murder. (Source: Manhattan District Attorney's Office)

(right) Rod Covlin leaving a Manhattan family-court hearing April 12, 2010, after the Office of Chief Medical Examiner ruled Shele's death a homicide. (Photograph by Steven Hirsch)

Assistant District Attorney Matthew Bogdanos in Manhattan Supreme Court during a pretrial hearing.
(Photograph by Steven Hirsch)

Assistant District Attorney Matthew Bogdanos watching his adversary, defense lawyer Robert Gottlieb, deliver his opening statement during Rod Covlin's trial.
(Photograph by Steven Hirsch)

Defense lawyer Robert Gottlieb delivering his opening remarks at Rod Covlin's trial. (Photograph by Steven Hirsch)

Defense lawyer Robert Gottlieb sitting at the defense table during a pretrial hearing in Manhattan Supreme Court. (Photograph by Steven Hirsch)

Rod Covlin's ex-girlfriend, Debra Oles, testifying against him during his murder trial. (Photograph by Steven Hirsch)

Marc and Eve Karstaedt's reaction to the jury's guilty verdict on March 13, 2019. (Photograph by Steven Hirsch)

Rod Covlin after a jury found him guilty of murdering his wife. (Photograph by Steven Hirsch)

Rod Covlin's parents, Dave and Carol Covlin, watching testimony during the trial. (Photograph by Steven Hirsch)

him, "Don't you ever touch that child in that fashion again, ever!"

The Covlins were also troubled by Rod's insistence on having Anna, nearly 12, sleep in bed with him and Debra. "We told Rod that Anna had reached an age at which her sharing a bed with him was no longer appropriate or acceptable and insisted that it stop," they wrote. "Rod rejected our demand, defending the 'family bed' practice as perfectly appropriate, as he had in the past."

While Debra did not find the arrangement untoward, she said Rod's judgment would often unnerve her. "A lot of times when he had Myles in bed [with us] he would want to have sex," she recalled. "I'm like, 'No! I'm not having sex with a 5-year-old boy in bed. It's just not appropriate.'"

Debra said Rod often exposed his children to situations and subject matter that were far too mature for their ages. He took them to see the R-rated film "Magic Mike," about a male stripper. "Why would you take them to see that?" she asked him.

"I'm honest with my kids," he replied.

The Covlins were appalled by Rod's vulgar excesses and limply tried to rein him in. But the more they tried, the more Rod resisted. "It was the most dysfunctional household I think I've ever seen," said Debra. "I did like his parents, but you're an adult, act like an adult. These are two traumatized children, particularly Anna. Don't have knockdown, drag-out fights in front of them almost every day."

Carol and Dave grew increasingly fearful of their son as his behavior degenerated. In late summer 2012, the senior Covlins defensively installed locks on the two doors leading to their room. "They were that much afraid of him," Debra recalled.

Desperate for a break from his parents, Rod took the kids to visit his sister, Aviva Quant, in Germany, where she lived with her husband. They spent a month there—and paid for the trip with money he had siphoned from Anna's college fund.

Despite a court order barring Rod from taking the children out of state pending the outcome of the custody case, he began to research a possible move to Texas. Rod's comprehensive vetting process included searches for both escorts and local synagogues.

Hoping to somehow wriggle free of his legal shackles, Rod conducted a dozen searches related to "texas guardian of the property of a minor" and "home in texas during bankruptcy."

Rod didn't limit his search for a quick financial fix to American shores. In September 2012, he clicked on an article about a Hong Kong billionaire who had offered a $65 million reward to any man who could marry his lesbian daughter. The fantasy was too delicious to ignore. He quickly conducted Google searches for "methods to learn Chinese" and "Chinese alphabet keyboard" before the delusion passed.

Meanwhile, his relationship with his parents continued to spiral out of control. On September 28, 2012, Rod ordered Debra to secretly record an argument he instigated with Carol and Dave to capture damaging behavior that could be leveraged against them.

In the audio, Dave can be heard suggesting to Rod that they start putting up the *sukkah* Saturday night to prepare for the weeklong holiday of Sukkot. During Sukkot, observant Jews erect small makeshift huts called *sukkahs* that are meant to resemble the modest tents their ancestors once dwelled in.

But Rod had little interest in weekend manual labor. Adding to the tension, Rod told his father that Myles wouldn't be joining him for synagogue that Saturday, citing a playdate.

To Rod's annoyance, Debra chimed in.

"I didn't think we had any plans," she said, hoping to defuse tensions. Skeptical about his excuse, Carol casually asked for the name of the friend's parents.

"They're very private," Rod said.

After a few more volleys, Carol could no longer suppress her anger.

"Monday I'm having people here for lunch," she told him. "Please don't be here. Okay?"

Dave then delicately returned to the possibility of taking Myles to synagogue as if traversing a minefield. "I mean Myles is supposed to go to *shul* with me tomorrow," he said. "We arranged it."

Debra can be heard wishing Anna goodnight in the background as Dave continued to prod his son. "You know shabbos [sabbath] we go to shul, do you not?"

"But did you ask me?" Rod asked. He then agitatedly turned to his son. "Myles, stay in my room tonight. You're in my room tonight. Okay?" Myles often slept in his grandparents' room.

With the argument turning petty, Rod told his father that he rescinded the synagogue visit because of Carol's lunch snub.

"Everything with you is an issue," Dave retorted. "You kiss everybody else's ass, and you shit on us!"

Intent on provoking his father, Rod further chastised him for clashing with a guest during a dinner party earlier that week. "You got loud because you were drunk!" he said.

"I was not drunk, you asshole!" Dave protested.

Carol then leaped back into the fray, accusing Rod of continually maligning her to the kids.

"You tell—you tell your children what pieces of shit we are!" Dave screamed.

"All the time!" Carol added in near tandem.

"Excuse me?" Rod turned to Myles amid the furor. "Have I ever said anything bad about Grandpa and Grandma to you? Have I ever said anything bad to you? Have I ever told you anything bad?"

Myles, who had turned 6 just two days earlier, can be heard muttering "no."

Dave continued to press Rod about setting up a supposed playdate that conflicted with the synagogue service.

"I am his father, and if I decide we're going to do something with people on a weekend, we're going to do it. That's it!" Rod declared.

"And you do it on Yom Kippur," said Carol, scolding Rod for making plans without his parents on one of the holiest days of the year.

"And you do it on Yom Kippur, and you fuck us, and you shit on us in our own house all the time!" Dave seconded.

Myles and Anna looked on helplessly, immersed once again in profane dysfunction. Carol picked up the attack and accused Rod of squandering the children's college money on frivolities.

"Look, you're screwing the kids out of their money," she said.

"How?" Rod said, in an injured tone.

"You are screwing the kids out of their money, because I know you are," Dave boomed.

"I went to the surrogate's [court], and I checked the whole file. I read it, and I made copies of everything," said Carol, referring to the money he had withdrawn from Anna and Myles' college funds.

"She read the whole file, and I know how much money you've taken from your children," Dave seethed.

"Excuse me?" Rod answered. He turned to Debra. "You see? They've gone, they've checked in surrogate's. You see what they're doing?" he said, casting himself as the aggrieved party.

"Because you steal from your children! You stole before!" Dave shouted. One of the kids whimpered in the background.

"They won't be able to get—to go to college by the time you're done with them, and you said you didn't care if they went to college," Dave yelled. "Why don't you tell Anna that every penny you're spending right now is her money and Myles' money?"

"That Shele worked her ass off for!" Carol added, in a cannon blast to her son's ego. "Because you haven't worked in five years—in the 12 years you were married you never—you never worked."

"Wait. Wait. Hold on. Hold on. Hold on a second. Anna, I'd like you to come here," Rod replied. "Hold on a second. Come here please?"

"Do I got to?" murmured Anna, then 11.

Carol's gloves came clean off as she turned to her granddaughter. "Your mother—your mother worked her ass off for every penny that he's spending. Let me tell you. The Danishefskys are not wrong. They may be wrong about some things but not the money. . . . Your mother worked and worked and worked, and your father sat on his ass like he's doing now. He refuses to get a job."

"He's spending your money—he's spending your money!" Dave said.

"You did it to us," Carol said bitterly.

Wounded by the accusations, Rod turned vengeful. "What you are saying now, in front of Anna and Myles, will ensure that you never see my children again," he said.

"You threatened us with your children for 11 years!" Dave replied.

Their tolerance had been exhausted.

"I want you out of the house by October 1st. Out!" Carol roared.

"Evict me. Evict me," Rod taunted. "File the papers. Evict me."

Dave turned to his granddaughter. "You know what, Anna, I spent a million dollars of my money to make sure you didn't go to the Danishefskys," he said, stressing his devotion to her. Then he turned back to his son.

"You're never gonna pay me back. You're going steal from me like you steal from your children!"

Rod would eventually spend more than $100,000 from his children's college fund.

The recorded brawl encapsulated Rod's twisted and now-broken relationship with his parents. He bled them of their money and weaponized his own children to assert control. Dave and Carol had come to harbor the same resentments as Shele—disgusted by his entitlement and adolescent tantrums.

After Carol ordered him to move out, Rod reacted in predictably extreme fashion. He vanished with the children on October 1, 2012. It was the same cruel maneuver that he had used to torment Shele when he felt his dominance wane.

He told his custody lawyers via email, "We will be getting a room/studio today," without revealing his location. Debra, Rod and the children checked into the Crowne Plaza in White Plains for one night, then switched to the Marriott Courtyard in Tarrytown. Debra picked up the bill.

The senior Covlins were panic-stricken. On October 3, Rod and Debra drove to his parents' home while they were at work. Rod asked Debra to take a video of the visit on her iPhone. Clutching a set of keys in his right hand, Rod could be seen grimly striding toward the front door as Debra trailed behind.

Rod tried to open the front door with his key—but it wouldn't turn.

"They changed the lock," he said, outraged.

He then marched to the garage and entered an electronic code into a keypad. It too had been changed.

His fury swelling, Rod returned to the front door. "I'm a resident—they have to evict me!" he said. Standing two feet from the locked door, he paused a moment before delivering a fearsome kick.

As he coiled his leg for another strike, Debra begged him to stop. "No, no, no! You're going to be arrested!" she implored.

Defeated, Rod walked away, his face pale and twisted, his breath labored.

"Rod, don't do anything you're going to get arrested for," Debra pleaded. "Please don't do anything you're going to get arrested for."

The cell phone video then cut out.

As Shele had done before them, the senior Covlins had changed their locks, desperate to keep Rod at a safe remove.

Deprived of free lodging, Rod and Debra quickly found an apartment nearby in New Rochelle on October 7 and signed a lease. With no income, bad credit and hair-raising Google search results, securing an apartment under Rod's name was a nonstarter. He persuaded Debra to put it in her name and promised to cover the rent using the children's college fund. With his reputation soiled, Rod had begun using aliases, including the surname Cazlen.

Dave and Carol grew so worried about the safety of their grandchildren that they called Joel Danishefsky for help despite the ongoing custody war over the kids. Carol told him that Rod had recently become "very wild" and was "beating up on Myles and abusing Anna." She said that Rod had taken off with the kids and they didn't know where they were.

Joel notified Marc, who immediately contacted their custody lawyer, Chinitz. The attorney called Child Protective Services in Westchester and the New Rochelle Police Department.

Around midnight, the caseworker reached Rod by phone, but he refused to let her stop by the apartment. He agreed to meet her at the New Rochelle Police Department the next day.

Dave and Carol were now so worried about the welfare of their grandchildren that, days later, they took the extraordinary step of suing Rod for custody. He was now faced with dual claims on his kids: one from Peggy and Philip's existing suit and now another from his own parents. Myles and Anna were being yanked in three different directions.

"From our point of view, our son's behavior is beyond control and will continue to be unless he receives professional help," the senior Covlins wrote in the filing. "Rod has become a danger to Myles, and is likely to become more so as Myles becomes increasingly independent, as Rod's violent assault on us portend."

They called his decision to continue sleeping in the same bed as Anna just shy of her 12th birthday "appalling judgment."

"Rod is not a fit custodian of the children, and the court must protect the children from him by removing them from his custody," they wrote.

However, the Covlins continued to argue that they were more deserving of custody than the Danishefskys, "with whom the children never had a significant relationship and with whom the children have had no contact at all for over two years."

They neglected to mention that they had helped dig that trench themselves.

Instead, the Covlins asserted that the kids had become

attached to their New Rochelle friends and community. "Removing the children from Rod's custody, which the court must do to protect their physical safety and emotional health, will unavoidably take a great emotional toll," they wrote. "To send the children to live in a strange place, with relatives who are virtual strangers to them, would be contrary to their best interests."

Further, they asked the court to grant them an order of protection against Rod and suggested that he only be permitted monitored visits with his kids.

Rod soon deployed his signature tactic—defaming his enemies to their employers. This time, he targeted his own mother. "I reported my mother that night (I was pissed, as you might expect) for writing false prescriptions," he wrote in an email to a friend. "I told Jo Ann [the children's legal guardian] about it. Now, my father called me and said, 'I handed the children to the Danishefskys.' Perhaps, if everyone was honest about blame, my mother never would have made that call in the first place. While my reporting was unfortunate, my parents can't excuse their call to the Danishefskys as just a little thing and mine as a big thing and blame me for everything, as they always do. I did refrain from reporting them for about $1,000,000 in tax evasion, which was a good thing I suppose."

Desperate to seize back the advantage from his parents, Rod's schemes became increasingly unhinged.

"He told me to lie and say that I saw his dad choke him out," Debra said.

Judge Gesmer weighed the senior Covlins' emergency custody request at an October hearing. She was concerned that they had failed to alert the court to Rod's rampages earlier.

"If your clients' allegations are accurate, then what jumped out at me from the papers is whether your clients, by inaction, put the children in harm's way, and that is extremely troubling to me . . . because if, in fact, there was violence of the level they contend, in front of the children six or seven months ago, for them to do nothing is very troubling to me," Gesmer said at the hearing.

The Covlins' lawyer countered that the couple had tried "many interventions that included counsel, clergy, other people . . . and there were great efforts to work with their son for all kinds of obvious reasons, but the minute it was clear it was out of control, then something else had to be done."

Gesmer also questioned the argument that the Danishefskys were incapable of adequately caring for the children because of their lack of interaction since Shele's death. "Part of the reason for that is that your clients joined Roderick Covlin in doing everything possible to keep the Danishefskys out of their lives," Gesmer stated. "Based on your current papers, that may not have been such a good idea."

Anna's legal guardian, Jo Ann Douglas, was also present at the hearing. She told Gesmer that Anna wanted to remain with her father and girlfriend, where she said she felt "happy, safe [and] comfortable."

Despite having been provided a chilling portrait of the Covlin household, Gesmer granted Dave and Carol temporary custody on October 9. She also issued an order of protection against Rod and in favor of Dave, Carol and the children.

All parties involved in the custody battle, including Philip, Peggy, the senior Covlins, Rod and both children's legal guardians, formalized the interim agreement. Rod was granted supervised visitation and phone calls with the kids. Gesmer managed these communications minutely, ordering that any conversations with Myles must be initiated by the boy and take place out of Anna's earshot.

She capped Rod's calls with Myles at 20 minutes to allow for the reading of a story. Any texts, emails or calls with

Anna would be allowed "only to the extent authorized by the senior Covlins," she wrote.

Gesmer ordered Rod to feign enthusiasm for the new arrangement and to encourage the children to obey and respect their grandparents. In addition, Rod was told to begin regular therapy sessions and to take any medication prescribed by a mental-health professional.

Finally, Gesmer directed the senior Covlins to arrange a meeting with the Danishefskys to "initiate contact with the objective of creating an ongoing relationship."

Shele's family thought they would finally regain a modicum of access to the children nearly three years after her death. But the damage had been done—in the end, Joel and Jaelene would see their grandkids only six times between Shele's death in 2010 and their own passing in 2017.

On October 10, Debra drove the children to the senior Covlins' home in compliance with the court order. Eager to excise Rod from their home, the Covlins placed 10 boxes of his belongings in the front yard for Debra to retrieve. But they would not be rid of him that easily.

CHAPTER SIXTEEN

Retreat

On November 8, 2012, Shele's sister, Eve, and her husband, Marc, replaced Philip and Peggy in the petition for custody against Rod and the senior Covlins.

The Karstaedts lived on the Upper West Side of Manhattan in a historic luxury apartment building with their only child, David. Of all the Danishefskys, Anna, now 12, and Myles, 6, had always been closest to Eve and Marc, who had socialized frequently with Shele and Rod.

In their petition, Eve and Marc, still represented by Chinitz, wrote that "extraordinary circumstances existed requiring the removal of Anna and Myles" from Carol and Dave's dominion. The couple described the close relationship they had had with the kids prior to their mother's death, assuring the court that the children would be surrounded and protected by doting family and friends.

They stressed to Judge Gesmer that they feared for the children's fate as long as they remained with the senior Covlins and Rod. "Roderick is the only person who had a motive to kill Shele, and we are advised that there are no other suspects in her killing," the Karstaedts wrote.

To drive the point home, the filing included a copy of the

autopsy report. Rod had still refused to speak to the DA's office or provide "any assistance in finding the person who murdered the mother of his children."

They reminded the court that Shele told Eve and other family members that "should anything happen to her, or should she die, Roderick should be the first person to be investigated."

To buttress their appeal, Eve and Marc submitted a statement from Rose describing Rod's callous and continual abuse of Shele and the kids during her employ. The nanny asserted that Dave and Carol, when they supervised Rod's visits with the children before Shele's murder, were powerless to "contain his violent behavior."

The Karstaedts also catalogued Rod's long history of cruelty toward his family before Shele's death. They recounted an incident in January 2009 when Rod had erupted after the kids failed to awaken him from a nap as ordered. Anna was the prime target and later complained to her mother about his incessant screaming. "I can't stand his yelling," she said. "I do not want to see my ninth birthday."

Rod, they claimed, drew perverse delight in reminding Anna that her brother was conceived through a donor egg and was not her full sibling. He once took Anna to see "High School Musical 3," and when she failed to adequately praise the film, Rod boiled over once again.

"Roderick became furious with her because she had not provided him with specific reasons why she did not like the movie," the Karstaedts wrote. "He flew into a rage, grabbed her arms and violently shook her. Anna was terrified and begged him to stop."

Myles was also subject to abuse for violating Rod's innumerable domestic rules.

In one instance, "Roderick grew angry at Myles, and

locked him, naked, in the shower, while Myles cowered in fear," the report read.

Anna had described the abuse to her therapist, saying that she wasn't eating properly because "she was scared, nervous and sad" and could no longer absorb her father's tirades. Hoping to discredit the senior Covlins' petition for custody, the Karstaedts said that Rod's violent behavior toward the children had clearly continued after Shele's death "and, if anything, had become more extreme."

For years, the Danishefskys had sent care packages, Hanukkah gifts and birthday presents, without any response. They doubted that the children were ever given these tokens of distant love. After complaining to the court, they would get stiff thank-you notes likely penned by Carol and Dave.

The senior Covlins protected Rod at every turn—even at the expense of their grandchildren, the Karstaedts argued.

"They have failed to confront Roderick, even if necessary to keep Anna and Myles safe," they said. Eve and Marc acknowledged that the delay in reporting Rod's behavior was "perhaps understandable conduct for victims of abuse" but it nonetheless made the senior Covlins "unsuitable custodians."

To coax a ruling in their favor, Eve and Marc described their spacious 2,200-square-foot home and said they had ample room to take in their niece and nephew. The apartment is in a 24-hour-doorman building, which they described as a "lovely, prewar residence with outstanding security, friendly staff and a large playroom. There is a beautiful, large courtyard in the center of the building with a magnificent antique fountain, which the children love."

They lobbied the court to return Anna and Myles to the community where they had once thrived before their mother's death. "We share the same circle of friends as Shele," the couple wrote. "In addition, like Shele, we are modern Orthodox observant Jews and have a strong Jewish background. We attend services at both Lincoln Square Synagogue, where Shele and the children were active members, as well as The Jewish Center, which is 100 yards from our home."

The Karstaedts said they wanted to enroll Anna and Myles in the Ramaz School on the Upper East Side, a prestigious private Jewish school, where their son was a student.

Prior to her murder, Shele had planned to send them there and the Karstaedts had already initiated an application. Marc would take the children to school every day, as he did with his own son, and Eve, as a stay-at-home mom, would be fully devoted to raising the children.

"We believe that unless the court takes action, Roderick will ultimately destroy Anna and Myles in the same way that he destroyed and eventually murdered Shele," they wrote.

Meanwhile, Rod worked to widen the chasm between the children and his enemies-in-law. In early October 2012, Rod instructed Anna to purposefully torment her brother during visits at the Karstaedt home to cripple their case for custody.

A voicemail she left for her father revealed her twisted predicament.

"And Myles—and Myles was happy," she said guiltily, concerned that she had let her father down. "I—like, I'm trying to make him not happy but it's really hard. . . . It's really hard to make him unhappy. But I'm trying to—like— I'm going to try. I'm going to try harder."

In a filing supporting the Karstaedts' petition, Chinitz blasted Anna's legal guardian for stating that the child was thrilled to be living with her father.

"It is clear from her statement that Ms. Douglas has utterly abdicated her responsibility to her minor client and is ignoring the near-certainty that her client is terrified of her father and what he will do if she does not do what he says.

Ms. Douglas expresses no concern about the allegations," Chinitz wrote. "It is frightening to think that Ms. Douglas actually believes that a child can be 'happy' or 'safe' or 'comfortable' witnessing her father physically assaulting her grandparents and her baby brother."

Chinitz acknowledged the legal hurdle of a nonparent suing a parent for custody, but argued that the Karstaedts had standing based on "the complete unfitness of the father."

Meanwhile, the awarding of temporary custody to the senior Covlins had crippled Joel and Jaelene's suit for grandparent visitation. In November 2012, both parties submitted papers supporting their positions. But before ruling on the petition, Judge Gesmer dismissed the grandparents' case on December 16, 2012.

Gesmer said that now that the senior Covlins had custody instead of Rod, Joel and Jaelene would have to refile their visitation case against them.

The clock for the ailing Danishefskys was now rewound. They would have to submit a new petition, endure a new hearing, file supporting motions and wait, perhaps years, for the judge to render a decision. Their only hope of ever seeing their grandchildren again lay in the fate of Eve and Marc's custody petition. But despite their compelling case and the extraordinary circumstances of Shele's death, her relatives knew that they faced a daunting road. Courts almost always favor a parent, even an unfit one, in a custody battle.

On January 24, 2013, in a letter to Judge Gesmer, Rod asked her for a free lawyer to present his own petition for custody of his children. The disjointed filing was gratuitously vindictive and likely raised further concerns about his mental state.

Along with the letter, Rod submitted a statement of net

worth—or what could more accurately be described as net debt. "While you might not approve of my job selection, I do have one," he wrote, referring to the backgammon habit that Gesmer had previously dismissed as little more than gambling during the divorce. Given his status as the only suspect in a high-profile murder, Rod argued that he had few routes of remuneration.

"My inability to find work in my previous field (or any professional field, for that matter) left me with little choice," he wrote. Rod claimed that he made more money playing backgammon professionally—$3,000 a month—than he would at any of the menial jobs he would qualify for given his tabloid infamy.

But Rod would use the majority of the filing to demonize and discredit his parents and the Karstaedts.

In scattered and sloppily punctuated prose, Rod wrote that his parents had a history of making "fallacious allegations" and had lied to the IRS about their finances.

"Carol Covlin engaged in lies/prescription violations/misdemeanors for years for which she was finally fired recently, Dave Covlin's alcoholism for which after trying to hide/lie about for 40 years finally went to AA, only to stop and continue his drinking (and driving drunk—he even walked home 5 miles after Carol telling him he couldn't drive her home rather than admit he had been drinking not realizing that his slurring and smelling like alcohol were easy tip-offs), which were put in newspapers and online and which, to Carol Covlin's certain delight, have cost me many of even my most previously steadfast friends. Though, given the disparaging remarks that she has been making to Myles and Anna (in violation of the stipulation and of common decency), I can only imagine what she has been telling others."

Rod told the court that he would soon be ineligible to

receive the $1,500 a month in Social Security benefits for the children that he had come to rely on. Combined with his backgammon proceeds, Rod said he was making about $50,000 a year with annual costs of $80,000.

The rant then turned to his former brother-in-law Marc, accusing him of various bad acts and swindles without evidence. "I do not have millions of dollars that I am not disclosing to this court, hidden in Europe from an estate I inherited from a distant relative who I suddenly took interest in as she was dying and who left me everything, including a villa in the south of France, which prompted a lawsuit by all of her other relatives, which I was able to win somehow," he wrote.

"The Karstaedts live in a $10,000-a-month apartment for about $2,000 a month," he said. "Marc was fortunate to have a sister who cared for two elderly women until they passed away. His sister 'inherited' the apartment."

He then scolded Eve for having a "full-time nanny until her son was 8 years old . . . despite the fact that Eve did not work (she didn't work at all—no charity work or anything—as she had 'issues'—Marc didn't even allow her to bathe Dave alone until he was 4)."

But Rod reserved his most venomous attack for his mother. "I need to get my children back from a manipulative woman who has psychologically abused her husband for 40 years and her children and now is doing the same to my children," he wrote. "A woman who, in from [sic] of Myles, called my partner, Debra, 'a bitch and a cunt' simply because she felt threatened because she came to see herself as my children's mother. A woman who made my daughter feel, in my daughter's words (and her attorney is aware of this) 'worse than the day Mommy died' during one of her uncontrollable rages while I was out."

But, like many of his legal gambits, the letter would ultimately backfire. Just five days after he sent it, Gesmer issued a ruling that all but paralyzed his custody bid and forced him to consider extrajudicial solutions.

She ordered a psychiatrist to perform forensic examinations of Rod, his parents, Eve, Marc and the children to aid in her custody decision. Gesmer wanted the psychiatrist to assess Rod's stability and his impact on the children. It was a vetting he could not afford, given his status as a murder suspect—albeit in a stalled investigation. To avoid having to testify at a family court hearing and trial about his possible role in Shele's death, he had no choice but to withdraw his petition.

"I would have to testify and there is an 87 percent chance that I could end up in jail for my wife's death," he told a girlfriend.

On April 4, 2013, Rod finally surrendered custody to his parents. The fight had now contracted to just two parties—the Karstaedts suing the senior Covlins.

For Eve and Marc, this was more favorable legal terrain. Still, the Covlins had the advantage of already having Anna and Myles in their possession. Judges are hesitant to uproot children who have endured severe trauma.

As the conflict raged on, the senior Covlins approached the Karstaedts and told them that Anna had entered a dangerous psychological spiral. She had slit her wrists in an unsuccessful suicide attempt. The Covlins told the Karstaedts that the constant familial infighting had pushed her to the edge—and pleaded for them to concede custody. The Danishefskys were stunned by the revelation.

In retrospect, Marc said that Anna's desperate act was likely a reaction to what she had endured while living with Rod's parents.

But at the time, Eve and Marc worried that a continued pursuit of custody would ultimately place Anna next to her mother. Psychologists recommended an immediate de-escalation for Anna's sake. "We were going to win the case," Marc reflected with regret. "They said, 'You know, it's not worth it. The chance something happens to the child. Just, just pull back.'"

Tortured by the choice, the Karstaedts ultimately withdrew their petition.

On January 8, 2014, the senior Covlins were granted full physical and legal custody of Anna and Myles. "We entered into this agreement with this long and convoluted system of visitation," Marc recalled. "No sooner had we signed the agreement, we had problems."

As part of the final accord, the Covlins agreed to weekly therapy sessions for both Myles and Anna. The stipulation also required counseling sessions with both families to heal their rifts.

But the court failed to recognize that Shele's murder had created an unbridgeable divide. Therapeutic platitudes were bound to fail—especially after both sides had so ruthlessly denounced each other as unfit guardians.

The ruling outlined a plan to reintroduce the children to the Karstaedts in four phases. Eve and Marc would begin with monthly three-hour visits supervised by a social worker. After three of these meetings, the social worker would determine whether to have them graduate to unsupervised visits. The second stage would transition the Karstaedts to unsupervised five-hour-long daytime visits. After the third successful unsupervised visit, the parties would move on to phase three: unsupervised overnight visits one weekend night each month. Finally, after the sixth overnight visit, the parties could implement phase four, with monthly weekend visits.

Given Anna's advancing age, the court granted her the right not to participate in these visits. Myles would get the same privilege upon turning 12.

The order also allowed Rod continued supervised visits with the children, as long as a therapist and his parents agreed. But he was barred from living in Dave and Carol's home.

Gesmer ruled that all electronic contact between the kids and their father must be strictly supervised, and he was not to access their personal email accounts or phones. Given the allegations of Rod's abuse of Myles, Gesmer issued a five-year order of protection in the child's favor. The senior Covlins were also granted access to Shele's $1,625,000 Aetna life-insurance policy to use for their care of the children.

Eve and Marc soon began their visits with the kids, eager to rebuild the fractured relationship. But Dave and Carol seemed intent on impeding its repair. "[They] insisted that they come on every visit, even though the judge had not mandated it," recalled Marc. "They claimed that the kids wanted it, and eventually had the children saying, 'I want the grandparents to come.'"

The handful of visits between the children and the Karstaedts were often marked by tension and unease—due largely to the Covlins' brooding presence. While the Karstaedts felt that they were starting to forge a fresh bond with Anna and Myles, the Covlins did their best to disrupt the healing.

Marc suspected that they were concerned Anna might let something slip about the night of her mother's murder that could incriminate their son.

"We had one extraordinary visit here where they came back to the apartment," recalled Marc. The kids ate pizza since the senior Covlins had objected to the Karstaedts splurging on pricey food. "We were not allowed to show them up," he explained.

During the visit, the Karstaedts' son, Dave, was throwing a foam ball against the wall when Myles picked it up and tossed it against a window. Suddenly, Dave Covlin became furious and sharply admonished the boy.

Marc tried to restore calm. "It's a foam ball," he said. "Dave hits the windows all the time—and the lights and the television. It doesn't do any harm." But Dave Covlin later told the court that Marc's permissiveness promoted the boy's delinquency.

"[E]very visit had a zinger at the end where [the senior Covlins] would go back to the court" and report some contrived misdeed on the part of the Karstaedts, Marc said. Fed up with their antics, Eve and Marc finally asked the court to allow them visits without the grandparents present.

"We said absolutely no Covlins because there was this nonverbal communication," Marc said. "The children were not allowed to answer until they looked at the grandparents and Dave either said go ahead or don't. So we had this constant friction. We couldn't have a good relationship with the children when [Dave and Carol] were there no matter what we did." After just a few visits, Anna decided she no longer wanted to participate in the reconciliation.

Myles' visits continued—as did the Covlins' interference. In 2014, Marc recalled picking Myles up from Dave and Carol's New Rochelle home with the supervisor in tow. "Myles refused to get in the car," Marc said. "When he got in the car, he kicked the back of the seat. He was cursing at me. He was, he went ballistic, basically." Myles started yelling that he wanted his grandfather to come with them, according to Marc. "So that was the end," said Marc. "They were strangers to us because they had been kept away from us for so long."

The Covlins had prevailed in their war of attrition. After having spent years—and millions—trying to preserve a relationship with the two children who represented all that remained of Shele, the Danishefskys surrendered.

Rod's girlfriend, Debra, later said that she found the Covlins' victory unthinkable given their extreme dysfunction.

"I just never understood how his parents were able to retain custody."

CHAPTER SEVENTEEN

Hit List

Rod's hostility toward his parents began to escalate after they successfully wrenched away custody of the kids. "He hated both of his parents for taking his children away, even though it was his own fault because he couldn't control his temper," Debra said.

Dave and Carol had supplanted Shele as the locus of his rage and resentment. In Rod's perception, they had committed an unforgivable injustice by robbing him of two of his few remaining sources of joy. This was an offense deserving of the ultimate penalty.

Rod told Debra that he had "no issue or problem with killing his parents, because they did the exact same thing that Shele had done to him." He began to conjure grisly methods of death and disposal. He once looked longingly at an industrial meat grinder and later told Debra that he was remiss in not having bought it.

"He said multiple times that he hated his mother so much, his parents so much, but mostly his mother, that he wanted to kidnap her and take her down [to the basement]," Debra recalled. "It's a finished basement with a bathroom and he wanted to torture her and cut her limbs off slowly and then he wanted to put the pieces through a meat grinder and flush her down the toilet as if she never existed. Those were his words."

He derived a sadistic thrill from the airing of his fantasies but also seemed to question his own splintering sanity.

"Do you think I'm a psychopath?" he would ask Debra. She would assure him to the contrary. But, inwardly, Debra knew that she was witnessing her lover's mental disintegration.

He drew inspiration for his first murder plot from his favorite television shows, "Breaking Bad" and "Dexter." The former featured the violent misadventures of Walter White, a cancer-stricken high school chemistry teacher who begins dealing amphetamines to provide for his family. "Dexter" centers on a blood-spatter analyst for the Miami police, who lives a secret life as a benevolent serial killer who hunts down and kills other murderers. Episodes from the two shows depict the use of the poisons ricin and aconite.

On September 29, 2012, Rod and Debra stationed themselves at public computer terminals at the Greenburgh Library, near where they lived in the New York suburbs. Rod had Debra log in as an "out-of-town" guest. Manning the keyboard, Rod first searched for information on ricin, a substance found naturally in castor beans. Its use as a lethal poison was first widely publicized after the 1978 assassination of Georgi Markov, a Bulgarian political dissident. He was famously felled when an assassin stabbed him with the tip of an umbrella on Waterloo Bridge in London, injecting a dose of ricin into his thigh and eventually killing him.

But Rod had no interest in turning his murder plot into a labor-intensive scene from a James Bond film and soon turned to the next option. While their neighbors at the computer desks refreshed résumés and caught up on the day's news,

Rod and Debra punched in Google searches for aconite, a poison used by the character Hannah McKay on "Dexter" to kill her first husband. The poison is extracted from the purple monkshood flower. The ancient Romans called aconite the "queen of poisons."

Aconite has also had some more contemporary applications. In 2009, a British woman was convicted of slipping aconite into her lover's curry and killing him after he left her for a younger romantic rival.

The intricacies of lethal botany proved too much for effort-averse Rod, and he soon clicked out of that plan.

With these grandiose plots shelved, he settled on rat poison. Rod could simply head to a local hardware store and purchase the item off the shelf. Usually sold under the brand d-CON, rat poison powder contains the anticoagulant brodifacoum, which thins the blood. It quickly terminates mice by causing internal hemorrhaging—though it is far less efficient in humans, requiring repeated and prolonged exposure. As a result, rat-poison fatalities in people are quite rare.

But Rod was undeterred. He bought a box of the toxin and stored it in his living-room closet. Rather than administer the poison himself, he planned for Anna—just 11 at the time—to mix it into her grandparents' sugar bowl and spike their tea.

"He said that if Anna was able to kill his parents, because she was a child, if she got jailed at all, it wouldn't be for very long," Debra recalled. "I said, 'You cannot do that to your child. You cannot do that to Anna. You cannot put her through that!'"

Debra eventually convinced him to set aside the scheme. Rod, Debra maintained, did have a profound love and affection for his daughter—even as he manipulated her for his own ends.

"They were close," she recalled. "He used her to get what he wanted, but I think in some warped way he did love her." He was far closer to Anna than he was to Myles, and she, like most little girls, was eager to please her father.

While the poison scenario lost steam, Rod's rage toward his parents continued to bubble. Not a day passed without Rod mulling their elimination, Debra said. He told her they "stole his future, they stole his life and kids' lives."

On October 29, 2012, Superstorm Sandy walloped the East Coast and left New York City a drenched mess. The storm began as a hurricane in the Caribbean, hitting Jamaica and then Cuba before snaking its way north. By the time it reached Manhattan, it stretched 900 miles wide and was the region's second-largest on record. Winds up to 80 miles an hour thrashed the tristate region and a storm surge flooded low-lying coastal areas, ultimately causing 43 deaths, destroying 17,000 homes and wreaking $19 billion worth of damage.

With the East Coast disoriented by the disaster, Rod sensed an opportunity. He told Debra that the time was right for killing. She had gotten into town the previous night from North Carolina, after Rod had insisted on seeing her, despite the treacherous driving conditions. Governor Andrew Cuomo had declared a state of emergency, and the roads were empty. With wind and rain battering their windows and the electricity knocked out, Rod and Debra sat quietly in their drab and darkened apartment. Streetlight streaking in through the window served as their only source of illumination.

Debra recalled a fluorescent ray hitting Rod's face. "I want to go over there and kill my parents. It's the perfect opportunity," he told her. "There's no electricity, the alarm won't be on. I can go through a window in the basement then set the house on fire." With unnerving calm, Rod explained that he would be able to maneuver himself and the kids out of the home while Carol and Dave burned.

"How are you going to explain your presence? How are you going to explain how you happened to be at your parents' house?" she asked incredulously, reminding him there was a protective order still in place. "You're just going to miraculously be there during a house fire to save your children?"

Debra tried to dissuade him from the outlandish plot, and they spent 15 minutes discussing it before the clouds of irrationality dispersed.

"It was the first time I was ever really afraid of him," Debra recalled. "Even in the dark, he had this look on his face. It was so intense. I realized what he was really capable of."

Just a week after abandoning that plan, Rod excitedly approached Debra with a fresh inspiration. He planned to pose as an African-American canvasser in the run-up to the approaching presidential election pitting Barack Obama against Mitt Romney. Donning blackface, Rod planned to knock on the door, wait for Carol to appear and then deliver a lethal karate chop to her neck. He asked Debra to drive him to a costume shop in Yonkers to buy "a black man's wig and makeup," then drive to his parents' house when he knew his mother would be home alone.

Rod instructed Debra to leave her phone at their apartment so that they wouldn't be tracked.

Rod used cash to make the purchase at the novelty shop. After they got back in the car, he told Debra to drive him to his parents' home, drop him off and wait on a back street. He told her that, after delivering the fatal strike, he would sprint through the backyard and jump into what was now a getaway car. Debra was so troubled by Rod's derangement that she considered calling the police. But, again, as they sat in the car with snow falling outside, she persuaded him to return to reality, and the makeup and wig went unused in the back seat.

Debra was now beginning to fear for her own safety. She told Rod that she had begun to worry that he was capable of killing her.

"No, I only want to kill the people who try and take my children away," he replied.

Surely, a piece of Rod ached for the company of his children, but he also missed access to their money. Without custody, he could no longer petition the court for use of their funds. "With the kids not being with me, I potentially run into financial issues at some not too distant point down the road," he wrote to a friend on November 14, 2012. "I've started playing backgammon for money again (though there isn't a lot of it out there) and giving lessons (though I haven't found students yet)."

With his cash melting and his debts mounting, Rod began to fear destitution—and a permanent end to his playboy dreams.

When the murder plots proved too onerous, Rod came up with perhaps his most disturbing scheme yet to regain custody of his children.

He hatched a plan to frame his father for the rape of Anna, then 12 years old. Out of fright, Debra said, she pretended to participate in the scheme.

On January 14, 2013, Rod handed Debra a handwritten letter and gave her precise instructions on how to deliver it to Anna. He made her promise that she would not read it. Debra agreed and drove alone to Anna's school.

Overcome by curiosity, Debra disregarded Rod's commands and opened up the letter while waiting for Anna. She took photos of each page before placing them back in the envelope.

Anna eventually climbed into the car, and Debra handed her the letter, which the child immediately read. Rod deliberately wrote the message's paragraphs out of order, and scribbled a series of numbers, letters and arrows in the margins to decode the proper sequence.

Dear Little Love,

I wish I could discuss all of this with you more to make sure I know it would be ok forever with you. But I'll have to trust what you've told Debra and Debra's understanding of how you feel. I trust Debra and you 100%. This letter or anyone ever knowing about this would be very very bad. I ONLY thought of this because you told Debra you wanted to poison g [grandma] and g [grandpa] and I am afraid that you might do something like that at some point. That would be worse for you (and me and Debra and Myles). You and/or I would be the suspects and you might end up in jail forever. This thing that you will be doing is terrible but is better than you ending up in jail forever.

In barely legible penmanship, Rod falsely indicated that Anna had conjured the rat-poisoning idea on her own, clearly attempting to deflect blame in case he was ever caught. The rest of the letter laid out his explicit instructions, starting with the father and daughter's chats on a self-deleting, encrypted messaging app called Wickr. They were under orders not to communicate unsupervised.

1. Wickr—you have written some stuff that might be not great if people had the ability to see it. I don't think anyone does. But if anyone saw, "I think I could do it Tuesday"—if they ask, say you just meant seeing Debra. "It might hurt but I guess I might enjoy it when I'm older"—just say that referred to bowling. You hurt your thumb the last time but you'll be bigger and stronger when you're older. DO NOT Wickr important stuff about any of this!!

2. If anyone EVER finds out I had anything to do with this I won't see you or Myles for a long long long time.

3. ALWAYS stick to your story. ALWAYS. No matter what!!!

Next Rod outlined the false narrative.

4. Your story is:

A few weeks ago I took my grandfather's ring (his star sapphire ring) and I started feeling bad about throwing it away. So, before I was going [word cut off in Debra's photo] shower I told him I did it. Then he got really really angry. He said "that's it! I've had enough of this nonsense!" He grabbed me and threw me in my bathroom and told me to stay there. He came back in with something he had his pants off and I got really scare[d]. I tried to get out but he forced [me] down. I fought and fought but . . . but . . . he. . . . [words crossed out and not legible]. Then he told me that if I told anyone he would make sure I never saw my dad again. I called my dad and told him . . . i was so scared . . .

5. Today you must do 2 things:

A. Myles MUST know that he had to say he wants to be with Daddy if anyone asks him. If they say he can't but who else he must say Debra. He MUST say no to ANYONE else. Make sure he knows he must say

*no if asked about Marc and Eve or any Danishefsky.
He MUST know to not say you told him this.*

*B. Try putting 1 condom (the other will be used to-
morrow) on your finger properly (slippery side out)
and disposing of the condom AND the wrapper. The
condom can be wrapped in 1 tissue and flushed. The
wrapper should be cut into 4 separate pieces. Each
piece should be scrunched up. Each piece can then be
wrapped in separate tissues. They can be flushed together.*

Rod told Anna that on her way from school on January
15, 2013, she must follow these explicit instructions:

*A. On the bus home email Jo Ann [Anna's legal
guardian]. Write that you took grandpa's star sapphire
ring and threw it out because you were mad at him but
now you feel bad about it and wanted to ask her about
it. Do NOT answer a call from her. Do NOT speak to
her before the rest of this happens. She might tell you
not to tell grandpa and then the whole reason for him
doing this disappears.*

*B. Take the cucumber, the condom a pair of shorts,
and a pair of scissors into your bathroom. Put the condom on the cucumber. Make sure the condom goes all
the way down. When you use this make sure the condom stays on—condoms can (but shouldn't) come off
and go into you. It can be difficult to get them out.*

In the prior days, Rod and Debra had visited a Stop &
Shop grocery store to select the proper produce.

*C. Use it. You will need to push it in slowly but force-
fully. It will be painful. You will be breaking your hy-*

men (do not do internet searches about any of this stuff) and you will bleed. This is necessary. It is the bad part. Try to make sure some blood ends up on the bath mat.

D. Leave the blood on you. Take a bunch of tissues and put them around your vagina, and put your shorts (and undies on).

E. Dispose (flush) the condom and wrapper as you practiced.

F. Cut the cucumber up into little pieces. Small enough to flush down the toilet also. Flush the cucumber pieces down the toilet. Make sure it all goes down.

G. Clean the scissors with soap and water. The blades must not have any trace of the condom.

H. Press the shower button in as far as possible so that the water doesn't come out proper[ly].

I. Put a towel around you, with only your shorts on—no top.

J. Tell grandpa that you want to take an early shower but the shower isn't working properly. Make sure he comes to the bathroom. If you can't get him to come that's ok but it will be better to do the rest in there, too.

K. Tell him you took his ring and threw it away. Start scratching his face. You MUST get his face scratched and get his skin and blood under your nails. He will grab you. Probably your wrists.

L. Eventually (after you are quite bruised) calm down. Do NOT wa[sh] your hands or your body.

M. Call me. Tell me. "I told grandpa I took his ring and he got really [word(s) cut off in image]. And then he raped me. And he told me if I ever told anyone he would make s[ure] I never saw you again."

Anna silently read the letter, then handed it back to Debra. The nauseating contents weren't a shock to the girl, as she had previously discussed the frame-up with her dad, who had told her to grow out her fingernails to better mar her grandfather's face. She asked Debra to clarify what she should tell her legal guardian. "I think I can do this," she told her.

Sick with guilt, Debra said she tried to talk Anna out of it. But the girl's initial hesitation hardened into resolve. "I don't want to disappoint Daddy," she said.

Debra took the letter, tore it into small pieces and dropped them into a thermos of orange juice as instructed by Rod. But it wasn't acidic enough to dissolve the paper, and Rod later dumped the contents down the toilet.

On January 15, 2013, Anna emailed her legal guardian at 3:50 P.M. from her iPhone: "Hey Jo Ann I wanted to know weather [sic] to tell them that I stole their rings? Thanks, Anna."

Douglas emailed back 10 minutes later, "WHAT????? I really don't know what you're talking about. Please call me when you are able to discuss, ok? Thanks." Anna did not reply.

Meanwhile, Rod was inside his New Rochelle apartment with Debra, eager to learn from his daughter and the police that his plan had been executed.

"He was waiting and pacing. Pacing and pacing and waiting for a call for the police to say that his father had been arrested," Debra remembered.

The phone didn't chime until nearly 9 P.M., but it wasn't the police, it was Anna.

"Daddy, I couldn't do it," she said, adding that Carol and Myles had both been home and that the task was impossible.

Rod was furious that yet another scheme had crumbled, Debra later said.

The next day, Anna messaged Jo Ann to stanch any suspicions about her email and told her that it had been meant for a friend.

Rod's criminal lawyer, Robert Gottlieb, later argued that the warped plot was born out of a sincere concern for Anna's welfare. "Knowing that his daughter had tried to kill herself three times, she's acutely suicidal, and that she was desperate to be reunited with her father. . . . That's the beginning and the end of the significance of the letter," Gottlieb said.

It was the third time Rod had tried to manufacture a false sex-abuse allegation against a family member to create a legal advantage.

Rod knew he was the only suspect in Shele's murder, and that the DA's office was keeping a close eye on his every movement. The next knock at the door could be from an NYPD detective waving an arrest warrant and a pair of handcuffs.

"It appears that the criminal investigation has been pushed into high gear again," he told Debra in a voicemail on April 16, 2013. "So, I don't want to speak about anything on the phone of any importance whatsoever. No backgammon stuff. I don't want to text about backgammon. We can text innocuous things. You can tell me how you're doing, and I'll tell you how I'm doing in general, you know, but that's about it, because clearly there is somebody who is now actively monitoring my phone and my texts and all that shit, so I don't want to fucking, I don't want to—it's just fucking crazy, probably from the Danishefskys pushing because of the shit that my parents said about me. That's my guess. That's what my criminal attorney thinks is the most likely scenario, anyway."

Knowing his communications were being monitored, and desperate to save himself at any cost, Rod wrote a false confession to Shele's murder and attributed it to Anna. He later remarked to Debra, "If [Anna] confesses to killing Shele or killing her accidentally then the suspicion would be off me, and I would get custody."

Rod had previously set up a Gmail for his daughter, which gave him access to her account. Early in the morning on June 25, 2013, Rod logged in to Anna's email and synchronized an Apple note that he had composed remotely. The entire message was written in the email's subject line. It sat in her draft email box and was addressed to Jo Ann Douglas. Rod hoped the note would eventually be discovered by investigators who were now tracking his every move.

Dear Jo Anne, as u may have realized it has come time for [me] to start thinking about my bat mitzvah and now that I have realized that it made me realize that's its not only about the party but doing the right thing and that includes telling the truth. All of these years I have been so incredibly afraid and guilty about the night my mom died. I lied. She didn't just slip. That day we got into a fight about her dating and I was still mad when I went to bed. I herd her go into her room and run the bath so I went in and argued some more and she told me to go back to my room and I got mad so I pushed her, but it couldn't have been that hard! I didn't mean to hurt her! I swear! But she fell and i heard a terrible noise and the water started turning red and I tried to pull her head up but she remained still so I took Myles crawled into her bed and cried myself back to sleep hoping I would wake up to see her right next to me. But when I woke up she wasn't so I called daddy and he tried CPR and all sorts of stuff like that but it didn't work at which point he called the police and you know it from there. I didn't tell daddy what happened up until when we moved out of my grandparents house and I told him to keep it a secret

*and if he told I would kill myself. I'm sorry for Lying
but I felt so guilty!*

Prosecutors would later contend that Rod had authored the
note because he had misspelled the legal guardian's name as
"Jo Anne" instead of "Jo Ann." Anna knew how to spell her
guardian's name, as evidenced by their prior emails and letters. Tellingly, Rod misspelled Jo Ann's name the exact same
way the very next day when he emailed her about a schedul-
ing matter.

CHAPTER EIGHTEEN

Mexico

While Debra had begun to fear Rod's erratic behavior, her closeness to his children kept her from ending the relationship.

One interaction in August 2012 exemplified her connection with Anna. Debra was driving Rod and Myles to pick Anna up from summer camp.

On the ride back, the conversation turned to politics and Rod skewered Debra for her conservative views. "He called me a fucking moron and he jumped out of the car," she said. Debra kept driving to their destination—a local mall—with Anna and Myles.

Rod called her and demanded that she drive back to retrieve him. "They're my children," he barked. "We're done!"

The threat of a split deeply distressed Anna, who began sobbing at the thought of losing one of the few remaining adults she trusted. "Anna was hysterical," recalled Debra. "She wouldn't let go of me the rest of the day."

Debra eventually returned to get Rod. "Please don't take another mother away from me," Anna begged her father.

Once the shouting subsided, they decided to go to a movie. "It was dark and I had these tears streaming down my face. She's just so amazing," Debra said of Anna. "She was holding on to me and she just happened to notice [my tears] and she says, 'You know, everything will be okay.' And it just made me cry harder. Here's this wonderful little girl who has been subject to all this craziness and is still such a loving, young girl. I mean, she's just a wonderful little girl."

Debra said she often winced at Rod's treatment of his daughter. "He would just sit there and berate her," she said. "He would go on this diatribe for like an hour. I thought he was really rough and I thought he was a bully."

Rod's treatment of Debra was also becoming abusive. While walking to a pizzeria in Larchmont from their apartment on November 6, 2013, Rod once again began raving about the litany of people who were betraying him.

"Everybody is fucking me over," he told her. "The attorneys, the judges, the legal guardians, my parents."

Then, with a sinister look on his face, he turned to Debra and said, "If you ever fuck me over, I'll come after you."

Debra chuckled nervously.

He grabbed her by the arm and snarled, "Seriously. I will."

They continued to clash on the walk home. Rod's anger intensified to the point that a terrified Debra punched 911 into her phone but did not place the call.

After seeing what she had done, Rod exploded and raced back to their apartment, several minutes ahead of her. As she approached, Debra saw that Rod had tossed some of her belongings in the driveway.

"Get out!" he yelled, even though the lease was in her name. An unfortunate tenant who had been subletting a room from the volatile pair let her in and hurriedly left for work. Once inside, Debra watched as Rod snatched the keys to her car and headed for the door. He had already been involved in two accidents while using her vehicle and she didn't want a third.

When she tried to take the keys from him, Rod's eyes flashed with hatred. "He grabbed me so hard by the arms," Debra said. "He picked me up, and he ran me back and shoved—and shoved me really hard into the wall."

He let her go, but then clutched her elbows and pushed her onto the bed. "He was on top of me and I thought for sure he was going to choke me or strangle me," she recalled.

But Rod then got up and walked out. Minutes later, he reappeared in the doorway, and began chucking her clothes and toiletries down the stairs, stopping only after she called their landlord.

She texted her daughter, who begged her to call the police. But Debra said it would only worsen his rampage.

"I'm all jittery and having a hard time walking," Debra wrote her daughter. "It's going to take me a long time to pick all my things up out of the stairwell."

"I knew he was a fucking monster," her daughter replied.

In keeping with their cycle of dysfunction, Rod later gave her a heartfelt apology and Debra extracted a promise of better behavior.

Just days after the blowup, Rod and Debra traveled together to a backgammon tournament in Washington, D.C.

But as a precaution, Debra began recording their conversations.

In December 2013, Rod concocted yet another farcical scheme to regain control over Anna and her money. He called Debra from a hotel room in Tampa, Florida, where he was frittering away more of his scarce funds on a backgammon tournament. After reprimanding her for failing to answer his prior calls, Rod introduced his latest far-fetched plot.

Debra recorded the exchange.

After an incoherent and lengthy preamble, Rod finally

got to his point. "In Mexico, girls with just parental consent can get married at the age of 14. Boys can't get married until they're 16," he said. "But girls can get married when they're 14."

"So where are you going with this?" Debra asked.

"Well, I have a passport for Anna," he said. "I mean I'm sure for $10,000 there's some 18-year-old who would be willing to marry her and remain married, and just not, obviously, live with her. And sign a prenup and whatever, but just get $10,000 and maybe even another $10,000."

Debra now understood Rod's nefarious intention. If he married off his daughter in a sham wedding to a complicit groom, she would assume control of her own fortune. Rod, in turn, could manipulate her into letting him access it.

"And how—and how would you propose to do that? She's 13!" Debra exclaimed.

Missing the larger point, Rod cut her off. "When she's 14," he said.

Debra countered that police would be searching for Anna the moment she was reported missing by Carol and Dave. Rod, however, had already considered this, and said he would arrange for Anna to attend a sleepover at a friend's house, creating a 24-hour window to get to Mexico.

"That's a really colossally bad idea," Debra said in disbelief.

"Well, first of all, people do it all the time," he replied.

"So what happens to her?" she pressed. "Suppose she carries out this harebrained scheme, and what is she going to do after the marriage—after the wedding is over, then what? Where does she go?"

"Just come right back and live with me," Rod replied. "It would work. I mean, it's not a matter of what I think. It would."

"Oh goody!" Debra responded facetiously. "Then her name could be in the New York Post again, 'Married at 14' . . . but not living with her husband, living with her father."

"Yeah," Rod replied.

"Excellent scheme," Debra said sarcastically.

"Right—well—so let me ask you something. I mean what's better? I mean, Anna is suffering horribly," he said, referring to her life with his parents. "I mean, she's basically getting psychologically abused daily. I mean if it's not daily, every other day for sure, and it's not getting easier. So what's better? What's better? Suffering through, you know, bad publicity or, you know, constantly being abused, and not being able to be with me?"

Debra warned Rod that his parents would seek retribution and cut him off from Myles.

"I understand that," he said. "I mean, I feel terrible about it, but Myles and I, we don't have the same bond that Anna and I have."

Rod stressed that there were few options to remedy Anna's misery of living with her grandparents. If she complained about Carol and Dave's abuse to her therapist or the police, she could potentially end up with the Karstaedts—an unthinkable outcome.

"Anna has to suffer in silence," he said. "My dad called my daughter, a teenage girl, fat. He called her fat. That's the sickest fucked-up thing that I have heard."

Rod continued to denounce his parents. "They can't understand that what they did is wrong, and they haven't been able to apologize," he said. "For destroying really—really destroying—my life. Every day I feel like killing myself. I do. The only reason, seriously, that I don't kill myself is because I know Anna would kill herself if—if I did. Like, my life is misery. . . . When you're here with me, it's better. I can survive. It makes my life palatable, but if not, I—really, I feel like killing myself every day."

"Don't talk like that," Debra admonished. "Stop it—that's not healthy."

He replied, "I wouldn't do it, because I know Anna would kill herself. As a matter of fact, she would kill Myles and then herself, is what she told me."

Rod told her that he and Anna had made the pact together.

"I've changed over the years. Okay? I've changed tremendously. Okay? I've made myself change. Okay? But I am still fucked up. Okay? Quite a bit. But I'm not as bad as I used to be. Okay? I'm not like—like I was when I was 18. I was extremely psychologically abusive to girlfriends."

Rod then resumed his diatribe against Carol and Dave. His parents, he said, constantly unloaded their own personal psychodramas onto Anna.

"Which is why she should have gone with your wife's sister instead. I'm sure she wouldn't have been abused by them," Debra argued. "Your parents are horrible, horrible people."

"The only problem with Eve and Marc is that everybody just felt that in short order they would just turn around and say that Myles shouldn't have time with me," Rod said.

But Debra expressed doubt that the Karstaedts would exclude Rod and his family from the children's lives.

"Look at what my in-laws have done. At every step along the way they have tried to, like, fuck me over, like my parents," Rod said.

After he hung up, Debra mumbled under her breath, the audio still recording. "The most horrible, horrible person. He's gonna give himself a pass. Really? For the violent raging, terrible way he behaved, he's going to give himself a pass? He was worse than his parents. He's fucking worse than his parents. He can't get his daughter to kill his parents.

He's asked her three times, and he can't get his daughter to rape herself—oh, God, he's horrible. Awful. Horrible."

Rod made an entry on his Gmail calendar to email a Mexican law firm.

Meanwhile, Rod's finances continued to crater, and he was forced to detach from his computer screen and join the workforce. In February 2015, the Ivy League graduate landed an unglamorous position as a debt collector at Pearl Capital in Manhattan. He worked there for at least six months. Aware that his Google results would out him as a suspected killer, Rod applied for the job using the fake surname Sommer, according to an article in the New York Post.

Rod even used the alias to set up a LinkedIn profile, but omitted any prior work history or education to mask his identity. With a criminal probe inching toward his front door, the article reported that Rod was coming unglued. Troubled coworkers said he arrived at work "reeking of booze" and was "living out of a hotel room and prone to furious outbursts." One colleague called him a "psychopath."

Those qualities, however, dovetailed nicely with the often merciless craft of loan collection. Rod, who arrived at work at dawn and left at dusk, seemed to delight in tormenting and threatening debtors.

"In one case, this man said he had cancer and couldn't pay his loan immediately," a colleague recalled. "Rod was furious. He had no compassion. He would say, 'I don't give a fuck if he has cancer. I want the money!'"

CHAPTER NINETEEN

Flight Risk

In the summer of 2013, Detective Mooney, Roadarmel's partner on Shele's murder case, boarded a flight out of New York to pay Debra a visit at her North Carolina home for the second time. It was Fourth of July weekend and Rod was away at a backgammon tournament. Sweating in the Southern humidity, Mooney rapped on Debra's door and identified himself. Startled, Debra accepted his business card but nervously told him she had company and couldn't speak. She closed the door and immediately dialed the subject of the detective's interest.

Prosecutors and police had ramped up their investigative efforts after Shele's exhumation, reinterviewing family members and friends to loosen leads. Over the years, they canvassed anyone associated with Rod—even flying cross-country to quiz his most tenuous associates. After securing search warrants, detectives had scoured his email, Facebook account and phone records in the hunt for clues. While their pile of suspect correspondence was now considerable, direct evidence was nil and Rod remained just out of reach. Prosecutors had reached an impasse.

But Manhattan Assistant District Attorney Ann Prunty and her team would get their pivotal stroke of fortune when

Rod made the ill-fated decision to end his relationship with Debra in the summer of 2014. Debra said she didn't initiate the split but insisted that there were no tearful protests.

Freed from Rod's tyranny, she began to reflect on their chaotic time together. Weeks after the breakup, she retrieved Detective Mooney's card from a drawer and took a long look at the New York number. While she still had residual feelings for Rod, the glow of her affection had dimmed and she began to appraise him in a far harsher light. Debra could no longer stifle her suspicions about his possible role in Shele's death, and she felt a growing obligation to cooperate with the investigation. She finally mustered the courage to dial the detective.

Just days later, authorities flew her to New York to meet with Mooney and Prunty, who huddled with Debra over the course of three full days. The senior prosecutor was particularly interested in several of Rod's hard drives that he had given Debra for safekeeping. She turned them over to the DA's office, along with a few of her own devices.

It took prosecutors a year and a half to examine the trove of documents, emails, messaging applications and other records obtained from the hard drives. Investigators had to pore through millions of digital files—nearly all of them immaterial.

In circumstantial cases, prosecutors do not enjoy the advantage of direct evidence. There are no eyewitnesses to dramatically point at the defendant in court, no confessions and no videos of the crime to lubricate a conviction. Instead, prosecutors must weave often disjointed bits of evidence together into a persuasive narrative of guilt. It is a painstaking and often tedious process. A stray communication on a messaging app might illuminate an email correspondence that had flummoxed an investigator six months prior. A search warrant for one email account might reveal the existence of two others and prompt a fresh round of legal motions to access them.

From this sprawling digital morass, Prunty and her team finally gathered enough evidence to bring the case to a grand jury. The office was under immense pressure to obtain an indictment. Back in 2012, Rod, Philip and the public administrator had entered a stipulation barring Rod from laying any claim to the Shele D. Covlin Trust, unless the Manhattan DA provided a written letter stating that he was no longer the prime suspect in his wife's murder—or if six years had elapsed without his being charged. The trust held about $2 million in life-insurance proceeds and $1.6 million in assets, plus interest. The total would be split evenly between him and the children.

Since Rod had not been charged, he could apply for his share on December 31, 2015—exactly six years after Shele's death.

But as prosecutors were presenting their material to the grand jury, Manhattan District Attorney Cyrus Vance Jr.'s confidence in the case began to buckle. Vance was scarred by his recent calamitous attempt to bring sexual-assault charges against former International Monetary Fund director Dominique Strauss-Kahn. His office was subjected to international derision for rushing to arrest the Frenchman on charges that he attempted to rape a housekeeper during his stay at the Sofitel hotel in Manhattan.

In that case, the DA's office had hurriedly obtained a seven-count indictment against Strauss-Kahn but was forced to drop the charges just three months later, after the accuser's credibility crumbled into pieces.

The New York Times called the debacle a "devastating anatomy of a case collapsing" and said that Vance's minions had relied on an accuser who was "persistently, and at times inexplicably, untruthful in describing matters of both great and small significance." It was a global humiliation for his office and would become a blot on an already-uneven legacy.

Now, Vance was fearful of bringing another high-profile case to trial without enough evidence to assure victory. On October 23, 2015, he summoned Prunty—who had worked on the Strauss-Kahn case—into his office as she prepared two witnesses to testify before the grand jury weighing Rod's murder indictment.

According to published reports, Vance questioned whether the circumstantial case was sturdy enough to take to trial. He was particularly concerned that a judge would refuse to admit evidence of Rod's damning behavior not directly related to Shele's death. While the hard drives that Debra turned over had provided an abundance of evidence related to Rod's psychopathic tendencies, including his internet search history, the murder plots against his parents and the false sex-abuse allegation against his father, the materials would be useless if a judge deemed them inadmissible.

Prunty, who had earned the forbidding moniker Ice Queen among her colleagues, was outraged by Vance's apparent retreat and stormed out of the room. She went directly to her office and drafted a resignation letter. Her then-boyfriend, Dan Rather, the son of the famed TV news anchor, also quit his DA job in righteous solidarity. They walked out of the Lower Manhattan office and never returned.

But under unrelenting pressure from Shele's family and the press to bring a case before Rod could legally access Shele's estate, Vance was compelled to pursue a conviction. He tapped one of his most senior prosecutors, Matthew Bogdanos, to fill the breach left by Prunty. The veteran attorney hurriedly brought himself up to speed and secured a murder indictment.

Nearly six years after Shele's neck was snapped, Rod's day

of reckoning had arrived. On Sunday, November 1, 2015, detectives Mooney and Roadarmel were sent to arrest him in Scarsdale. They spotted Rod exiting his car at the local train station and approached his vehicle.

"What's going on?" he asked.

The cops were uninterested in conversation. They slapped on handcuffs and placed him in the back of their police cruiser.

The detectives drove to the 20th Precinct and put him in a cell. At about 11:30 A.M., Rod questioned Detective Roadarmel about the fate of his personal property.

"Are you keeping my phone?" he asked.

"Yes," Roadarmel replied.

"I have privacy issues with my phone," Rod said. "How am I going to call my attorney?"

Roadarmel let Rod dial his lawyer, Robert Gottlieb, from the precinct line.

The following day, Rod was marched before Justice Bonnie Wittner, where he was arraigned on two counts of second-degree murder. Wearing a beleaguered expression, Rod pleaded not guilty. Eve, Marc and Shele's other relatives looked on from the gallery. Wittner ordered the defendant held without bail.

The New York Post reached out to Jaelene Danishefsky, then 84 and in failing health. "It's about time," she declared to reporters. "I hope he gets what he deserves. There will never be closure. She's gone, and that's all there is to it. I think of her every day."

The belated arrest was covered in every major newspaper, including the New York Times and the Wall Street Journal. Local TV stations carried the story on the evening news, flashing pictures of a beaming Shele into New York City's bars and living rooms.

Gottlieb told the press in those early hours that Rod had been blindsided.

"We're stunned by the arrest," Gottlieb said. "We know that his ex-wife's family has continued to place enormous pressure on the DA to bring these charges. Now we will begin the process of really seeing whether or not there is credible evidence to support a murder indictment."

After a week behind bars, Rod returned to court on November 9, 2015, for a bail hearing. Judges rarely grant bail in murder cases, and Wittner, an older judge known for a fixed scowl and prosecutorial favoritism, was unlikely to buck that unwritten rule. But a murder arraignment rarely arrived six years after the commission of a crime.

Matthew Bogdanos, a former military man and hobbyist boxer, clashed with Gottlieb over bail. Nicknamed the Pit Bull, the veteran prosecutor had forged a reputation as one of DA Vance's most reliable courtroom lieutenants. The son of Greek-immigrant restaurant owners, Bogdanos grew up on Manhattan's hardscrabble Lower East Side. Instilled with an iron work ethic by his mother and father, he joined the Marines before attending Bucknell University and eventually earning his law degree from Columbia University. Cultivating a lifelong interest in the military, Bogdanos also received a master's in strategic studies from the United States Army War College.

He left active duty to join the Manhattan DA in 1988 and soon established himself as a dogged legal soldier. Moved by the 9/11 attacks on his hometown, Bogdanos temporarily swapped his suit for fatigues and was deployed to Afghanistan in 2001 and Iraq in 2003. While in Iraq, he was tasked with hunting antiquities looted during the chaos of Saddam Hussein's ouster.

Bogdanos would eventually coauthor a memoir about the operation called "Thieves of Baghdad: One Marine's Passion for Ancient Civilizations and the Journey to Recover the World's Greatest Stolen Treasures." In 2005, his efforts earned him a National Humanities Medal from President George W. Bush.

He returned to the DA's office in 2010 but continued to aid in the search for stolen artifacts and would sometimes don full military regalia during repatriation ceremonies.

While stern in comportment, the prosecutor had a weakness for verbal opulence, often peppering his arguments with allusions to Greek mythology and literature. Colleagues sometimes sniffed that the style showed more concern for displaying his intellect than his legal acumen.

Gottlieb had grown up in suburban Hicksville, Long Island, the son of a furrier and a school secretary. "I was the only kid on my block with a real Davy Crockett coonskin hat," the attorney liked to joke. An activist as a student, Gottlieb attended Cornell University and took a year off to serve as student coordinator for Shirley Chisholm, the nation's first black presidential candidate. He earned a law degree from New York University before becoming a Manhattan prosecutor under legendary District Attorney Robert Morgenthau. After four years spent securing convictions, he switched sides, becoming a sought-after New York defense attorney. Gottlieb's extensive client list, which spans decades, includes Al Qaeda subway bomb plotter Adis Medunjanin, noted exoneree Marty Tankleff and fallen sports radio host Craig Carton.

With reporters from more than a dozen news organizations swarming the gallery at the bail hearing, Bogdanos pushed to keep Rod caged for the duration of the trial. Appearing in his standard court uniform—a sober, form-fitting suit just taut enough to accentuate his slight but toned physique—he outlined the case against Rod, who faced two counts of second-degree murder and life in prison.

The prosecutor acknowledged that the evidence against Rod was entirely circumstantial but argued that such cases are frequently "more powerful and compelling than those buttressed by direct evidence." Rod's motive, Bogdanos said, was as simple as it was timeless: greed.

"He was desperate, and the financial situation that the defendant was facing at the time, coupled with the custody battle, was truly looming over him like a Damocles sword," the prosecutor told the court. He inventoried Rod's unseemly history, from the violation of protective orders and the physical abuse to the false sex-abuse allegations and frenzied infidelity.

"Based on the evidence, Your Honor, it's the People's position that the only person who had the unparalleled motive, unfettered opportunity and undeniable means, to the exclusion of everyone, is the defendant," Bogdanos said. He blamed Rod for misleading police and emergency medical personnel at the scene. Those distortions, he said, delayed an autopsy that would have triggered a near-instant arrest.

Bogdanos also sought to preempt the defense's argument against Rod being a flight risk, telling Judge Wittner that Rod had remained in New York despite the swirl of suspicion around him only to maintain a proximity to Shele's estate. But the arrest made him ineligible for those funds and he now had every reason to vanish.

Bogdanos pointed out that Rod had habitually ignored judicial orders in the past, citing his illicit correspondence with Anna on messaging apps and the Mexican marriage plot.

In closing, Bogdanos told Wittner that he suspected Rod of passing coded messages to Anna through Gottlieb and demanded that all of his correspondence—even letters to his attorneys—be vetted. He also pushed to limit his contact with the outside world, asking that Wittner bar all jail visitors—including Myles and Anna—save for his lawyers.

Irritated by Bogdanos' prolonged denunciation of his client, Gottlieb immediately fired back. The defense attorney cut a starkly different figure than his adversary. In contrast to Bogdanos' sedate sartorial style, he favored custom suits and flamboyant pocket squares. He radiated an avuncular warmth with the refined slickness of a luxury-car dealer.

"Your Honor, there is much that was said just now that is just downright wrong and misleading," Gottlieb began. "I know you have had cases where there is a merger of matrimonial custody battle and criminal cases. What happens in the context of matrimonial and custody battles oftentimes can just defy logic and common sense. It doesn't mean that the individual committed murder."

Rod's case, he argued, "cries out for bail."

"He had six years to prove that he, in fact, will not flee," Gottlieb continued. "The heat was on right from the beginning."

Rod stayed, the lawyer said, because of "his love and concern for his children."

Wittner then referenced the recorded call with Debra wherein Rod plotted to kidnap his daughter and marry her off in Mexico. "The telephone conversation doesn't seem—"

"It had nothing to do with money," Gottlieb interjected. "His daughter was suicidal."

The veteran defense lawyer then began to dismantle the DA's case, casting it as little more than circumstantial speculation. "We didn't hear anything to justify the sudden new arrest based on any new direct evidence or smoking guns," he said. "In fact, we know there's no confession, no DNA, no video, no eyewitnesses."

After Gottlieb concluded, the parties headed to Wittner's chambers to discuss a topic too sensitive for public disclosure—Rod's plot to have Anna fabricate rape charges against her grandfather. Gottlieb tried to minimize the scheme, telling Wittner that it was the last resort of an anguished dad. "It was done in the context of a desperation of a father trying to do everything in his power to regain custody," he said.

Wittner had heard enough. She soon returned to the bench and tersely ordered Rod held in jail without bail. She also granted Bogdanos' motion to bar Rod from communicating with anyone other than his lawyers. He was now completely isolated.

CHAPTER TWENTY

The Jury

The draconian terms of Rod's imprisonment infuriated Gottlieb, who argued that Wittner was purposefully seeking to place his client in a legal straitjacket. Her ruling compelled the Department of Correction to remove Rod from the general jail population and place him in isolation at the Brooklyn Detention Complex, a forbidding structure set amid the borough's downtown bustle.

Rod was deposited into a grim 23-hour-lockdown cell. He was barred from any contact with fellow inmates and received food through a metal slot in his cell door. He was only released from his box for one hour of solitary exercise and a 15-minute shower. That arrangement made it easier for prison officials to ensure that he didn't violate Wittner's near-total ban on correspondence.

Prosecutors, hoping to call Anna as a witness, feared that Rod would discourage her from cooperating against him if allowed contact. Bogdanos and his assistants were also concerned that Rod would convince prior girlfriends—especially Debra—not to take the stand.

Gottlieb countered that there was no evidence Rod had attempted to tamper with the case and that he shouldn't be presumptively punished. He eventually swayed Wittner, who loosened her original order. She conceded that the conditions on Rod's confinement were excessive and instructed the DOC to permit visits with a limited list of family and friends, including his mother, father, Myles and two friends. She preserved the internet ban and limited mail correspondence to his lawyers.

But despite the order, the DOC failed to implement Wittner's new rules. Rod was moved to the general population, but all of his communication and visitation privileges remained suspended. For weeks, despite a flurry of letters and phone calls from both Gottlieb and Bogdanos, Rod was still unable to place a phone call or receive a visitor. It would take a full two months to resolve the matter.

But that delay would prove minimal compared to the three years Rod had to wait for his day in court. He moldered behind bars as the DA's office sifted through millions of files on the hard drives Debra had turned over, a process that took well over a year.

As is customary before trial, both parties filed a dizzying variety of motions. In March 2016, Gottlieb notified the court that Rod was now penniless and that the senior Covlins could no longer foot his mounting legal bills.

The highly paid and sought-after attorney agreed to represent Rod for free before eventually receiving limited compensation from a taxpayer-funded panel that covers legal costs for indigent defendants. By the end of the trial, Gottlieb's billable hours and expenses would total more than $2 million. While his final payment fell far short of that sum, the vast publicity the case attracted likely made the endeavor worthwhile for a veteran attorney with an affinity for headlines and hype.

In early 2017, Wittner retired, and Justice Daniel Conviser was assigned to the case. He presided over a pretrial proceeding, known as a Huntley hearing, to determine whether

Rod's incriminating and contradictory statements to police and investigators would be admitted at trial.

Both attorneys knew that the materials would likely be allowed, but the parley gave Bogdanos and Gottlieb a chance to browse each other's evidentiary arsenals.

That same year, time finally ran out for Shele's parents. Joel and Jaelene passed away just six months apart. The heartsick patriarch died on February 25, 2017, at the age of 85 from an aggressive cancer he was in no condition to fight. Jaelene had been in and out of a rehab facility after contracting a staph infection during a hospital stay. She would succumb on September 22 while in hospice care at the age of 81.

The legal stakes heightened in February 2018, when Bogdanos pushed Conviser to unseal Rod's letters to Anna containing the false rape allegation against her grandfather and her fake murder confession. Unsealing the two items would make them public—and available to the press.

Knowing that the materials would be insurmountably prejudicial, Gottlieb opposed the prosecution's request. He argued that the documents may not even be allowed in evidence at trial and Conviser agreed.

That same year, the case was reassigned once again to Justice Ruth Pickholz. The petite jurist was known for a lacerating wit, judicial independence and a genial manner on the bench. A native New Yorker from the East Village, Pickholz wore her gray hair in a stylish pixie cut and often donned silver jewelry embellished with colorful stones.

Among Manhattan defense lawyers, Pickholz was esteemed for never cowing to prosecutorial aggression and for issuing rulings based on merit rather than political pressure. That reputation was burnished in 2011 when the case of pedophile Jeffrey Epstein crossed her desk. He had just completed a year in jail in Florida for soliciting a female minor for sex in 2009 and appeared before Pickholz to determine his sex-offender status in New York, where he owned a mansion.

Despite evidence that the billionaire had systematically abused dozens of underage girls, Manhattan prosecutors inexplicably argued that Epstein should be designated a Level 1 sex offender—the lowest and least stringent tier. Assistant DA Jennifer Gaffney said that his offender status should be based only on crimes for which he had been convicted.

"I have to tell you, I am shocked," a stunned Pickholz told Gaffney.

The judge rejected the defense and prosecutors' positions—which were oddly aligned—and ruled that Epstein was a Level 3 offender, the highest tier available. Epstein later hanged himself while in prison on new sex-abuse charges.

In the spring of 2018, Bogdanos filed a lengthy three-part motion that presented the outline of his case against Rod.

Unable to tie the defendant to the slaying with forensic evidence, Bogdanos instead sought to persuade jurors that they were in the presence of a sociopath fully capable of committing the murder. To do so, he needed Pickholz to let him present evidence of Rod's misconduct both before and after the murder. In legal terms, uncharged behavior not directly related to a given crime but still peripherally relevant is known as Molineux material.

The name stems from the case of Roland Molineux, an esteemed chemist who was convicted and sentenced to death for the cyanide poisoning of Katharine Adams in 1900. Molineux's intended target was Harry Cornish, a man with whom he had a power struggle over their positions at the prestigious Knickerbocker Athletic Club in Manhattan. At trial, the prosecution was allowed to introduce evidence of a prior uncharged murder: the cyanide poisoning death of a romantic rival that was uncovered during the investigation of the Adams case.

The defense appealed Molineux's conviction, arguing that the prosecution should not have been allowed to introduce evidence of the prior murder, for which he was not charged, to prove a subsequent crime. In 1901, the Court of Appeals agreed and overturned the verdict. Molineux was acquitted in a retrial.

But the ruling also defined when Molineux material could be admitted. If its value as background information outweighed its prejudicial impact, a judge could consider allowing it.

In this case, Bogdanos contended that it would help to establish that Rod had the motive, means and personality to kill Shele. Gottlieb countered that Rod's misconduct revealed an irrelevant propensity for poor behavior and little else.

Pickholz ruled that evidence related to Rod's trysts with other women before and after Shele's death, his request for an open marriage and backgammon habits were admissible. Critically, she also allowed in his hacking of Shele's email accounts, the false drug-abuse accusations he made to her employer and the false sex-abuse allegations involving Myles. While she disallowed evidence of Rod's physical attacks on his parents, Pickholz ruled that Bogdanos could introduce his plots to kill them.

But in a blow to the prosecution, Pickholz barred mention of Shele's expressions of fear to friends and family that Rod would kill her.

In another significant win for Gottlieb, the judge nixed Rod's damning plot to frame his father for the rape of his daughter. "I do not believe that any jury could fairly judge the defendant after hearing such evidence, no matter how strong the limiting instruction," she wrote.

She also blocked the false confession that Rod had written in his daughter's email, and the Mexican marriage plot.

Even after the ruling came down, both attorneys continued to push their positions. As the trial proceeded, Pickholz repeatedly modified the ruling—usually in Bogdanos' favor.

Gottlieb later said that Rod's fate hinged on the sensitive material. "I knew from the beginning that the case was going to rise and fall on Molineux, and that's why we spent a month arguing these issues, and that continued even during the trial."

On January 7, 2019, the motions were unsealed to the public and distributed to reporters. Disallowed portions were supposed to be redacted—including references to Rod's attempt to frame his own father for rape.

But to Gottlieb's horror, the DA's press office—ostensibly in error—gave the unredacted version to reporters, who sank their teeth into the depravity.

Gottlieb was apoplectic. The next day, he dashed off a letter to the judge, demanding an emergency conference to "address the impact of the district attorney's office disclosure to the press of sealed material in violation of two prior court orders."

Gottlieb complained that "nothing [could] be done now to undo the harm and prejudice by the disclosure and dissemination of the sealed information that now jeopardizes Mr. Covlin's right to a fair trial."

The defense attorney's disgust was compounded by a simultaneous attempt by Bogdanos to shoehorn in an expert witness whom Gottlieb deemed laughably irrelevant.

Prosecutors had hired master diver Andrea Zaferes, who described herself as a forensic expert with a specialty in bodies found in bathtubs. She had previously participated in several murder trials—with decidedly mixed results.

To demonstrate that Shele's death was inconsistent with

a suicide or accidental drowning, Zaferes had staged the crime in the same tub and filmed it.

The footage, filmed two years after the murder, shows a female model, her face half-obscured by a snorkel, attempting various rigor mortis poses with her head submerged in water. With the camera rolling, a male model assumes Rod's role and tries to pluck her from the water in between contortions.

Bogdanos pushed Pickholz to let jurors watch a clip of the peculiar dramatization, while Gottlieb lampooned the exercise and said it could not reliably approximate the circumstances of Shele's death. Noting that Rod had told police he couldn't remember what position Shele's body was in when he found her, Gottlieb dismissed the B movie outtakes as "junk science."

"One must suspend reality to believe that the condition in which [Shele] was found unresponsive can be accurately simulated with certainty by a clothed, living, conscious human being who is breathing through a snorkel and intentionally contorting her body," Gottlieb wrote with contempt. "Everything about the video reconstruction is based entirely on guesswork and assumption, not facts."

Gottlieb also noted that Zaferes' reputation had sprung leaks in prior proceedings. She had been barred from contributing to trials in two other jurisdictions because of concerns over her unorthodox methodology and slapdash reconstructions.

"Once one overcomes the shock of the bizarre behavior demonstrated in the video, it is almost comical that the People plan to offer this reconstruction video and accompanying expert testimony from the so-called aquatic expert," Gottlieb wrote. "She's not a doctor, she has a certificate in scuba. She teaches people how to use a snorkel. . . . This is quackery."

The prosecution withdrew its request to introduce the video before Pickholz could rule on it.

On the first day of jury selection on January 14, 2019, Bogdanos fired a missile.

The prosecutor told the court that Rod had been captured on prison surveillance video demonstrating what appeared to be a martial-arts chokehold to another inmate.

Just one week prior, Gottlieb had insisted that karate expert Dan Anderson be disallowed from testifying because there was no evidence of Rod's martial-arts mastery. But the November 2018 clip from the Brooklyn Detention Complex law library appeared to suggest otherwise.

Bogdanos asked permission to show the clip to jurors to demonstrate Rod's familiarity with the type of maneuver that they say killed Shele.

Gottlieb resisted, telling Pickholz that the video "clearly falls under that cardinal rule, that black-letter law, that we all were taught, that is, you have got to be kidding me," he said. "There is no evidence he was taught that chokehold and knew about it at the time it was relevant to this case. . . . There is no basis. It's absurd, it's ridiculous and should have no part in this trial."

Bogdanos fought back. "We have him knowing it before the murder, we have it being the mechanism of the murder and have him knowing it after the murder," he argued.

Pickholz would eventually allow the soundless video into evidence.

With pretrial skirmishes finally settled, roughly one hundred potential jurors shuffled into the courtroom for vetting. Pickholz cautioned the random assortment of New Yorkers that the case was of intense media interest and that there would likely be daily coverage.

The judge asked if anybody had heard of Shele's death.

Several arms shot up. It soon became clear that many prospective jurors were eager to latch on to any excuse to avoid a trial that could last for more than six weeks. Some groused that they had vacations scheduled, while others said they lacked the impulse control to avoid press accounts that could taint their judgment. One potential juror told Pickholz that he used to work for disgraced movie mogul Harvey Weinstein, who was facing sex-abuse charges in the same courthouse and would later be convicted at trial and sentenced to 23 years in prison. The juror was dismissed.

On the third day of jury selection, Bogdanos accused Gottlieb of purposefully trying to purge females from the jury. "Women are being systematically deprived of that right [to serve on a jury] in this case," he roared righteously.

Gottlieb, in turn, had challenged the inclusion of a woman who worked with victims of domestic violence and also sought to dismiss a three-time divorcée. "Each time, I felt I had a new life," the woman told the court of her breakups.

Once the bickering subsided, 12 jurors and four alternates were selected, and both sides braced for trial.

CHAPTER TWENTY-ONE

Openings

On January 22, 2019, just over nine years after Shele Danishefsky died in a bathtub, her husband's murder trial commenced in a drab, windowless courtroom at 111 Centre Street.

This was not one of New York City's finer chambers of justice. It was bereft of the august opulence of the historic courthouses just three blocks south, featured in the opening credits of "Law & Order." There were no mahogany benches, no Latin phrases etched high above the gallery. The musty, unadorned courtroom was purely utilitarian, a grim processing center for the criminally accused.

The beige 12-story building was built in 1958 and looked more Soviet than sophisticated. The forgettable structure sits just north of Collect Pond, the former site of a miasmal swamp that marked the center of the city's most violent district in the 1830s.

Anticipating heavy attendance, Pickholz moved the trial from her small courtroom to a larger space on the fifth floor to accommodate press, family and gawking court buffs.

Nearly every seat in the gallery, furnished with stiff wooden benches, was taken. Shele's family sat in the front row. Their group included Eve, Marc, Philip, Peggy, Shele's brother Fred and his wife, Margaret. A Danishefsky family lawyer and other supporters were also present, positioning themselves in a row directly behind the prosecution's table. Bogdanos and his two young assistants, Anne Siegel and Nicole Drosinos, took their seats as the tension rose like a silent tide.

Rod's faction—consisting only of his mother and father— sat on the opposite side of the courtroom, behind Gottlieb and his assistants, Seth Zuckerman and Sarah Leddy.

Much of the anticipation for the trial stemmed from what promised to be a tectonic clash between two of New York City's top trial attorneys. Seated between them at a raised desk in the middle of the room, Pickholz held both a physical and figurative authority over the proceedings.

At 10:42 A.M., 12 jurors and four alternates filed into the courtroom and found their assigned seats in the jury box. After a few pleasantries, Pickholz delivered basic instructions to the panel, reminding them not to discuss the case with anyone, including their fellow jurors, and to diligently avoid media coverage.

Wearing a bland gray suit and blue tie, Rod sat stone-faced at the defense table, with the same inscrutable expression he had assumed since his arrest. Although his hair had thinned, especially at the crown, he remained tall, lean and handsome.

As the judge gave her instructions, media outlets that had been permitted in the well roamed freely, including cameramen from NBC's "Dateline" CBS' "48 Hours" and ABC's "20/20," along with newspaper photographers from the New York Post, the New York Daily News, the New York Times and other publications. One shooter crouched low in front of the defense table, his lens just two feet from Rod's face, and took over 100 frames in rapid succession. Another photographer stumbled as he traversed the crowded area between the defense and prosecution tables to take pictures of the Karstaedts and Danishefskys in the gallery.

Startled by their unruly presence, several jurors repeatedly toggled their gaze from Pickholz to the shutterbugs. Gottlieb, wearing a natty pinstriped navy suit, blue tie and purple pocket square—along with his signature black-rimmed spectacles—requested a sidebar.

The defense and prosecution teams clustered in front of the judge's bench to converse out of the jury's earshot. "Your Honor, I have a strong objection to the cameras," Gottlieb said. "They are very intrusive, quite frankly. . . . It makes it look like a circus."

For once, Bogdanos agreed with his opponent. The judge, the most press-friendly in the courthouse, said she would reassess the situation after the attorneys delivered their opening remarks.

As is customary, the prosecutor presented arguments first. Immediately assuming his dramatic air, Bogdanos greeted jurors and launched into his theory of the case: that a doting and industrious mother had been heartlessly murdered by a ruthless parasite.

"She was beautiful, universally regarded as a great mother, a great sister and a great daughter," he said of Shele. "Active and engaged in her children's lives, she had it all. She was the American dream. But she had a dark little secret, a secret that she kept from the world, a secret that she was ashamed of, a secret you don't talk about at parties and at Merrill Lynch, and at playdates, and at parent-teacher conferences, and at UBS. A secret she tried to hide for so many years. But we will talk about that secret, here in the courtroom, because that secret cost Shele her life. She was the victim of domestic violence, and not just a physical kind— and you'll hear about that—but the more insidious kind: the constant emotional and verbal abuse that is such a feature of what an expert will tell you is called 'the cycle of domestic violence.'"

He quoted for jurors a statement Shele had made to a friend: "I feel like I am at my wits' end, scared if I stay with this person with this kind of temper." The prosecutor described how she had finally summoned the courage to divorce Rod after his outrageous request for an open marriage on their 10-year anniversary.

Concerned friends and family, Bogdanos said, had applauded her newfound bravery and readied themselves for Shele's rebirth.

"But that decision was also to cost her her life," he told jurors.

Bogdanos described the morning of December 31, 2009, when Rod had called the first responders who found Shele faceup on the bathroom floor. The defendant proclaimed to everyone that it was an accident that she had drowned.

"Her bruised and battered body told a different story, but only if you listened," Bogdanos said. "And on that day, you will learn, no one listened."

Bogdanos told the rapt jurors that Rod stood to inherit $5.27 million from Shele's death, both directly, and indirectly through his children. "As you will learn, less than two days before her murder, Shele had made arrangements to change her will," said the prosecutor, pacing in front of the jury box and varying his tempo to keep their attention. "The totality of the defendant's conduct shows that his primary motive for killing his wife was pure, unadulterated greed."

Bogdanos claimed that Rod had hacked his wife's email and knew she planned to write him out of her will.

He described Rod's online skirt-chasing, causing several jurors to cast glances in the accused's direction. The defendant,

Bogdanos said, dedicated his whole life to bedding as many women as possible and becoming a nationally ranked backgammon player.

Bogdanos spiked his opening with contemptuous digs, portraying Rod as little more than a vicious lout. After painting in broad strokes, Bogdanos then began filling in his case in detail. The prosecutor pelted jurors with an unceasing—and, at times, disjointed—hail of facts. He spent a lengthy portion of his opening trying to discredit the defense theory that Shele had slipped and fallen. He told jurors about Shele's missing iPhone and how it reappeared beside her bed months after the murder. Although experts could not pinpoint the cell phone's exact location, it remained within a one block radius of the Dorchester Towers and was most likely inside the building from December 30 to June 2.

"Whoever returned it must have had access to the sealed crime scene—must have had a key," he said. "That person had to be the murderer. The person who had the iPhone and returned it had to be the murderer."

He described Rod's deteriorating relationship with his parents and their petition for custody of his children in 2012. "His parents became the new Shele, the new obstacle," he argued, summarizing Rod's abortive murder plots against them.

Bogdanos assured jurors that he wasn't presenting this stomach-churning material to prove that Rod was a bad son, husband or father.

"They are offered solely for a single purpose: to explain to you the defendant's motive in killing Shele Covlin," he said. "The only human being on the planet with the motive, the opportunity and the means to have done this is sitting just across from you here in the court: the defendant."

The marathon address ran into the 1 P.M. lunch hour and Pickholz excused jurors for their break.

The moment they exited, Gottlieb promptly leaped to his feet and demanded a mistrial, ripping Bogdanos' introduction as "outrageous."

With aggrieved intensity, he argued that Bogdanos had flagrantly ignored Pickholz's Molineux ruling by referencing Shele's statement to a friend that she feared Rod's worsening temper. The judge, Gottlieb said, had clearly barred Bogdanos from introducing any statements from Shele referencing Rod's capacity for rage.

"That was not ambiguous. That was not gray," he said.

Gottlieb called Bogdanos' team "a prosecution out of control," adding that "we can't unring the bell." Jurors, he said, were now irreversibly prejudiced against his client.

Bogdanos responded by reading the exact quote he used in his opening statement and stressed that he never mentioned "any threat to kill."

Despite Gottlieb's best efforts, the judge sided with Bogdanos and denied the long-shot mistrial motion.

Rejuvenated by the break, the jury was ushered back in for the defense's opening statement.

With his informal manner and disarming smile, Gottlieb stood as a counterpoint to Bogdanos' stern rigidity. He began by describing Shele's death as "tragic beyond limits. A young, bright, talented woman died, and two young, beautiful children lost their mother."

He acknowledged the pain of her loved ones, who were still grieving. But he called Bogdanos' narrative a "misleading distortion of the facts."

"The police, not Rod Covlin, the police who were involved in this case from the beginning, and who went there on December 31, believed that Shele Covlin's death was a tragic accident," Gott-lieb told jurors. The police, he said, had taken stock of the situation inside the apartment, inspecting the tub, the bathroom and Shele's body, and interviewing all parties present. In their professional opinion, Shele's death was "a tragic accident of slipping and falling in the bathtub."

The attorney emphasized that the initial law enforcement opinion was corroborated by an investigator from the Office of Chief Medical Examiner, who found that she had died under "benign circumstances."

Gottlieb ridiculed the police's belated investigation into Rod. "It was so sloppy, careless and cavalier that sadly, Shele Covlin's family will never know why Ms. Covlin died and neither will you, neither will you, by the end of this trial," he said. "The entire case is riddled with gaps as wide as the ocean." He argued that there was not "one scintilla of evidence" that Rod knew that Shele had planned to write him out of her will the day of the murder, calling the state's entire case "a prosecutor's theory of what happened and then a desperate but unsuccessful search for justification for that theory."

His remarks cast Bogdanos as something of a courtroom huckster who was playing keep-away with essential facts.

The prosecutor, who prided himself on his unimpeachable integrity, seethed in his chair as Gottlieb levied the attack. Gottlieb knew that his arrows were landing in the very center of his ego.

Bogdanos' argument, he said, was dependent entirely on "the dislike, the animosity, the intensity" of Rod and Shele's separation—but little else.

"The evidence will show that she apparently died after slipping, falling, grabbing on to that cabinet door right above the faucet, and then hitting her head and neck against something very hard, having nothing at all to do with Rod Covlin," he said.

Citing the Danishefskys' refusal of an autopsy, Gottlieb asserted that even her family initially thought her death was accidental.

It was a plausible scenario, he insisted. The hyoid break, which had been key to reversing the medical examiner's cause of death ruling, could have been sustained in a variety of ways, including a bathroom fall or during her burial.

Besides, Gottlieb asserted, even if the state could somehow establish that Shele was indeed murdered, there was absolutely no hard evidence that Rod was the culprit. He pinned Rod's arrest on an unremitting campaign by her family to coerce the DA into reopening the case through media pressure.

Gottlieb said prosecutors and police had spent six years compiling a record of Rod's personal degeneracy "in the hopes that you would convict Mr. Covlin not based on proof that he committed the crime of murder, but because you don't like him."

Repugnancy, he argued, "is not a basis for a guilty verdict."

Gottlieb noted that Shele was dating several men at the time of her death. The attorney's motive was clear—to insinuate that perhaps another love interest had accessed her apartment.

He told jurors that after the investigation was revived in June 2010, another man's DNA had been found on the zipper of a makeup bag at the murder scene. Despite having excluded Rod, police did nothing to determine whose DNA was on the item, Gottlieb said. They had tracked down approximately 20 men that Shele had met on Jdate, but didn't test any of their DNA.

Although Rod's apartment was across the hall, detectives did not conduct even a cursory search of the residence.

"Why was Rod arrested six years after Shele died?" Gottlieb asked. The stipulation over the life-insurance payouts, he told the jury, provided the answer.

"In order to prevent Rod from receiving any money from the life-insurance policies, Mr. Covlin, on November 1, 2015, suddenly is arrested without any notice or warnings," he said. There was no fresh evidence or new context in the case that would have justified the charges—save for the looming deadline that would have allowed him to collect the millions.

"The DA buckled, not based on evidence that Mr. Covlin committed a crime, but for reasons connected to the civil litigation involving Ms. Covlin's family," he said.

With that, Gottlieb concluded his two-hour address and Pickholz excused the fatigued jury for the day.

The Covlins and Danishefskys quietly exited the courthouse, studiously avoiding each other and girding for the slog ahead.

As the prosecution's first witness, Bogdanos called Eve Karstaedt. Shele's petite baby sister strode to the witness box wearing a black pencil skirt, elegant green tweed blazer and black pumps.

Following Bogdanos' lead, she told the panel that she lived on the Upper West Side of Manhattan with her husband and their 16-year-old son.

Bogdanos flashed a copy of a magazine cover on the courtroom monitor. The packed gallery swiveled in unison toward the image of Mann on the Street, a finance trade publication that chronicled the industry's major players.

The October 2008 edition had featured a story on the Danishefsky Group, the lucrative offshoot of Merrill Lynch Wealth Management run by Joel, Shele and her brother Philip.

The cover depicted Shele and Philip standing on either side of their father in a sumptuous office. Wearing a black blazer, Shele looked confidently into the camera.

In another photo accompanying the article, she wore a blue blouse with a low neckline that revealed a Star of David pendant dangling over her scarred chest.

The images captured Shele at the pinnacle of her career. For most of her life, she had purposefully chosen clothes that obscured her disfigurement. But in the months before her death, she had clearly shed that self-consciousness and was finally at ease in her own imperfect skin.

Throughout the trial, Bogdanos repeatedly flashed the photograph on the screen to remind jurors of the pedestal from which she had been shoved.

Eve answered Bogdanos' questions clearly but nervously, recalling her sister's career ascent and successful collaboration with her father.

Bogdanos then asked Eve about the last time she saw her sister.

"We went to a funeral together," she remembered, referring to a December 16 ceremony for the death of a neighbor near their childhood home in New Jersey. Bogdanos played a surveillance video from the night of her death, showing Shele walking into the Dorchester's service entrance shortly before 8 P.M., wearing a fur coat with her iPhone at her ear. It would be the last time she entered the building. She would exit in a body bag.

The prosecutor then had Eve narrate the deterioration of her sister's relationship with Rod. To preempt an inevitable line of questioning from Gottlieb, Bogdanos asked Eve about Rod's contention that Shele drank and used drugs to excess. "Did you ever know your sister to take any drugs?"

"No," she replied.

"Did you ever know your sister to drink to excess?"

"No," came the reply.

The testimony moved on to the aftermath of Shele's death.

"Are you aware in the Orthodox faith of the position about autopsies?" Bogdanos asked.

"Yes. In the event somebody dies as a result of an accident, you do not—in the Jewish religion, we don't perform autopsies. The body is supposed to be buried complete," she explained.

But Eve asserted that the family had wanted an autopsy from the beginning. "We were concerned there was foul play," she said.

After a 10-minute recess, Gottlieb began his cross-examination.

"I am sorry for your loss and your family's loss," he said by way of introduction, before swiftly moving on to the prescription bottles found in Shele's apartment: one for Ritalin and another for Adderall. He said that Marc later went to Shele's office, and found more bottles of Adderall in her desk drawer.

Eve was ignorant of her sister's prescription-drug use, but Gottlieb's repeated questions about her medicine cabinet suggested to jurors that Shele had a pill habit that could have impacted her bathtub balance on the night of her death.

Gottlieb questioned Eve about the autopsy waiver, testimony that Bogdanos splintered with repeated objections. The defense lawyer asked if anyone had told her there were signs of a struggle.

Bogdanos sprang to his feet. "Objection, Judge!" he barked. "This is hearsay!"

Pickholz permitted the line of inquiry, but Bogdanos continued to pop up from the defense table like a basketball coach barking at a referee. Frustrated by his constant interruptions, Gottlieb fired back. "If the DA is going to continue doing this, Your Honor, he can get on the witness stand," the attorney said.

"Okay, stop it please, gentlemen! Please," Pickholz said like an exasperated parent.

Gottlieb moved on, asking Eve if she knew at the time that "there was no evidence of forced entry or theft."

"I didn't get any of that information—that never came up," she replied.

Gottlieb looked pleased. With a theatrical air, he then produced an imposing stack of papers, which included Eve's signed affidavit from the custody fight for Anna and Myles.

"Do you recall swearing in the affidavit with regard to what you were told: 'We were advised that there was no evidence of forced entry or theft'?" he asked.

"I don't recall," she said.

Gottlieb marched to the witness box to hand her the document, and she conceded his point.

"Is it fair to say that, initially, the family thought Shele's death was an accident, specifically, 'a bizarre slip and fall in the bathtub'?"

"That is not what we thought, no," she replied.

Gottlieb recited a line from the same sworn statement: "Initially, the family thought Shele's death was an accident, a bizarre slip and fall in the bathtub."

"That's what we were told," said Eve, flustered.

Gottlieb asked if she agreed with the rabbi's ruling forbidding the autopsy.

"We were not comfortable, but we went with it," she replied.

"Ms. Karstaedt, but if you thought to the contrary, knowing your personality, your intellect, is it fair to say you would have said, 'I don't agree with that'?"

Eve said that the family agreed to the decision only out of respect for the rabbi's religious authority.

With that, court adjourned for the day. Rod was placed back into handcuffs, taken through a side door and transported to his cell.

The following morning, Gottlieb resumed his exchange with Eve, showing her a series of photos of Shele's apartment taken on various dates after her death. The images showed that many items had been moved in the weeks and months after Shele's murder. Gottlieb would repeatedly present these pictures to witnesses to establish the extent to which the crime scene had been compromised.

The defense attorney then abruptly turned the court's attention to Shele's dating practices after her separation from Rod. He suggestively asked Eve if she was aware of how many men Shele was corresponding with and meeting on Jdate.

She said she was.

Gottlieb concluded his cross-examination and returned the floor to Bogdanos.

The prosecutor immediately sought to bandage the most consequential wound Gottlieb had inflicted—the introduction of a sworn statement that the Danishefskys initially thought Shele's death was an accident.

"So when you learned that Shele Covlin, your sister, was dead, what did you think?" Bogdanos asked simply.

"I thought 100 percent that it was not an accident. It was foul play by the defendant," she answered.

"Did you agree with the rabbi's decision?"

"I didn't agree with it."

"Then why didn't you protest? Why didn't you speak up?" asked Bogdanos.

Eve suddenly exploded in tears. "It goes back to following the laws within Judaism and respecting my father for his decision," she said.

Bogdanos asked her if she regretted the decision.

"Objection," Gottlieb shouted.

"Sustained," the judge ruled.

Still weeping, Eve climbed down from the witness stand and walked wearily back into Marc's embrace in the gallery. One by one, the Danishefskys rose to comfort her.

After the jurors were excused, Gottlieb told Pickholz that the display of emotion in front of the jury was highly inappropriate.

Bogdanos agreed and said he would warn the family. "Don't hug her, don't put your arms around her. You can't do it," he scolded.

CHAPTER TWENTY-TWO

Water Hazard

As her personal life was caving in, Shele had sought solace in a small circle of confidantes, including her laser hair-removal technician, Stephanie Goldman. Shele had been the beautician's client since 2002 and they had become close friends. Shele sometimes invited her to the Friars Club or treated her to dinner at the posh Campagnola restaurant on the Upper East Side. Goldman, whose own marriage was running aground, was especially receptive to Shele's marital complaints.

On the witness stand, Bogdanos asked Goldman to read jurors a foreboding text message that Shele sent her on January 4, 2009, a year before her murder.

"Thank God he will be away this weekend," she wrote. "I feel like I am at my wits' end. Scared if I stay with this person with this kind of temper that something very bad could happen in the future to my kids or me."

Bogdanos paused to let Shele's words resonate. He then asked Goldman if Shele had known about Rod's girlfriends.

"She knew he had cheated and that he—in Las Vegas or at backgammon tournaments, he cheated."

"Did she ever talk about whether or not backgammon was a source of marital strife?" he asked.

"Yes. He was gone a lot, but that was the least of it. He

was making no money and she was the one working, making the money, had the money, and he was just playing backgammon," she said. Shele's family members nodded their heads in agreement.

Goldman said that Shele was so fearful Rod would vanish with the kids that she kept their passports with her.

She had last seen Shele the month of her death, in December 2009. They had planned to have a New Year's lunch, but there would be no more appointments with Shele—either professional or personal.

After a weekend break, the trial resumed on January 28, 2019. Bogdanos called one of Rod's brief flings, Patricia Swensen, to the stand.

Dreading her courtroom cameo, Swensen's eyes were frozen wide as she walked unsteadily to the stand. She wore baggy jeans and a hoodie with her long blond hair down. A pair of poorly drawn-in eyebrows accentuated her weathered visage. From the stand, she glanced briefly at Rod and trembled.

Swensen told jurors that she lived in Upstate New York and owned a highway-construction business. She had encountered Rod online and they first met in person on March 4, 2009, at his favored date venue, Lure Fishbar. He admitted that he was married in the early stages of the evening.

"I told him that I don't date married men, so until he was separated, he would never see me," she recalled.

Rod reached out to her that summer to report that he had separated from Shele and they agreed to meet once again at Lure. Their final outing came that August, when Swensen picked Rod up at his apartment in her car and drove to Gettysburg for a weekend getaway. He recorded videos of her driving, as she playfully turned away from the camera and giggled.

The intervening years had taken their toll on Swensen, as the comely blonde depicted in the decade-old video bore little resemblance to the witness on the stand.

They stopped at Soldiers' National Cemetery to visit the site of Abraham Lincoln's Gettysburg Address before checking in to a hotel that night. The couple strolled through the historic hamlet the following morning before settling on a quaint eatery for brunch. They conversed breezily until the topic turned to Shele, and Rod's face tightened.

"He was very angry, very angry, talking about that she took all of the money out of their safe and that she completely looted their bank account," Swensen said.

Rod turned red with anger and his rising voice began to perturb fellow diners.

"You're getting way over angry than the normal person should be," Swensen recalled telling him. "You need to get psychiatric help."

"Mind your own business!" Rod had yelled at the glaring patrons.

On the stand, Swensen began weeping as she recounted the nightmarish meal. "He was getting so mad at me, more and more angry," she said. "It was so embarrassing."

But despite the public spectacle, Rod's wrath spiraled.

"He said he wanted Shele dead," Swensen told the jurors in a low voice.

It wasn't the first time he had made the shocking comment—but this time was different.

"His face, his eyes, his eyes—they were, like, glossy. They were getting glossy, like almost psychotic," she recalled.

Over eggs and orange juice, Rod then said he wanted to send a pair of goons to kill his father-in-law and "make it look like an accident" because he controlled Shele's funds. "My money is all tied up with him," he seethed.

As the casual brunch devolved into a homicidal tirade, Swensen grew panicked.

"I was in shock, I was in disbelief and I was scared," she said, telling jurors that she excused herself and went to the restroom to hatch an exit strategy. She returned to the table and falsely claimed that her teen daughter had fallen ill and she urgently had to rush home.

"He was really angry as we were walking back to the hotel, telling me how much money he wasted," she recalled.

Rod's mood brightened after he managed to browbeat a clerk into refunding the remainder of their stay. Despite her phantom pretext, he still tried to coax Swensen into extending their date so they could attend a romantic candle-making workshop that afternoon.

But Swensen was now immune to Rod's clumsy seductions, and she insisted that they drive home. She still had to endure his gloomy silence on the return trip to New York.

The prosecutor, having extracted what he wanted from Swensen, now wanted to shore up her credibility before Gottlieb took his swings. Bogdanos broached her 2012 drunk-driving arrest.

"Would you call yourself an alcoholic?" he asked.

"A functional alcoholic," she replied candidly, telling jurors that she drank between six and 12 Coors Lights each evening starting at 5 P.M.

"Do you drink before 5 P.M.?" Bogdanos asked.

"No, never," she replied.

"Have you had a drink today at all?"

"No," she said.

As Bogdanos had expected, Gottlieb immediately sought to cast Swensen as an unreliable sot. He interrogated her at length about her drinking habits until she admitted to indulging on a daily basis since her early 20s.

Smelling blood, Gottlieb asked Swensen if she had ever experienced blackouts, hangovers or other symptoms of advanced alcohol abuse. He snidely inquired if she ever experienced headaches after a particularly vigorous bender—but he got an answer he wasn't expecting.

"The only time I actually had a headache," she suddenly exploded, "was after my date with your client! I believe he drugged and raped me!"

The allegation stunned the courtroom into silence. Swensen's sobs pierced the quiet and her hands quaked violently.

Pickholz quickly interjected, telling jurors to disregard the accusation before ordering a brief sidebar. She told Bogdanos that the rape allegation was clearly inadmissible and that he should warn the erratic witness not to mention it again.

But Gottlieb's offensive continued unabated as Swensen squirmed in her seat.

"How much did you have to drink last night?" he asked.

"Five beers, five and a half beers," she answered.

"Have you had any blackouts?"

"Yes," she replied, telling the court that she checked herself in to rehab a month and a half after her first date with Rod.

She admitted that on that night she had had at least one martini, and possibly more, before switching back to beer. "I couldn't remember how I got home," she said.

"And you got drunk, correct?" Gottlieb asked.

"I wouldn't call it drunk because I am able to handle a lot of alcohol—I drink daily."

"Did you have sex with him?"

"I can't remember, because every time I went on a date with him I ended up drunk, so I don't know if he raped me or not," she replied, ignoring the judge's order to avoid the topic.

"You were so drunk you couldn't even tell us whether or not you had sex with Mr. Covlin, correct?"

"I believe I was drugged, not drunk," she said bitterly.

Swensen also couldn't remember if they had had sex in Gettysburg, and she repeated that she suspected that Rod had drugged her on the trip.

On Bogdanos' redirect, Swensen testified that Rod had pulled out a bag of prescription drugs and offered them to her on their first night in Gettysburg.

"I told him that I was feeling nervous," she told jurors. "He reached in and took out this black bag that had a bunch of different-colored pills in it and I said no."

Gottlieb had another go at the witness and pressed the admitted alcoholic on whether she had simply had too much to drink on those dates. He also questioned why she would agree to a second and third meeting if she thought Rod had drugged her.

Swensen said she didn't realize what had happened until the Gettysburg trip when he presented the pills to her. "I didn't believe he had drugged and raped me until I put two and two together," she said.

In closing, Swensen said that before she and Rod parted for the last time, she had offered him some simple counsel.

"Talk to God and ask for help," she had told him.

To undermine Rod's claim that Shele had died while taking a bath, Bogdanos called her longtime hairdresser, Adam Aminov, to the stand.

The Uzbek immigrant, speaking in a heavy accent, testified that he had given her a keratin treatment that same day—and cautioned her not to wet her hair.

Aminov first met Shele in 2006 at a Manhattan salon. She soon entrusted him with maintaining her treasured locks and often had him tend to her entire family at her apartment.

Shele saw Aminov at least once a week but would sometimes pay him additional visits for blowouts if she had important meetings or events. She had her hair colored every three to four weeks and eventually began keratin treatments, the stylist said.

"What are keratin treatments?" Bogdanos asked.

"Her hair originally is very frizzy, very volume. A lot of volume on. Hair so poofy, another way to say that," he said.

"Poofy?" asked the judge.

"Poofy. She doesn't like it very poofy," he replied. "So she likes the hair to be more straight and not frizzy and silky smooth. That's why keratin treatment make the hair flat and straight and silky."

"When you gave Shele the keratin treatments, did you give her any instructions?" asked Bogdanos.

"Yes. Of course. It has instructions on the bottle of the keratin," he said. "So the most important part after you finishing is not to get the hair wet or any humid because . . . it's not going to get the right result, so the hair is not going to be silky, not going to be straight, because this product doesn't like humidity and wet."

"So you said don't get the hair wet?"

"Right," he said. "Even no gym, no sweat, nothing making humid and wet." He said that he told Shele not to dampen her hair for three days.

Aminov told jurors that he had performed a keratin treatment on Shele December 30 at her apartment—the day before Shele was found dead.

Bogdanos asked again whether he had reminded Shele not to get her hair wet during that visit.

"She knows that," he replied without hesitation. "Everybody knows that."

This was a critical pillar of Bogdanos' case. He asked Aminov to repeat his exact instructions that morning.

"No wash, no shampoo, no gym, be careful from the rain. Put hoodie and umbrella," he testified.

Reporters covering the trial noted a parallel to the 2001 film "Legally Blonde," in which a lawyer, played by Reese Witherspoon, discredits a witness who claimed she didn't hear a gunshot because she was washing her hair. Witherspoon's character, Elle Woods, points out on cross-examination that the witness had undergone a perm that morning and would never have taken a shower, knowing that moisture deactivates the curling treatment.

Aminov had cut Myles' hair that day, and Bogdanos showed the court a tender picture of the hairdresser snipping at the smiling boy's locks.

He also counted Rod as a client, and told jurors that he had once played backgammon with him in the deli next door to his salon.

Hoping to limit the damage of Aminov's testimony, Gottlieb asked him during cross-examination if he ever explicitly told Shele not to bathe for three days.

"No," Aminov said.

He was followed on the stand by a friend of Shele's from the Friars Club, Warren Handelman. He testified that they chatted there a few days before the New Year.

Handelman told jurors that she was anxious over an upcoming meeting with a lawyer scheduled for December 31 to expel Rod from her will.

He saw her at the venue again on the eve of her death and they planned to meet for dinner the following night.

"I'll call you in the morning," he said and bade her goodbye.

On February 4, 2019, hotelier and businessman Neal Rothenberg, whom Shele had been dating at the time of her death, entered the witness box.

Rothenberg, who met her on Jdate, testified that he had prospered in the Florida hospitality industry for 20 years before returning to Manhattan to work in real-estate development. Tall with a graying beard and hair, Rothenberg wore a knitted yarmulke, glasses and a sober gray suit.

He told jurors that Shele had expressed her deepening fear of Rod and said she was worried about his martial-arts expertise. She also mentioned that he had keys to her apartment.

Gottlieb had fought to bar the latter disclosure before Rothenberg's turn on the stand. Pickholz had eventually allowed it in, but agreed to lighten its impact with what is known as a "limiting instruction" to the jury. "I just want to make clear to you, the fact that he stated that she said something to him regarding a key does not mean it's true or it is not true," she told jurors.

The judge said the information was being offered only to explain why Shele was in a hurry to get home before 8 P.M. Shele did not want Rod entering the apartment if she was late.

Gottlieb argued that the judge's hazy qualifications were unlikely to register. If jurors knew that Rod had a key, the lawyer reasoned, they would know that he had access to Shele's apartment the night of the murder. It was a significant blow to his defense.

At the end of the direct examination, Bogdanos asked Rothenberg about his surprising criminal past. As he had done with Patricia Swensen, the prosecutor opted to introduce the material himself, rather than afford Gottlieb the benefit of a dramatic unveiling.

Rothenberg admitted that in 1970 he was arrested and later pleaded guilty to criminal trespass after participating in a demonstration as a college student to protest persecution in the former USSR.

Bogdanos then asked him about a far more serious episode three decades later, in December 2001. Rothenberg said there had been an electrical fire in his apartment while he was out.

Upon his return, the doormen told him that there were firemen in his unit.

When he got upstairs, he discovered that they had called the police after finding guns in a lockbox under his bed.

"Did you, in fact, have five pistols in your apartment?" Bogdanos asked as the jurors straightened in attention.

"Yes," he replied.

He explained that when he sold his hotels in Florida to return to New York, he did so in a rush and let his attorneys and managers handle the transition.

The firearms, he said, had actually been confiscated from hotel guests and staff, and their reappearance was an ill-conceived prank.

"When [my employees] sent me everything from my personal office, they thought it would be funny if they sent me some of the pistols that were taken away," he said.

The guns were tucked into a desk drawer. When he found them, Rothenberg said he called his lawyer, who advised him to unload the guns and lock them away until they figured out a solution. But the firemen had discovered them first.

Rothenberg's justification had fallen on deaf ears in New York City, which has some of the toughest gun laws in the country. The hotelier was arrested and eventually pleaded guilty in 2003 to misdemeanor possession of a pistol.

Gottlieb, eager to diminish the impact of Rothenberg's testimony, immediately seized on the bust.

"The case wasn't dismissed because it was so funny, right?" Gottlieb shot back caustically.

Rothenberg tried to minimize the incident as little more than a practical joke. "I asked my lawyer to attempt to have the case dismissed because I thought it wasn't a case," he said. "I wasn't a criminal with a gun shooting people."

Gottlieb shifted topics. After Shele's death, Rothenberg had met with the Danishefsky family, who put him in touch with their private investigator, Michael Swain. During their meeting on January 24, 2010, Rothenberg did not mention Shele's remarks about Rod's martial-arts expertise or key possession. Gottlieb noted that he had again omitted mention of these seemingly crucial disclosures at a subsequent meeting with investigators in April 2010.

The attorney suggested that Rothenberg may have gleaned these details from Shele's family and retroactively attached them to his narrative.

"Is it fair to say that your recollection of what Ms. Covlin said to you when you went on these dates in 2009, that your recollection was clearer in 2010 than it is today?"

"It would seem that way," Rothenberg conceded.

Bogdanos then summoned Shele's friend Jeffrey Kanter to the stand. They had met at the bar of the luxurious St. Regis hotel in 2008 and would occasionally have a drink there to converse and commiserate. They connected over their high-pressure jobs in finance, as Kanter was a partner in a consulting firm that specialized in executive compensation.

"She was very smart," he recalled. "We started chatting, predominantly about business." Kanter, a married man, said their relationship was platonic.

He testified that Shele often complained about Rod and told him she was never late to retrieve the kids so that her estranged husband wouldn't have grounds to enter her apartment.

Bogdanos hoped to brand into the jury's mind that Rod had a key. But, once again, the prosecutor was forced to address a checkered episode in his witness's past to preempt Gottlieb.

Kanter, who has a law degree, had been punished by the

New York Bar Association for financial misconduct while working in estates and trusts.

"I had presigned checks by the executive, and I ran into a financial issue, and I was desperate and stupid, and I wrote two checks to myself, wrote a promissory note, and that's a serious no-no. And as a result, I was disciplined," he explained.

Kanter had committed the frauds in his 30s, and Bogdanos did not press him about the exact nature of his punishment.

Gottlieb, of course, was happy to fill in the blanks.

"You took money that belonged to individuals who entrusted their money to you as their lawyer, correct?" he drilled down on cross-examination.

"That's correct."

"The punishment for stealing your clients' money was to be disbarred, correct?" Gottlieb asked.

"That's correct," Kanter admitted. His license had been revoked and he could no longer practice law.

Having successfully humiliated yet another prosecution witness, Gottlieb turned to Kanter's statements to detectives after Shele's death.

Like Rothenberg, Kanter was forced to admit that he didn't note Shele's purported complaints about Rod during those initial interviews, and only mentioned them after visits with the prosecution.

That afternoon, Bogdanos called AT&T radio frequency engineer Denishkumar Patel to the stand. In prolonged technical testimony that appeared to test the jury's eyelids, he described the basic functioning of cell phones.

Patel explained that Manhattan has roughly 400 cell sites perched on roofs throughout the city. When an AT&T user places a call, the phone connects to the company's cell site with the strongest signal. Normally, but not always, this is the one closest to where the phone is located. AT&T keeps records of calls and the cell sites to which they connect.

Bogdanos then introduced Shele's phone records into evidence and ended his direct examination of Patel. He would call another expert to examine those records—particularly those produced after her murder.

Gottlieb's co-counsel Seth Zuckerman handled the brief cross-examination.

"If you were to look at records of cell sites where a phone call was placed from, that would be indicative of where you're located. Is that accurate?" he asked.

"That's usually the case," Patel replied. He explained that records can identify the sector—the area surrounding the cell site—where the call connected or other phone functions were used.

Each sector usually consists of a few blocks. But unlike GPS, cell-site data cannot place the exact location of a cell phone.

"So because you can't tell which specific building someone is located in, is it also fair to say you can't tell which specific apartment within a building someone is located on that phone?"

"Yes," Patel answered.

CHAPTER TWENTY-THREE

Thin Blue Line

On February 6, 2019, prosecutors called Rose Reid to the stand. In her thick West Indian accent, she described her tumultuous decade-long tenure as a nanny for the troubled Covlin family.

She had cared for their children for nine years, from the time Anna was born until Shele's death, when Rod fired her. From her intimate vantage point, Rose authoritatively depicted the family's corrosion and collapse.

Rose told jurors about Rod's escalating abuse and Shele's anguish. She said Shele became especially distraught during a conversation several days after the disastrous Mother's Day outing with Rod and his parents. On May 12, 2009, the nanny returned to the apartment after dropping off the kids at school and could see that Shele was disturbed.

"I asked her what happened and she could barely hold back the tears, and she said she and Rod had a fight Sunday," Rose recalled.

"What did she say to you?" Bogdanos asked.

"She said, 'Rose, Rod said if I ever tried to take the kids away from him, he is going to move me permanently,'" the nanny said. Her awkward phrasing appeared to frustrate Bogdanos and confuse the jury.

Rose continued, recalling that she had asked Shele what she had meant. But Shele turned away and walked to her room. The nanny said she was so shaken by the cryptic remark that she jotted it down in a notebook and dated it.

Pickholz stepped in to try to clarify the statement and asked Rose what she meant by the phrase "move me permanently."

"She told me that Rod said if she ever tried to take kids from him, he's going to move her permanently," she repeated.

Bogdanos' face turned red. He was clearly expecting a different answer.

Rose added that Shele then burst into tears when she asked what Rod had meant by "permanently."

Now at full boil, Bogdanos handed Rose the note she had written that day and instructed her to read it silently to herself, so that jurors couldn't hear her. *May-12-09. Came to work, Shele told me what he said, that if she tried to get custody of the children he will get rid of her permanently,* the note said.

To make the document admissible, Bogdanos needed Rose to tell the court that the note helped her recall that exact phrasing on the stand. He needed her to tell the jury that Shele said Rod would "get rid of" rather than "move her" permanently.

"Does that refresh your recollection as to the exact words Shele used to you?" Bogdanos asked with irritation.

Clearly confused as to what he wanted, Rose stared down at the scrap of paper. "I don't remember now."

"Do you remember now what she said?" the judge asked.

"No, I don't," she replied.

Had Rose simply answered in the affirmative, the critical note would have come into evidence. But, perhaps confused by Bogdanos' technical diction, she failed to comprehend what he was prodding her to do.

As a result, the jury never heard Rod's ominous threat to Shele, and Bogdanos was livid. He stormed out of the courtroom at the next break, putting his hand up when members of Shele's family tried to approach him.

When court resumed, Rose returned to the stand. She testified that Shele never took baths. Whenever she cleaned the bathroom, the soap and shampoo were always in the shower stall. The morning Shele's body was discovered, the items were, uncharacteristically, sitting on the rim of the bathtub.

After Rose had botched the most critical portion of her testimony, Gottlieb conducted a limited but impactful cross-examination. The nanny told jurors that Rod did not have a key to Shele's apartment, contradicting several other witnesses and undercutting Bogdanos' claim that he had easy access to the crime scene.

Having completed her uneven turn on the stand, Rose stepped into the gallery and embraced members of Shele's family before leaving the courthouse.

Two days later, on February 13, 2019, prosecutors called doorman Albert Battle-Figueroa to the stand. He narrated surveillance video of Rod exiting the Dorchester Towers through the lobby on December 31, 2009, just after 4 A.M.

On his way out, Battle-Figueroa said that Rod asked him if he wanted anything from the drugstore.

"It kind of struck me as strange," the doorman said, explaining that he had never made that offer before.

Taking advantage of the odd burst of largesse from the normally quiet resident, Battle-Figueroa placed an order for a Snickers. Rod returned 10 minutes later with the candy bar.

Surveillance video showed him exiting the building through a service entrance about an hour later and returning through the main lobby not long after.

Another doorman whose shift started later that morning, Louis Melendez, said he had received a call from Anna at 7:11 A.M. saying an ambulance was coming for her mom and to send them up to the apartment.

Bogdanos then called several first responders.

Retired FDNY Lieutenant Matthew Casey had been the first to enter Shele's bathroom and find her on her back with Rod kneeling beside her.

Rod barked, "Do something!" but Casey knew it was too late. The FDNY veteran was well acquainted with the appearance of rigor mortis, and Shele's awkwardly curled limbs indicated she had been dead for hours.

Jurors were once again shown the graphic photos of Shele lying half-nude on the floor beside a tub filled with bloody water.

Police Officer William Irwin arrived after Casey and ended up spending five hours with Rod. He told jurors that the pants Rod was seen wearing in the surveillance video on his 4 A.M. store run differed from those he had on when first responders arrived.

At the scene, Police Officer Sean Noce had noted to himself that Rod's clothes were completely dry. He told the jury he'd assumed that first responders had taken Shele out of the water, and the judge asked him to elaborate.

"I've removed children from a tub and gotten saturated," he explained. "To take any sort of object out of a tub, a small child or a full-grown woman, you're bound to get wet. I noticed that Mr. Covlin wasn't wet."

A procession of dour firemen, NYPD officers and other investigators strode to the stand to offer brief testimonies. Crime scene detective William Brown, who had snapped photos of the apartment, testified that he had planned to return the next day, after an autopsy, to dust for prints and collect DNA. But he never got the call. "It was my understanding that an autopsy would be performed because it was a suspicious death," Brown said.

On cross-examination, Gottlieb asked whether Brown had asked the detectives that day if they believed a crime had been committed. He said that he had.

"Isn't it true that they told you that they didn't believe a crime had been committed?"

Brown replied, "They felt it was suspicious."

"How about just a C-R-I-M-E?" asked Gottlieb, spelling out the word.

The judge scolded, "Mr. Gottlieb, that's not necessary."

To highlight the slovenly probe, Gottlieb barraged Brown with questions he was forced to answer in the negative. Brown admitted that he had not taken DNA swabs, looked in the hamper for any towels, taken pictures of the floor of Shele's room, searched the building's trash compactor, examined Rod's apartment or bagged a single piece of physical or forensic evidence that day.

He acknowledged that time of death was a critical detail to record. The attorney then asked him to state the time of death as he had written it in his report. After several awkward minutes, Brown looked up from the document.

"I don't seem to have that in my report," he admitted before backpedaling. "It really doesn't do anything for my investigation. It's more for the ME's office. That time helps them."

His thin summary described Shele's injuries, including bleeding from her mouth and nose and a possible bruise on the upper left side of her lip.

"Isn't it true that you didn't write anything about the scratches or anything like that?" asked Gottlieb, referring to the marks on Shele's face.

"They were self-evident," Brown replied defensively.

Gottlieb reminded him that he was supposed to document all the injuries he had observed.

Bogdanos then called "Rabbi" Meyer Weill. Wearing a dark gray suit, velvet yarmulke and round glasses, he stepped into the witness box.

"Could you tell us what you do for a living, please?" the prosecutor asked.

"I sell medical supplies," he replied.

Weill told jurors that he had cofounded Misaskim, the organization that helps Jews bury their kin in accordance with their faith and provides resources to those in mourning. Weill said that one of Misaskim's main objectives is to prevent autopsies of Jewish decedents.

"I have called you a rabbi. Are you in fact a rabbi?" Bogdanos asked.

"Yes," he answered hesitantly.

"Are you ordained as a rabbi?" Pickholz interjected.

"No, I am not ordained as a rabbi," he replied.

Weill testified that he had gone to Shele's home at about 12 P.M. the day after her death with the NYPD's permission. He told jurors that he traipsed through the apartment unsupervised and gathered the blanket and pink sheet that Shele had been found in. Weill then splayed them on Shele's bed and checked for blood specks. Unable to find any, he left the items strewn there.

Wearing his regular clothes with booties and gloves, Weill got on his hands and knees in the bathroom, spilling peroxide across the tiles, allowing it to penetrate and then scrubbing the surface with a toothbrush before wiping it up with a towel.

Weill said he did not recall moving or taking a pair of black pants bunched up on the floor near the toilet. The pants were in the December 31, 2009, crime-scene photos, but had subsequently disappeared.

With his task complete, he called the Danishefskys to see if they needed any assistance and was told of the impending autopsy.

Weill said he was so distraught that he rushed to meet them at Eve and Marc's home, where the family was sitting shiva. The family members told him they suspected foul play, which Weill quickly discounted. He relayed that the police had assured him that Shele died of an accident and insisted on speaking to the rabbi who had granted permission for an autopsy. After the conversation—in which Weill introduced himself as a rabbi—Joel's rabbi revoked his blessing.

On cross-examination, Gottlieb facetiously asked how he should address the unofficial holy man. "Now let me just clarify, it's rabbi? Should I call you rabbi?"

"You can call me Meyer," he answered.

"I'm not going to do that," Gottlieb replied with a slight smile. "You're not ordained?"

"Correct."

"You didn't go to rabbinical school?"

"Not to become a rabbi," he replied evasively. "I went to regular yeshiva."

"So even though you're not an ordained rabbi, you're permitted to call yourself rabbi?" asked Gottlieb.

"I don't call myself rabbi, they call me rabbi," he said. "Call me Meyer."

"I mean, not everybody can be called rabbi, right?" Gottlieb pressed.

Having painted Weill as a bungling bit player whose only role in the case was to sully the crime scene and hamper the investigation, Gottlieb closed his questions.

The next day, prosecutors called psychotherapist Kristen

Slesar, a domestic-violence expert, who had never met Shele or Rod. She spoke generally about the cycle of domestic violence. Bogdanos introduced the testimony to help explain why Shele gave Rod a key and cosigned his lease while claiming to be so fearful of him to her friends and family. Slesar told jurors that domestic-violence victims often try to appease their partners to prevent an eruption of temper.

She stressed that the riskiest decision domestic-violence victims can make is to leave their abusers.

The lead detective in Shele's case, Carl Roadarmel, lumbered to the witness box on February 21, 2019, and would remain there for three grueling days. The hulking cop's deeply creased face reflected three decades spent picking through the rubble of human wickedness. He had labored for 18 years as a detective and had recently been named the NYPD's investigator of the year for his work on the horrific case of Yoselyn Ortega, a deranged Manhattan nanny who killed two toddlers.

The laconic detective—no stranger to courtrooms—spoke in a flat and fatigued monotone. Roadarmel walked Bogdanos through his first moments on the scene, his interviews with Anna and Rod and his subsequent investigation. Bogdanos showed Roadarmel an autopsy photo of Shele's battered face.

"Did you notice the scratches and bruises on December 31?" Bogdanos asked.

"Yes, I did."

Bogdanos asked whether these injuries had aroused any suspicions as to her manner of death.

"Yes, I was waiting for the medical examiner's decision, which would follow the next day," Roadarmel said.

"What was your concern at the time of seeing her face?"

"That it was suspicious," he said.

Given Roadarmel's lethargic probe, this was a dubious claim. Roadarmel had been skewered in the press for failing to vet Rod's version of events, and he knew that Gottlieb was preparing to carpet-bomb him on the stand.

In all of their initial reports, Roadarmel and his colleagues had gulped down Rod's explanation—that Shele had slipped and fallen in the bathtub.

Bogdanos asked if he had searched the building's garbage compactor, the incinerator or any common areas. He had not.

"Because at that time, I just had a suspicious death. I had no probable cause to look through anything at the time," he pointed out.

After a five-day break, the trial resumed on February 26. Roadarmel plodded back into the courtroom and onto the witness stand.

He told jurors he'd learned that the family had forbidden an autopsy, and Shele was interred on January 3, 2010. Roadarmel insisted that it was the lack of an official homicide finding that stymied his investigation. In gunshot and stabbing cases, he said, a murder investigation can proceed without an autopsy. But in Shele's case—with no obvious signs of lethal trauma and no indications of forced entry—Roadarmel claimed he was all but powerless to pursue the case. He added that he had been assigned to at least 40 other cases at the time.

Bogdanos then broached the faux rabbi's brief but damaging crime-scene intrusion.

"What was your reaction to that?" the prosecutor asked.

"I was shocked," he said.

Roadarmel told the court that he didn't get around to interviewing the Dorchester doormen for more than a month after the discovery of Shele's body. They told him about Rod's early-morning convenience-store excursions, and Roadarmel attempted to retrieve the corresponding surveillance footage from the shops. But it was too late. Managers told him the video was erased automatically after a week.

On February 9, 2010, Roadarmel and his partner, Frank Brennan, went to Shele's apartment to search for her cell phone, after getting permission from Joel.

Bogdanos showed him photos taken the day Shele's body was found and on the day he returned to the scene. Several items were in different places—and Roadarmel had no explanation for their being moved.

During that same visit, Roadarmel seized Shele's laptop, an empty bottle of vodka and several of her prescription medications. But he neglected to voucher the items as evidence until weeks later, after the ME's homicide determination.

With no sign of the phone, they locked the door and Brennan affixed a new police seal.

In March, Roadarmel received the judge's order to exhume Shele's body and two checks from the DA's office to pay for the macabre task. Looking on in a heavy overcoat in the early-morning frost, Roadarmel watched as Shele's casket was removed from her burial plot beside her twins and placed in a metal box. He escorted the hearse to the ME's office and watched as Dr. Hayes dissected Shele's corpse atop an examination table.

After Hayes located the snapped bone in Shele's neck and declared her death a homicide, Roadarmel and Brennan were compelled to revive their flagging investigation.

More than two months after Rod's 911 call, Roadarmel and his partner finally began canvassing the entire population of the Dorchester Towers—640 apartments in total. They asked tenants whether they had seen or heard anything irregular in the hours before Shele's death. The exercise—which took days to complete—produced little more than shrugged shoulders.

The detectives moved down a checklist of basic tasks

that had been neglected. They obtained building surveillance and a list of Dorchester employees. They even visited nearby martial-arts studios in an unsuccessful bid to find anyone familiar with Rod.

Roadarmel and Brennan finally obtained a search warrant for Shele's apartment and entered on June 2—more than five months after her body was found on her bathroom floor. The prior searches were conducted with the Danishefskys' permission, while this one was court-ordered. The detectives were startled to find that someone had injected glue into the front-door lock. The team was forced to use a battering ram to enter a space that civilians—including the 'rabbi'—had already been waved into.

They combed the apartment and vouchered evidence for what was now a murder investigation. There, in the master bedroom, they spotted Shele's elusive cell phone attached to a white charging cord, as if it had been there all along.

The scene had changed in three other notable ways: there was a *mezuzah* ripped off the wall and lying on the floor; a makeup bag that had been on the upper shelf of the bathroom was now lying in the tub; and an order of protection barring Rod from contacting Shele was on the floor, partially torn.

Prompted by Bogdanos' questions, Roadarmel said they did not take prints or DNA on June 2 because the prime suspect had had access to the apartment. At that point, the Manhattan DA had taken over the case and Roadarmel and Brennan were largely sidelined.

Now it was Gottlieb's turn.

"Good afternoon," he said with unsettling warmth.

"Good afternoon, sir," Roadarmel replied.

The niceties ended there.

Gottlieb immediately challenged Roadarmel's specious claim that he needed a search warrant or autopsy to process evidence at the scene.

"Is it your testimony that unless there's a search warrant, you are not authorized to direct Crime Scene to seize property that you see in plain view at the scene of a potential crime? You need a search warrant?"

"We would like to get a search warrant, yes," replied Roadarmel.

"I didn't ask you what you would like to do," Gottlieb said.

The judge interjected. "You keep saying you'd like to. What does that mean?" Pickholz asked. "Is it at your discretion?"

"It's not at my discretion, Your Honor, it would be with the boss on the scene to make that call," he said.

"It's their discretion?" asked the judge.

"Yes, it would be their discretion."

"So it's discretionary, it isn't required? It's discretionary whether you could dust for prints?" she pressed.

"Yes," he replied.

Gottlieb continued, forcing Roadarmel to admit that, as the lead detective, he could have ordered crime-scene officers to voucher evidence, dust for prints and swab for DNA. Contrary to his previous statements, he did not have to obtain a search warrant to conduct a more robust investigation.

Gottlieb asked if he could point to any official NYPD directive that established this limitation. Roadarmel said he couldn't. Gottlieb added that he could have simply asked Shele's family for consent to search the apartment.

The pummeling continued. "Detective, as part of your training and your experience over the years, you would agree, would you not, that speed is very important in undertaking any criminal investigation, correct?"

"Yes, sir," he replied.

"And on December 31, 2009, as the lead detective, did you make any handwritten notes of any of the interviews you took that day?" asked Gottlieb.

"I don't believe so," said Roadarmel, who then asked to check his file. "I don't see any handwritten notes of the interview that day, no," he admitted.

"And as you told us, it's important to keep accurate records of those interviews, correct?" asked Gottlieb, extending the spotlight on Roadarmel's blunder. "And you do not have any notes for any of those interviews on December 31, correct?"

"Not that I recall, sir," he said.

The judge broke for lunch and Roadarmel shuffled out of the courtroom, clearly worn from an interrogation that had only just begun.

Back in the witness box, Gottlieb reminded Roadarmel that he had told the jury the previous week that he had not checked the building's compactor, garbage or any of the surrounding areas.

"You didn't need a search warrant or subpoena to search the building's garbage, did you?" Gottlieb asked.

"No."

"You just decided not to do that?"

"Correct," said an increasingly resigned Roadarmel.

He admitted that he had learned of Shele and Rod's strained relationship, the order of protection and the impending divorce soon after responding to the scene on New Year's Eve.

"Did it ever cross your mind, based on everything that you saw that day, that it might be important to search Rod Covlin's apartment, if you could?" asked Gottlieb.

"Not at that time, no," he replied.

"Did you consider that it might be a good investigative tool while you're there to ask Mr. Covlin whether or not he had any problem with you going into his apartment?"

"No, I didn't consider that."

"You actually entered the bathroom, looked over her and saw her face, correct?" the lawyer continued.

"Yes," he answered.

"Is it fair to say that you considered that this could potentially be a homicide, yes or no?"

"No," he replied.

"So based on everything you learned from police officers Pagano and Irwin, and including everything you observed, yourself, and how Shele Covlin appeared, nothing led you to believe that this might be a homicide?"

"Not at that moment, no," he said.

Gottlieb walked Roadarmel one step further. "Is it fair to say in your judgment, in your opinion, it could have been an accident?"

"Could have been, yes."

"Did you believe that Mr. Covlin was a potential suspect in a homicide?"

"No," said Roadarmel, evincing skeptical looks on several jurors' faces.

For the rest of the day's bludgeoning, Gottlieb enlisted Roadarmel's help in documenting his own investigative negligence.

Gottlieb showed a photo of Shele's makeup bag that had somehow moved from the shelf above the bathtub to the tub sometime between February 9 and June 2 of 2010.

"That makeup bag was removed, was taken, wasn't it, for forensic testing?" asked Gottlieb.

"I believe so," said Roadarmel, who had vouchered the bag and ordered the DNA testing.

Gottlieb concluded his assault the following morning by asking Roadarmel his impressions of Debra Oles, Rod's former girlfriend and the prosecution's star witness.

To the courtroom's astonishment, Roadarmel said he didn't know who she was.

"As you sit here today, you do not recognize the name Debra Oles?" Gottlieb asked incredulously.

"I do not," he replied.

On redirect, Bogdanos scrambled to recover ground, but the damage had been done.

Eager to shift momentum back in his favor, the prosecutor asked Roadarmel an incendiary question he knew would draw an immediate reproach from the bench.

"Did you know at the time that Rod wanted his wife dead?"

Gottlieb sprung to his feet. "Objection!" he thundered.

"Sustained," Pickholz said, glaring at the prosecutor.

After a three-day mangling, Roadarmel exited the witness stand like a beaten boxer from a ring.

CHAPTER TWENTY-FOUR

Debra

Senior Medical Examiner Jonathan Hayes, a forensic pathologist, took the stand on February 27, 2019. The portly Briton wore a dapper green olive suit with a checkered blue shirt, green tie and a navy pocket square. He sported a full head of shaggy graying hair, along with a bushy, overgrown goatee and mustache. While the ensemble had an eccentric air, Hayes wore a stern expression befitting his vocation.

After having been subjected to Roadarmel's hapless drone for several days, jurors seemed enlivened by Hayes' exotic articulation. The pathologist had worked for the ME's office for 26 years. He had retired at one point and moved to Florida, but eventually tired of sunny idling. Longing for the somber intrigues of the Manhattan morgue, he returned to his former job.

Hayes told jurors that he had received Shele's body on January 1, 2010, and immediately urged the family to allow an autopsy after seeing the scratches on her face. He recounted the back-and-forth pleas to his boss, Chief Medical Examiner Charles Hirsch, to waive the religious objection, which he refused to do.

"Why did you cave?" Bogdanos asked.

"He had the power and I did not," Hayes said simply.

Hayes then summarized his initial external examination and eventual autopsy while Bogdanos showed corresponding photos to the jury. The panel stared at several shots of Shele's face marred by bright red scratches and cuts on her nose, lower eyelids, cheeks and lips.

She had bruising and a scrape on her right elbow and on her flank. There was a cluster of four dime-size bruises on her right wrist and a larger bruise on the base of her index finger. The images also showed the contusion on her upper left lip.

"When could this have happened?" asked Bogdanos of the lip bruise.

"This is a fairly fresh injury," Hayes replied. "The split hasn't started to heal yet."

Bogdanos then showed jurors a close-up of Shele's right eyeball, the eyelid pulled back to expose the whites.

"You see a hemorrhage—actually two—in the eye," Hayes said. The pivotal marks were subtle: two little red specks the size of pen points. He told jurors that these were petechiae and explained their importance.

"If there is pressure applied to the neck, the flow of blood to and from the brain is interfered with," he said, causing blood vessels to burst. If pressure is applied quickly and evenly to the neck, blood stops flowing within seconds. Tunnel vision sets in six to 10 seconds later, then the victim passes out. If pressure is applied unevenly, blood continues to flow into the brain, building up pressure and causing petechiae.

Hayes described the three basic types of strangulation. In a manual throttling, the hands are used to apply pressure to the neck, leaving localized areas of bruising. The pressure is applied unevenly, delaying death and leaving more petechiae, primarily in and around the eyes and in the mouth.

The second method involves the use of a ligature, often a rope or wire, which usually leaves a distinct imprint of the weapon. The third variant is a chokehold, which uses pressure applied by the upper arms to evenly and quickly cut off blood flow.

"The findings are extremely subtle," Hayes said of the chokehold. "Blood is not flowing to the face and you see relatively few petechiae."

Jurors were shown pictures of Shele's awkwardly twisted limbs. Hayes said that this was rigor mortis, the stiffening of the muscles and joints that usually occurs two to four hours after death. The muscles of the face and neck are usually the first to be affected, followed by the extremities.

In a temperate climate, Hayes said, rigor mortis takes from three to six hours to set in. In colder temperatures—or in the case of a violent struggle—the process can accelerate. Based on the state of Shele's rigor mortis, she was killed sometime between 1 A.M. and 4 A.M., he testified.

Jurors were then presented with extremely graphic photos of the March 2010 autopsy. Several of them winced when the images flashed on the courtroom's monitor.

"The body has begun to break down, so the skin is somewhat discolored," he told jurors of a close-up photo of the right side of Shele's neck. The skin had been peeled back to expose her Adam's apple.

The gore was too much for Juror No. 8. His eyes fluttered before he suddenly flopped forward in his seat and fainted.

"He needs medical help!" shouted another panelist. Hayes asked the judge for permission to tend to the stricken juror.

Moving briskly despite his girth, he maneuvered out of the witness box. Another juror, who happened to be a nurse, rushed to his side.

Hayes crouched beside the man, took his pulse and softly

questioned him. The juror seemed to float in and out of consciousness before stabilizing and waving off help. Pickholz called for an early lunch and replaced the juror with an alternate.

After the dramatic interlude, Hayes resumed his testimony and described the bone that broke the case. Tucked protectively behind the jaw and under the base of the tongue, Hayes said the hyoid was an "unusual bone" that keeps the airways and larynx open to ensure free breathing. He pointed to the monitor, which displayed an image of Shele's hyoid bone, preserved in formaldehyde and stripped of tissue.

"It's a U-shaped bone, it's fairly delicate, and it's like a wishbone—but a small wishbone—and sits just above the Adam's apple," he said. "There are two horns on either side and you can see the right side of the horn is snapped. It's completely fractured."

Hayes explained that the nearby tissue in Shele's neck showed bruising, which meant the hyoid was fractured while she was still alive.

The forensic pathologist stressed that while the break did not directly cause Shele's death, it indicated what had. The injury showed that a great deal of pressure had been applied to her neck.

"The cause of death was neck compression," Hayes said. "The manner of death is homicide."

He added that Shele's other injuries also indicated the presence of a malevolent hand.

"The more striking thing was the scratches on her face," he said. "If a person is put into a chokehold, they fight back by trying to claw the arm away from their neck and they do so by clawing at their own face."

Bogdanos asked whether her injuries were consistent with a fall or drowning.

"No to an accidental fall," he said. "If she has an accidental fall and breaks her hyoid, there's no reason for her not to survive."

Excluding a drowning, he said, was more complicated.

"I can't say whether she was choked to unconsciousness and placed in the bathtub or killed completely by neck compression and placed in the bathtub."

Bogdanos asked if he had indicated on January 1, 2009, whether drowning was a possible mechanism of death.

"I was speculating," he said.

With the unsettling images of Shele's flayed neck still fresh in the jury's mind, Bogdanos introduced Rod's jailhouse chokehold video into evidence. Pickholz read a limiting instruction to the jurors, telling them they could consider the footage only to determine whether the maneuver was consistent with the manner of death.

"You may not speculate that Mr. Covlin was confessing to killing Shele Covlin or demonstrating the manner in which she was killed," Pickholz told the panel.

Jurors swiveled to watch the one-minute clip of Rod's interaction with an unidentified inmate in the Brooklyn Detention Complex's law library on November 9, 2018.

He can be seen standing on one side of a round table across from the man, bending forward and bringing his left arm toward his chest. He then turns and demonstrates the same move with his right arm.

"Are you able to tell the jury whether that action was consistent or inconsistent with the mechanism of death?" Bogdanos asked Hayes.

"This gesture is the gesture I've been describing when I've been showing how a chokehold would be applied, and this folding of the arm and elbow is exactly how a chokehold is done," he said.

On cross-examination, Gottlieb tried to dismantle Hayes'

determination of death, suggesting that the pathologist was making one logical leap after another.

"You don't know in this case if she scratched herself, do you?" he asked.

"I don't, but I don't have any other explanation for how it happened."

"Can you agree with the following: There's no basis to conclude Mr. Covlin is showing what he did to Shele Covlin?" Gottlieb asked of the video.

"I was struck by how similar this action was to what would be required to place a chokehold on an individual," Hayes replied deftly.

Gottlieb's line of questioning suggested that Rod may have simply been demonstrating the prosecution's theory of the case, which had been established four years prior.

The attorney confirmed through Hayes that Shele kept a medley of potent pills in her medicine cabinet. He also asked whether the scratches on Shele's face could have been caused by her skin grating against a rough surface.

"No, I don't think so," he said.

Gottlieb ended his cross-examination by asking the pathologist if a hyoid bone could break in the absence of a homicide.

"Potentially," he acknowledged.

Eager to convince the jury of Rod's lethality, Bogdanos called martial-arts master Dan Anderson to the stand to demonstrate a variety of chokeholds on a skeletal prop that had been hauled into the gallery.

The heavily muscled and moussed black belt described a range of strangulation styles, from wrestling and judo to classical karate.

"A chokehold can be done in two ways: a blood choke, which is cutting off the carotid artery or jugular. Then there is a wind choke or an air choke . . . that's the larynx or the Adam's apple, or attacking the trachea," he explained.

Bogdanos then asked him to commence his abuse of the mannequin. The jurors appeared to perk up at the prospect of dramatized violence.

Anderson began by wrapping a beefy arm around the skeleton's throat from behind and latching his hands together in a maneuver known as the Gable grip.

"The Gable grip was actually named after the Olympian Dan Gable," he said reverently.

"The hardest part is to clear the chin," Anderson continued, explaining that recipients of the deadly move instinctively tuck their chins in toward their chest. This impedes the ability of the attacker to secure a cinch.

"I pull the top of your head back and get in deeper, or I can pull the chin and inch in deeper," he said, manhandling his inanimate costar.

Suddenly, the skeleton's lower jaw dislodged and fell to the floor.

"Oh, I think I broke it. I'm sorry!" exclaimed the red-faced witness, drawing chuckles from the jury.

"I can't believe you just did that," Bogdanos said in mock outrage. "Don't do it again!"

A court officer dutifully scooped up the skeleton from the gallery floor—but it flopped sideways and accidentally head-butted court reporter Denise Huntington. The absurdity of the scene sent the entire courtroom into a rare bout of laughter.

Anderson finally returned to the stand once the wounded prop exited the stage, and resumed his testimony. He told jurors that a properly executed chokehold can cause unconsciousness in as little as five seconds and brain damage or death in just 10.

Bogdanos replayed the November 9, 2018, surveillance

video of Rod's jailhouse demonstration. With exacting technicality, Anderson identified the first maneuver as "the rear-naked choke with the Gable grip."

"Is this consistent or inconsistent with a chokehold taught in martial arts?" Bogdanos asked.

"Yes," replied Anderson. He said the second move Rod had performed for the inmate is commonly referred to as the less distinguished "bouncer chokehold."

Once Bogdanos finished, Gottlieb rose to the podium and applied a few holds of his own.

With a tinge of relish, the attorney asked Anderson about his criminal history in his home state of Arkansas—a record that appeared to catch Bogdanos completely by surprise.

"Did you run into any troubles with the law in 1994?" asked Gottlieb.

"Objection!" Bogdanos barked. "Troubles with the law?"

"I'll allow it," the judge ruled.

"Yes," Anderson answered, to Bogdanos' chagrin. "I stole baseball cards out of a baseball-card shop with my friend and we got into trouble."

"You were charged with residential burglary?"

"Yes, it was a baseball-card shop in the back of a guy's house," he said dismissively.

"No big deal?" Gottlieb asked sarcastically

"No big deal," said Anderson, now grinning awkwardly.

Prolonging the moment, Gottlieb had Anderson reveal to jurors that he had pleaded guilty to burglary and theft and was sentenced to one year in prison.

Anderson's vaudevillian cameo came to a merciful close and he stepped off the stand and back into anonymity.

With the outline of his case against Rod established, Bogdanos was ready to call on Debra Oles to sew his circumstantial strands together.

During a break, Bogdanos briefly stepped into the hall at the same time as Rod's father. Clearly stewing in hate for the prosecutor, Dave strode toward Bogdanos and delivered a stiff shoulder check before continuing on as if nothing had happened.

But Bogdanos ignored the cheap shot—as a far more urgent issue had emerged. After seeing a pack of photographers waiting to barrage her at close range, Debra was threatening to bolt. Bogdanos conveyed her displeasure to the judge and asked that cameras be prohibited during Debra's testimony. Pickholz refused.

It appeared that the lynchpin to the prosecution's case was in danger of popping out. It took Bogdanos and his team nearly half an hour to compel her participation.

Debra, 60, finally took the stand on March 5, 2019. She would be put on display for three unpleasant days. Wearing a theatrically haughty expression, Debra marched into the courtroom donning oversized sunglasses, a long black trench coat and a white scarf tied snugly around her neck.

With wavy blond hair that fell to her shoulders and clear blue eyes, Debra had retained her beauty despite years of unrelenting stress and poor health.

As if describing the contraction of an illness, Debra said she had first met Rod at a backgammon tournament in Michigan in July 2009.

She said their relationship was sporadic, ebbing and flowing for years and dictated primarily by their backgammon schedules. The union cooled considerably after Shele's passing, but eventually resumed.

As his anxieties spiraled, Rod began to give Debra several of his computer hard drives, which held all his online and offline activities, to take with her to North Carolina. Confident of his ability to control her as he had controlled other women in his life, he likely never imagined that those same devices would end up on the desk of a Manhattan prosecutor. While they didn't contain direct proof of his guilt, they provided enough peripherally damaging information to finally bring the case.

Before Bogdanos waded into the muck of Rod's custody battle with his parents and his various plots to kill them, Pickholz gave jurors instructions on how to treat the startling allegations. She told them that the information was being introduced only to the extent that it might help shed light on his motive to kill Shele.

With an air of belated repugnance at what she had participated in, Debra recounted Rod's ludicrous murder schemes—including the plot to execute his mother in an Afro wig and blackface.

"He wanted to drive to his parents' house when he knew his mother was going to be home, and when she opened the door, he wanted to karate chop her in the throat and kill her," she recounted, as Dave and Carol looked on from the gallery.

"What he said frightened me very much," she said. He even begged her to join in his parents' slaying, Debra recalled.

"It's indelibly etched in my mind," she said, describing Rod's mental and moral descent. "I'll remember it until the day I die."

That afternoon, Gottlieb began his cross-examination, immediately casting Debra as a vindictive shrew bent on burying Rod for dumping her.

"When did Mr. Covlin break up with you?" Gottlieb asked.

"Sometime in 2014. I don't even recall because I don't care," she replied.

"You told us that Mr. Covlin initiated it, correct?"

"Yes, but there are more details than that."

Debra grew more agitated as Gottlieb continued his provocation.

"Is it fair to say you have a history and have admitted to being a habitual liar?" he asked.

"That is disgusting and false! That is not true. There is not even a glimmer of accuracy to that!" Debra seethed.

"Do you have a history of lying?" the attorney pressed.

"I do not!" she protested, drawing out the word "not."

"Do you recall telling Detective Mooney that, 'I mean, I've lied to my husband, I've lied to my friends, I've lied to my family'?"

"You don't know what that's about," she shot back, her face pinched with rage.

Pickholz intervened. "Did you say that?" she asked.

"I did," Debra reluctantly admitted.

Gottlieb repeated her statement to Mooney for effect—and then asked if her dishonesty stemmed from a taste for extra-marital thrills.

"No," she replied.

When asked, Debra said she had married her husband in 1979 and that he worked for the federal government. The position required periodic background checks—one of which revealed a secret bank account she had opened with Rod. Her husband confronted her and she had admitted to the betrayal in December 2013—more than four years after their relationship began.

"At the time you met Mr. Covlin, you were having an affair with someone else?" asked Gottlieb.

"Briefly," she replied, telling the court that she had had a dalliance with another backgammon acquaintance.

"When did that affair begin?" Gottlieb asked.

"It was 2007," she said. "I really don't recall."

Gottlieb asked if Rod had ever admitted killing Shele.

"He did not say he killed his wife," she confirmed.

"You do not know anything or can tell the jury anything about the night his wife died?"

"I do not."

The trial then broke for lunch.

As Debra reentered the courthouse, she spotted Eve standing in front of her in the metal-detector line.

"I really hope you get justice for Shele," Debra told her. "I'm trying my best."

Eve smiled appreciatively, knowing that there would have been no case without Debra's involvement. "You're amazing," she said. "You're doing an amazing job."

When Debra returned to the stand, Gottlieb began to parse out the intimate details of her relationship with Rod. He confronted her with numerous adoring messages she had sent him.

"All I feel for you is love," she told him in one note. "I've never met a man more loving or caring to his children than you," she gushed in another.

In the letter, Debra called him the "sweetest, nicest, kindest, most loving man I have ever met."

She continued to express her love for him until they broke up, she admitted.

Gottlieb asked her about a March 2013 Facebook message to Rod that accused him of pursuing a "bevy of women" and using a dating app.

"It doesn't take a genius to figure it out," she said. She had also noticed that he'd deleted their history together on Facebook and removed tags that showed they were a couple.

"Were you jealous at the thought he may have been looking for other women?" Gottlieb asked.

"I don't know how to answer that," she said. "I was mad at him. I was just angry with him."

"You were angry with him because he was looking for other women?"

"No, I was angry with him in general."

Gottlieb asked Debra if she ever called the police on Rod when he threatened to murder his parents.

"I didn't have enough evidence," she said.

The judge instructed her to answer the question without commentary.

"No," she sniffed.

"You're saying that you need evidence to put a call to a police officer?" Gottlieb asked.

He reminded the jury that Debra was besotted with Rod to the very end of their time together. "I love you," she wrote him in March 2014.

The trial broke for the day, and the brutal cross-examination continued the next morning.

"For years, you lied to your friends, your family and your husband, correct?" Gottlieb asked.

"It's more complicated than that," she replied.

Gottlieb tried again. "Did you tell Detective Mooney that you lied to your friends, family and husband?"

"I did but it's misleading," she answered.

Gottlieb, having finally drawn the answer he needed, ceased his attack.

"I have no further questions," he said.

On Bogdanos' redirect, Debra told the jury that she was indeed intoxicated by Rod during the early stages of their relationship. But as his true personality revealed itself, her rapture waned.

She said she had delayed going to the police about Shele's case out of deference to her husband and to spare her family embarrassing media scrutiny.

"I felt like I owed him because I didn't want it in the press and all that," she said. "But I changed my mind."

"Why didn't you leave him?" Bogdanos asked.

"I was worried about his parents," she said. "I was concerned about Anna. I was also very frightened. I loved Anna and she loved me, and I was always concerned about Anna. It was very hard because I didn't want to be with him, but I wanted to be there for her."

Bogdanos asked Debra why she finally pulled Detective Mooney's card from a drawer on August 19, 2014.

"It was time. It was the right thing to do. It was the moral thing to do," she said.

With the prosecution's witness list finally exhausted, Pickholz turned to Rod.

"You understand you have a right to testify?"

"I do," he replied.

"And you do not wish to testify?" she asked.

"That's correct," he answered.

Gottlieb informed Pickholz that he would not be presenting a defense. With the burden of proof on the prosecution, defendants and their criminal attorneys often choose not to put on witnesses of their own—especially if they think the DA's case is weak.

CHAPTER TWENTY-FIVE

The Last Word

The parties convened for a pre-deliberation conference on March 8, 2019, to determine whether jurors would consider both intentional murder and felony murder counts—each of which presented differing theories of Shele's death.

The intentional-murder charge required that Rod had intended to kill his wife that night. The more nuanced felony-murder charge is applied when a slaying occurs during the commission of a separate crime, and does not require intent. In Rod's case, under the felony theory, he committed burglary by entering the apartment with an order of protection in place.

Both crimes are second-degree murder and carry the same sentence. If the jury found Rod guilty of intentional murder, the second count would become moot. But if they acquitted him of that first count, jurors would be able to weigh the second charge.

Bogdanos pushed to preserve the latter option as his legal safety net. Gottlieb argued that Bogdanos had provided no evidence to support the felony-murder count—and Pickholz agreed.

"Based on the evidence you presented here," Pickholz told Bogdanos, "I can't imagine you think he came in and didn't really want to kill her and just wanted to scare her and he didn't understand his own expertise and she ended up dying. . . . This is a murder, an intentional murder, and nothing else."

Still, she ruled that jurors could consider the second count. "I think this is a mistake for you," she cautioned, waving a finger at Bogdanos.

On March 11, Gottlieb began his closing remarks to a courtroom packed with more than 200 spectators. Shele's family sat in the front row behind the prosecution, while Rod's mother and father took their usual seats on the opposite side of the gallery behind the defense. Dozens of friends and members of Shele's community attended the closing act.

Drawn by the trial's outsize drama, three judges, longtime friends of Pickholz, arrived early to secure prime seats. A buzzing throng of reporters, photographers and TV producers occupied the front rows.

Gottlieb, wearing a red and blue tie, navy suit and a blue pocket square, walked solemnly to the lectern in front of the jury and placed a three-ring binder before him. He adjusted his signature black-rimmed glasses and smiled amiably as he lifted his gaze to the panel.

Rod, Gottlieb knew, was not an appealing character. Bogdanos had largely succeeded in presenting him as a manipulative menace with a cracked moral compass. Any chance of an acquittal would hinge on the jury's ability to subordinate their aversion and focus solely on the evidence.

He opened with an appeal to the jurors' sense of civic duty.

"Even if you think somebody is guilty, even if you believe in your gut that someone is guilty, a juror is the person who makes sure that in this country, at this time, in this courtroom, you put the government, the state, to its burden of proving a case beyond a reasonable doubt," Gottlieb said.

Bogdanos, just a few feet away at the prosecution table,

sat with his back ramrod straight and intently listened to his adversary's climactic push. At the table behind Gottlieb, wearing a pleading expression, Rod scanned the strangers who would soon determine the course of his remaining years on earth.

"Not only do you not know, the state does not know, and the state won't be able to tell you what in fact happened based on the evidence that the state presented in this case," the defense attorney continued. "Just remember, when the prosecutor gives you his summation and begins to tell you emphatically what happened and points his finger or raises his voice or walks around, I suggest that you keep in mind, and you think and you ask yourself, 'Mr. Prosecutor, where is the evidence that supports what you are telling us?'"

Bogdanos, he said, had failed to produce any proof that Rod was in Shele's apartment before 7 A.M. on December 31, 2009.

"Ladies and gentlemen of the jury, make no mistake about it, the fundamental basic reason why you cannot and will not ever be able to know what really happened and why it happened is because of the most botched, incompetent and disgraceful police investigation in the history of the world," he said. "It was frankly shocking to learn that detectives from the distinguished, respected New York Police Department were so cavalier, so sloppy in their approach, so sloppy in their attitude and their willingness to do absolutely nothing, nothing to investigate. They failed miserably at doing their job."

The attorney conceded that his client had behaved despicably during their split—but argued that divorces are usually ugly and produce aberrant behavior.

"Make no mistake about it, the state was intent on eliciting every nasty, bad thing Mr. Covlin has ever done or said, and by doing that the prosecution is hoping, is banking on you to convict Mr. Covlin because you don't like him," he said. "You may detest him, you may not even be able to stomach him, you may strongly believe he has a terrible and a bad character, and in some ways you can almost be suffocated by all of that evidence that was presented to you, but it has nothing to do with the evidence, the testimony or any proof that was introduced to answer the question of what happened on December 30 and 31."

During the three-and-a-half-hour summation, Gottlieb painstakingly combed through every element of the prosecution's case.

He zeroed in on one of Bogdanos' evidentiary pillars—that Shele would not have taken a bath after her keratin treatment. Gottlieb argued that it was possible that she did so without wetting her hair. In fact, Marshall Baron, Rod's friend, had testified that Shele took frequent baths to soothe chronic pain.

The defense attorney moved on to Rose's claim that Rod asked if she planned to sleep over at Shele's apartment the night of the murder. Gottlieb told jurors that Rose did in fact stay there on occasion, and that Rod's question was nothing out of the ordinary.

Then there were Rod's convenience-store jaunts the night of the slaying. "You can't assume anything sinister or sneaky or even suspicious by this action," Gottlieb said.

Even Rod's immediate call to his lawyer after finding Shele's body was not suspect, the attorney contended. "Here you have to think about the circumstance," Gottlieb told the jury. "He's involved in a very contentious divorce."

The lawyer dismissed the testimony of first responders who had pointedly noted that Rod's clothes were dry minutes after he claimed to have pulled Shele's sodden body from the tub. "You don't know if he went back to his apartment and changed," Gottlieb theorized.

It was also unsurprising that Rod objected to Roadarmel's initial attempt to speak to Anna out of earshot. The father, he said, was trying to shield his daughter during an intense trauma.

Gottlieb stressed that not one officer observed any blood or bruising on his client, arguing that a mortal struggle with Shele would have left visible marks. None of Shele's neighbors reported hearing any troubling noises the night of her death. The initial investigator on the scene said that there was no sign of a struggle or forced entry and had quickly concluded that Shele's death was likely a tragic mishap.

"The state does not have sufficient proof that Ms. Covlin's death was nothing more than a horrible accident, slipping in the bathtub," he said.

The police told the family it was an accident—even though they were fully aware of the acrimony between Shele and Rod. Her family initially accepted that determination and waived an autopsy, he said.

Dr. Hayes' contention that he was immediately convinced of foul play was dubious, according to Gottlieb. He read to jurors notes the medical examiner jotted down after first receiving Shele's body the day after her death. Hayes had written that it was entirely possible she slipped and fell, and suggested intoxication or illness as potential causes.

He reminded jurors of the egregiously contaminated crime scene and the bungling "rabbi" whom police had authorized to enter the apartment.

"If evidence is forever lost and unreliable, then the impact is, you, the jury, are deprived of the proof that you need to answer the question: What happened?" he said.

Shele's broken hyoid bone—the fulcrum of the case—could easily have snapped from a fall. The attorney mocked Bogdanos' motley parade of witnesses, reminding jurors of

Jeffrey Kanter's disbarment, Neal Rothenberg's gun collection and Dan Anderson's burglary caper.

Building momentum, the attorney strode confidently back and forth in front of the engaged panel, gesticulating for effect. Several jurors studiously leaned in during his address.

The attorney argued that there was no demonstrable evidence of Rod's karate prowess, and that Bogdanos' attempt to portray him as a Jewish Chuck Norris was baseless. Having adequately cuffed the junior characters, Gottlieb then turned to Patricia Swensen and Debra Oles.

"There has never been a trial in the history of the world with as many misfits and malcontents that you had the opportunity to see testify on that witness stand," Gottlieb said, pointing to the now-vacant box.

He called Swensen an admitted alcoholic whose entire testimony was "absurd, preposterous, inconsistent, illogical, bizarre and worthless."

Gottlieb had equally harsh words for Debra, whom he likened to an actress who "performed her role well, read her lines and followed her script perfectly."

On cross-examination, he said, Debra betrayed her lack of credibility.

"She was evasive. She was shifty. The bottom line is, she cannot be believed for anything."

He reminded jurors that Debra was brazenly cheating on her husband during her time with Rod and had habitually lied to those closest to her.

"The easiest thing to do is to testify if you're going to tell the truth, because you never get tripped up," Gottlieb said, jabbing a finger in the direction of an especially attentive juror. Debra was little more than an embittered former lover who "exacted her revenge" by going to the police.

Gottlieb rejected the prosecution's claim that Rod repeatedly snuck back into Shele's apartment, arguing that there was no direct evidence to support it. He said there was also nothing to back Bogdanos' assertion that Rod had taken possession of Shele's cell phone or that it had even been removed from her apartment.

As the hours ticked by and Gottlieb's phrases piled on top of one another, the jury began to fade. Even Rod's father dozed off in the gallery.

But Gottlieb plodded on. He pointed to DNA-testing results of the makeup bag found in the tub on June 2, 2010. A male's DNA was found on the zipper—but Gottlieb said investigators never pursued the potential lead, because it didn't comport with their theory of the case. Perhaps one of Shele's love interests had paid a visit that night, Gottlieb speculated, noting that surveillance footage was checked only for Rod's appearance, not anyone else's.

Bogdanos appeared to bristle at having to listen in silence as Gottlieb leisurely belittled his case.

Finally, the defense attorney pointed to the timing of Rod's arrest, just weeks before he was set to collect Shele's inheritance. That onrushing deadline, he said, shoved his client into the back of a police car. He told jurors that the only reason there were two counts of murder was simple: "Just in case you don't like the first theory, go with the second theory." Bogdanos, who was staring at Gottlieb's back, shook his head.

As Pickholz had predicted, Gottlieb argued that the DA's need to present the second murder count showed "that their theory all along is weak."

In a final appeal to the jury, Gottlieb gravely lowered his tone. There was no evidence of Rod's presence in the apartment, he said. There were no witnesses to Shele's death. First responders thought it was an accident. Mere distaste for Rod was not sufficient grounds for a conviction.

"You're bound by the law," he said. "You're bound by the burden of truth. If the truth isn't there, it's right, it's noble, it's the highest tradition of this country to stand up and say, 'State, you failed to meet your burden.' Our obligation, our responsibility is to uphold the law and to say, 'Not guilty,' even if it hurts, even if it's difficult."

Pickholz called for a brief adjournment after Gottlieb's address. In hushed tones, impressed spectators murmured that the lawyer's closing performance was both thorough and persuasive.

Given the near-total lack of direct evidence linking Rod to the crime and the laughable police investigation, many courtroom observers viewed a unanimous guilty verdict as unlikely.

"Sure, he probably did it, but where's the evidence?" mused reporter William Gorta, a former NYPD captain turned journalist who covered the trial for the Daily Mail.

"They'll be out for one week then come back hung," predicted a veteran judge in the gallery.

A court officer led the jurors back to their seats. District Attorney Cyrus Vance Jr. was in the audience for Bogdanos' closing—a gesture reserved for his office's most significant cases.

The prosecutor rose, then shuffled a stack of papers on the podium. The weight of the moment was apparent. Gottlieb, he knew, had likely punctured the jury's certainty as to Rod's guilt, and those holes needed plugging if his case was to remain afloat.

"There's only one person in the universe, to the exclusion of every other person on the planet who could have done it," he said. "There's only one person who had the motive, the opportunity and the means to have done this, or else she'd still be alive."

Bogdanos warned jurors not to be seduced by Gottlieb's personable air.

"Think of all the things that are not relevant. For example, the tone, voice, demeanor, the performance, if you will, of the lawyers," he said. "Mr. Gottlieb is a good man, he's a good, decent, honorable lawyer. But he's not on trial; the defendant is." Bogdanos' exaggeratedly polite tone suggested a purposeful insincerity, and Gottlieb smirked to himself at the defense table.

The prosecutor then zeroed in on the flaws in Gottlieb's argument.

He told the jury to dismiss the medical examiner's initial notes that indicated an accidental fall as a possible cause of death. That theory, he said, originated with Rod and had been funneled to responding cops and conveyed to Hayes.

"Think about the irony," he said. "The defendant is the source of the vast majority of the information that the medical examiner used in justifying not doing an autopsy."

He conceded that the case had moldered needlessly after Shele's death.

"That's a legitimate complaint," he said. "As you walk through each of the things the police didn't do, you have a moment of outrage. I get it. I'm there."

He agreed with Gottlieb that no one, except maybe Rod, would ever know exactly what transpired in the apartment that night.

"To suggest that you need to have more eyewitnesses is to reward the murderer for choosing well, which is why the law permits circumstantial evidence," he argued. "Which is why the law recognizes that in some cases, circumstantial evidence is more powerful than direct evidence. Than direct eyewitness testimony."

He reminded jurors that Shele was the lone obstacle to Rod's dreams of backgammon celebrity, financial security and sole custody of his children.

Rod, he said, was not on trial for domestic violence, serial womanizing, idleness or any other vices.

"What is he on trial for?" he thundered, as a radiant picture of Shele flashed on the monitor.

"He's on trial for taking this and turning it into that!" he continued as the shot was abruptly replaced by an autopsy photo. The graphic close-up showed Shele's eyes closed, her hair matted with blood and scratches marring her face.

"The question was never, 'Is he going to kill Shele?'" the prosecutor said. "The question was always when. Always. There's the tragedy."

Bogdanos again inventoried all of Rod's repellent conduct, rendering him more monster than man.

"Is he on trial for propositioning over 1,000 women in a year?" Bogdanos asked. "Absolutely not."

The prosecutor said he had presented these episodes to demonstrate Rod's increasingly manic state in the period before the murder. "He's trying to fill a void, the emptiness of his nowhere life."

Rod was all but insolvent, Bogdanos stressed.

"He had 5.27 million reasons to kill Shele Covlin," the prosecutor said, pointing to a summary of her life-insurance policies displayed on the monitor.

"On the very day that she was going to write the defendant out of her will, she has a fatal accident. Are you kidding me?" Friends gave slightly differing testimony for the date of the appointment, with some saying it was set for December 31 and others recounting that it was scheduled two days later.

He then played the surveillance video of Rod walking through the building lobby at 4:15 A.M. and chatting with the doorman. "He's creating an alibi," Bogdanos argued.

"I don't believe in coincidences," the prosecutor said. "I

believe in the Trojan War, I believe in King Arthur, I believe in a whole lot of things. I don't believe in coincidences!"

He then ran through each of the critical phone calls placed that morning. At 7:04 A.M., Shele's landline called Rod's cell phone.

"Mr. Gottlieb, a good man, wants you to believe that Anna made that call," he said tartly. "Other than the defendant's own statement, where is the evidence Anna made that call?"

At 7:11 A.M., Anna used the intercom inside apartment 515 to call the Dorchester lobby and told the doorman to expect an ambulance for her mother.

At 7:12 A.M., Rod called his divorce lawyer Luis Penichet's pager.

At 7:14 A.M., Rod called 911.

"You might be asking yourself why 911 is the third call, not the first," Bogdanos said.

He again referenced a firefighter's observation that Rod's shirt was dry, despite his claim that he had hoisted Shele out of the bathtub. That inconsistency, Bogdanos said, cast doubt on the entirety of Rod's narrative.

Knowing he would be an immediate suspect, Rod had a script at the ready, the prosecutor argued. But he couldn't keep his story straight. He told detectives and first responders different versions of how his daughter alerted him to the incident. In the first, she rushed across the hall and banged on the door. In the second, she called him on his cell phone.

"Unfortunately, police officers bought it," Bogdanos said. "There's no running away from that. They did."

Rod's version, he said, had been a hastily mixed concoction. Shele never took baths, and Bogdanos noted the absence of towels in the bathroom and water around her body.

"Where did the water go?" he asked. "Dry. Dry. Dry." He presented photographs of the bathroom taken on December

31, 2009. In the pictures, Shele's hair is wet and a halo of red-tinged water surrounds her head—but there is no liquid around her body.

Rod's online activity ceased from 1:13 A.M. to 4:13 A.M., an oddity for the night owl, he continued. Bogdanos reminded the jury that Dr. Hayes said rigor mortis set in roughly three to six hours after her death, which meant that she died between 1:25 A.M. and 3:25 A.M.

"Does that time period sound familiar?" Bogdanos asked. "It's when the defendant went dark."

Citing this combination of circumstances, Bogdanos presented his specific theory of Shele's murder for the first time. He displayed a photo of Shele's bed taken December 31, 2009, that showed a pair of five-inch tears on the sheet and a dark stain about six inches long at its widest point. In photos of Shele's room taken days later, the damp spot is gone.

"We know she bled, we know she took a shot to the mouth, we know she bled from the nose," he said. "I respectfully submit that that wet spot is where the attack began."

He said Rod went on a second trip to the store that morning at 5:02 A.M. and returned with two two-liter bottles of seltzer to clean up the blood.

"I grew up in my family's Greek restaurant," he said. "My mother told me the way to get red wine out is seltzer."

"Was she ever in the tub at all?" Bogdanos asked. "Based on the evidence, you can infer that the only part of her that was in the tub was the face, the part that was bleeding."

He put up a photo from the morgue of Shele's legs taken January 1, 2010, showing blood splatter on them.

"Why weren't they washed off in the tub if her body was in the tub? Now you understand why there was no water on the floor. Now you understand why he was bone-dry."

Bogdanos added that there was no way Rod had time to

change his clothes between his alleged discovery of Shele's body and the arrival of first responders.

The sun had dipped low outside the windowless courtroom and it was getting late. Bogdanos had to adjourn his closing for the day, saving his grand finale for the following morning.

Pickholz excused the jury.

As the packed gallery exited the courtroom and flowed toward the elevator banks, an unidentified Danishefsky partisan suddenly accosted Dave.

"He should have killed you too!" the man seethed.

The incident was reported to the judge and Pickholz addressed the confrontation the next morning before admitting the jury.

"This was a very intense trial," she said. "I know emotions are high on all sides. If I hear of any interaction between the parties—gestures, faces, outright threats—I will not tolerate that, and anyone who does that or engages in that conduct will be excluded from the courtroom."

Barely refreshed after a night's respite, the jurors took their seats.

Bogdanos resumed where he had left off, stressing the inconsistencies in Rod's story.

He had told some people that Anna had initially knocked on his door after discovering Shele's body, while insisting to others that she called him.

"Shakespeare once said, a liar has to have a very good memory because you actually have to remember both what happened and what you say happened," Bogdanos said.

The prosecutor moved on to the jail video of Rod performing an apparent chokehold for another inmate. Both Dr. Hayes and Anderson, the martial-arts expert, had testified that the maneuver was consistent with Shele's manner of death.

Bogdanos alleged that Rod had applied the chokehold from behind, wrapping his left arm around Shele's neck and using his right arm to hold down her right hand, leaving four finger-size bruises as he squeezed her into oblivion. Suffocating, Shele used her free left hand to dislodge his arm and clawed her face in the process, leaving her own DNA under her nails. It was near impossible that her fractured hyoid bone, Bogdanos argued, was sustained from a fall.

Having established the motive and means for Shele's slaying, Bogdanos proceeded to the question of opportunity.

He reminded the jury that several witnesses testified that Shele told them Rod had keys to her apartment. Rod's access, he argued, was cemented by his alleged possession of Shele's cell phone.

Police and family vainly looked for the device numerous times after Shele's murder—before it reappeared in the very location they had searched. Bogdanos said that returning the device to Shele's apartment was Rod's most significant blunder.

The prosecutor returned to his theory of the murder, walking the jury through the last minutes of Shele's life, dramatically acting out the scene in a one-man show.

With the photo of the wet spot on Shele's bed on the monitor, Bogdanos assumed the role of Rod.

"You're a calculating, evil woman, you controlling, malicious woman, hell-bent on laying waste!" the attorney bellowed.

He told the jury that Rod then placed Shele in a chokehold and dragged her into the bathroom as she struggled.

"She started clawing at her face," Bogdanos said. "He drops her on the floor, then grabs her by the hair and plunges just her head into the water, pulls it out and puts her back on the ground. He goes to the store, gets the seltzer, cleans up the scene.

"What is the defense to this? I can do this in 30 seconds," he said loudly. "Everyone is a liar. I mean everybody. Liar, liar, liar, liar, liar, liar, liar, liar!" he shouted.

Bogdanos took a pause and apologized for his volume. "Our job is to speak for those who no longer speak for themselves, and sometimes when you speak for the dead, you have to speak loudly," he said in a subdued tone. "Now is the time, here is the place and you are the people to do justice, to do justice for Shele."

CHAPTER TWENTY-SIX

Verdict

After a short break, the judge prepared the jury for deliberations, offering them guidance on how to evaluate the credibility of witnesses. She explained the law and the difference between the two murder counts, and that if they found Rod guilty of the first, there was no need for them to deliberate on the second.

She also reminded jurors that she had permitted the prosecution to introduce evidence about Rod's misconduct for which he wasn't charged solely to shed light on his motive and intent with regard to Shele's murder.

"Even if you believe this evidence, you may not infer that because Mr. Covlin planned these crimes or committed bad acts, he must have had a propensity or a predisposition to commit crimes and that he was therefore also likely to have killed his wife," she said.

The jurors filed out of the courtroom just before 1 P.M.

Shele's family nervously milled about the gallery and prepared for what was likely to be an extended courthouse wait. Reporters and TV crews chatted in the hallways, with some quietly taking wagers on the length of deliberations and the verdict. The consensus was that the panel would require at least a week to wade through the evidence—most of it circumstantial.

A little less than two hours later, at 2:50 P.M., the jury sent a note to the judge requesting a dozen exhibits, including Dr. Hayes' autopsy report, the chokehold video, the photo of the master bedroom's bed with the wet stain and ripped sheet, the Dorchester visitor log for Rod's apartment and the entirety of Rose's testimony.

In addition, the panel asked for all testimony about Anna's discovery of Shele's body.

Bogdanos paced, while Gottlieb wore his default expression of genial calm.

As jurors are not allowed to read trial transcripts, any requested testimony is instead recited by the court reporter in open court. This process swallowed most of the afternoon, and the judge ordered the panel back the next morning.

They resumed on March 13 and began deliberating at about 10 A.M. At 11:30 A.M. they sent another note requesting any stipulations related to Anna, Myles and Surrogate's Court.

At 12:25 P.M., the jury sent a request to Pickholz that likely turned Bogdanos' stomach. They asked for clarifications on reasonable doubt, circumstantial evidence, intent versus motive and the definition of burglary—a legal element that would apply only to the second murder count.

Gottlieb and his partner could barely hide their glee. After the judge reread the relevant section of her instructions, the pair sat on the hallway benches outside, radiating cautious optimism.

Bogdanos looked stunned. He approached the Danishefskys in the front row and uneasily told them not to worry. Even if the jury declined to convict on the intentional-murder count, Rod could still go down on the second charge, he said.

Since the judge had explicitly told the jury to consider the second count only if they acquitted on the first, the implication was devastating for the prosecution. It suggested that the jury had deemed Rod not guilty on the first count—the theory most compatible with Bogdanos' exhaustive presentation.

Less than an hour later, at 1:15 P.M., jurors issued a fourth note thanking the judge for answering their questions and relaying that they had no additional requests.

The Danishefskys huddled together on one side of the gallery while Carol Covlin sat alone on the other side, her face fixed in a ghostly stare.

At 3 P.M., the jury sent its last note, "We have reached a final verdict. Thank you."

There would be no protracted deliberation. Considering the length of the trial and amount of evidence presented, the breakneck turnaround was astonishing.

Jolted reporters immediately alerted their editors that a verdict was imminent and opened laptops to finalize prewritten copy—both guilty and not-guilty versions.

As word rocketed through the building and into DA Vance's office, the gallery began to fill once again. With the benches packed, it took several minutes to retrieve Rod from the innards of the courthouse. The extended delay pumped tension into the room like an invisible gas.

Jurors filed in wearing grave expressions.

"Will the foreperson please rise," said clerk Jeanine Ferguson-Bridgwater. "How say you to the first count of this indictment charging the defendant, Roderick Covlin, with the crime of murder in the second degree: guilty or not guilty?"

"Guilty."

The clerk then polled each of the jurors, who confirmed their decisions.

Rod's granite veneer finally cracked under the crushing weight of his conviction. He appeared shell-shocked, bowing his head in abject surrender.

The Danishefskys sat in the same row they had occupied during the trial, directly behind the prosecutor's table. The moment the verdict came down, they grasped one another's hands and sobbed tears of relief, some looking skyward in communion with Shele, Joel and Jaelene. Marc turned to Eve, who was weeping audibly, and enveloped her in his arms. Peggy hugged her husband and her brother-in-law Fred. It was a subdued joy.

Meanwhile, Carol, sitting alone on the opposite side of the gallery, looked dumbstruck as tears streamed down her face.

Bogdanos did his best to mute his jubilation. In the hallway, the Danishefskys wrapped their arms around the victorious prosecutor and thanked him profusely. Vance arrived in time to bask in the glory of his office's much-needed triumph. He delivered a brief statement outside the courtroom flanked by Bogdanos and his team.

Later, outside the building, Marc Karstaedt spoke to reporters for the first time since the trial began. "The wheels of justice turn very slowly, and we always had confidence that ultimately this day would come," he said. "Finally, after nine years, we have justice for our beloved Shele. She was a beautiful person both inside and out, extraordinary in so many different ways and angelic, and she was brutally murdered in a way that no one could imagine nine years ago, and our lives have not been the same since."

He continued, "Our emotions are just—they're all over the place. You never want to send anybody to prison for second-degree murder, but in this case, we felt that it was absolutely warranted."

CHAPTER TWENTY-SEVEN

Reckoning

During the trial, Rod had walked into court each day with the presumption of innocence. He was able to present himself as the aggrieved target of overzealous prosecutors and inept investigators. Buoyed by the support of his children, Rod could still carry himself with the pride of a beloved father. Even during damaging stretches of testimony, he had maintained an air of imperturbable defiance, glaring at hostile witnesses and conferring assertively with his legal team.

But on April 10, 2019, Rod entered the courtroom as a convicted killer—permanently exiled to society's most damnable rung.

With his hands cuffed behind him, he was led to the defense table, wearing a defeated expression that reflected his new reality. Rod's already-sunken eyes appeared to recede still farther into their sockets. As he had during the trial, he wore a rumpled white button-down shirt, dark slacks and discount dress shoes that gave him the look of a mattress-store clerk on a smoke break.

To afford them a final say, victims are allowed to address the court before the judge renders a sentence. Eager to confront Shele's killer directly for the first time in years, nearly every member of Shele's family asked to be heard.

Peggy Danishefsky, Shele's sister-in-law, was the first to approach the lectern.

"Like many great women in modern society, Shele did it all," Peggy began. "But at the end of the day, the only job that truly mattered to her was that of being a mother to her darling Anna and Myles. Shele was a modern woman with her feet firmly on the ground and planted in core values of family and tradition. But let's not forget that Shele was terrorized by the father of her very own beloved children."

Peggy told jurors that Shele's killing tore asunder what had once been a vibrant and joyous family. Not only was Shele erased from their lives, but Myles and Anna, under the influence of the Covlins, became strangers.

Rod, she said, was like a horror-film villain who had crashed through the screen and into their lives.

"During the trial, in the middle of the night, one of my children, who is six feet tall and basically an adult, a man, woke in the middle of the night in a cold sweat, because he had a nightmare that the defendant escaped from prison and was chasing him down and trying to kill him," she told the court. "When my children were toddlers and they would come to bed with a nightmare, I could rock them back to sleep and tell them it was just their imagination. But that is no longer the case, because this nightmare is our family's reality."

Peggy pleaded for a life sentence. She said that Shele's devastated parents were looking down from the heavens.

"Losing Shele broke them. And further losing Anna and Myles destroyed their spirit and put the final nail in their coffins," she said. "The defendant is a heartless monster."

Shele's older brother, Fred, struggled to compose himself as he arranged papers at the lectern. Once steadied, his rage burst forth.

"The existence of Rod Covlin is the strongest argument there is for the death penalty," Fred said, his voice breaking.

He glared at Rod—who remained expressionless and stared straight ahead—while recounting his offenses against both the Danishefskys and his own family.

"I beg you to think of the early-morning hours of December 31, 2009, in apartment 515, when the six-foot-two defendant had my beautiful sister, Shele, five-foot-four, in a chokehold like the one this bastard proudly demonstrated in the video from the prison! Please think about how he applied the lethal pressure to the neck of the mother of his own children! How Shele was struggling and clawing for her life!"

Philip, the youngest sibling, followed. In a wrenching address, he described the wreckage Rod had left in his wake.

"Our sages teach that when one saves a life, you save an entire world," he said. "And when one takes a life, you take the life of an entire world. The defendant brutally and unconscionably murdered Shele and murdered an entire world."

Philip juxtaposed Shele's modesty and dignity with Rod's dissolution.

"By living her life in the proper, upright manner, Shele was literally an agent of God. And it was her way of bringing God into a God-challenged world. She was a fine woman. She was elegant. Shele's world was a world of honor, love and productivity."

Her "fiendish" spouse, he railed, "had no right to decide whether Shele lives or dies. No right!"

Philip blamed Rod for plunging his parents into a haunted darkness.

"The defendant is also responsible for my parents dying in the saddest possible way because they lost their daughter," he said. "My parents were simple, modest, God-fearing people who went to work every day to support their family. This overwhelming horror and grief were too much for them."

He added that the Covlins' campaign to keep the kids from their maternal grandparents had reduced them to living apparitions.

"My father, as we all did, loved them so much," he said. "And that ended up bankrupting him and my mother. And they in essence died penniless."

And Rod's black hole of destruction eventually swallowed up Anna and Myles as well.

"In the middle of the night, the defendant beat, bloodied and choked to death a young, innocent woman who was half his size," he said. "And then left her naked, distorted body in the bathroom only so these poor children could find her, scarring them for life."

The shockwaves from Shele's death, Philip told the court, would reverberate across generations. Echoing Peggy, he said that his children—who were mere babies at the time of the killing—eventually came to fear Rod as they would a storybook goblin.

"This is what was thrust upon them," he said. "Little kids being enveloped in our cloud of mourning and horror. And they have had to suffer and live their lives in fear and terror with nightmares and sleepless nights."

Eve followed her brother. She exhaled deeply to settle her nerves before speaking.

There were moments, she said, in which she nearly fled the courtroom when graphic images of her sister flashed on the monitor.

To cope, Eve trained herself to find glimpses of Shele's life in these poses of death.

"In that close-up picture of her bruised hand, I saw the hand that helped me dress my dolls. That baked Grandma's cookies with me. And held my son the day he was born."

Eve said that Rod had become an unwelcome visitor in her dreams.

"I have recurring nightmares about her final moments as he squeezed that final breath out of her," she said, trembling. "How helpless she must have felt along with the panic and terror, knowing death was imminent despite her valiant effort to fight back."

But perhaps the most moving statement came from Marc, who had become Joel and Jaelene's earthly representative. While alive, Joel had counted on Marc to pursue justice for his beloved daughter and to safeguard her children. The son-in-law dutifully fulfilled that role to the best of his ability.

"They died in 2017," Marc said. "But their deaths began on December 31, 2009, when they lost their daughter, their granddaughter and their grandson. Joel and Jaelene were shattered by Shele's murder."

The patriarch had no longer been able to muster the strength to return to his office, where he was forced to stare at Shele's unoccupied desk. "Joel gave up, a broken man, ending his long and illustrious career on Wall Street," Marc said.

"Joel and Jaelene then mindlessly stared at the television," he recalled. "Joel stopped reading, learning and following the markets." The old man pined for his little girl.

"Often he dozed off," Marc told the court. "And sometimes he would have a garbled conversation with Shele—groaning and grimacing as he wrestled with the demons that haunted him."

Jaelene's state deteriorated in sad concert with her husband. Their once-mirthful home had taken on a funereal atmosphere.

"Jaelene spent her days huddled in the alcove area adjacent to the kitchen," Marc said. "There she wrapped herself in an afghan, sat in a dark room illuminated by one light.

She surrounded herself with many photos of Shele, Anna and Myles—a small shrine which she looked at constantly and wept."

They sank deeper and deeper into a silent agony.

"Things were unraveling and ominous signs were everywhere," Marc recalled, choking up. Prescriptions weren't being picked up. Mail was ignored. Phone calls from creditors went unanswered. Light bulbs that burned out weren't replaced.

The only remaining ember of hope was the prospect of seeing Anna and Myles one more time. In March 2015, Marc invited the Covlins and the children to attend a dedication ceremony at Shele's old synagogue, where a wing was being named in her memory.

Although they were bound to wheelchairs and largely confined to their home, Joel and Jaelene strained themselves to attend the function in order to see Myles and Anna.

Accompanied by Dave, the children entered the Lincoln Square Synagogue—but were quickly ushered away from the Danishefskys. The elderly couple could see the children from afar and dissolved into tears.

"They were whisked away suddenly, with no goodbyes," Marc said. "Jaelene cried, commenting on how beautiful Anna was and how much she resembled Shele." It was the last time the grandparents laid eyes on their grandchildren.

"Rod destroyed their lives and he destroyed the lives that Anna and Myles might have had," Marc said. "So many lives taken, so much life lost. Your Honor, were Joel and Jaelene here today, I think they would look up and say please, God, no more."

His lower lip trembling, Marc made his way to his seat in the gallery and tearfully reached for his wife.

Bogdanos let the statement hover in the silent courtroom for a minute before rising to speak.

Calling for the maximum sentence of 25 years to life, the prosecutor once again unfurled Rod's rampages that culminated with his entry into Shele's home on New Year's Eve.

"From the moment the defendant entered the apartment, she had no shot. No chance," he said. "When she opened her eyes and saw him for the first time, she had to know it. She had to know she was going to die. And however fast it was—and we all hope it was—the bruises and scratches tell us it wasn't fast enough."

Rod departed the bathroom and returned to his studio across the hall, knowing that Shele's bruised and battered body would be discovered by one or both of her beloved kids.

"I close the way I started," Bogdanos said. "With hope. The hope that one day the pain to Shele's family will soften and become bearable. The hope that Shele, in death, can find peace and comfort the defendant denied her in life. And the hope that Rod Covlin will never again breathe free air."

The defendant showed little emotion during the parade of denunciation, occasionally leaning over to whisper to his lawyers.

It was now the defense's turn to speak. Carol Covlin, wearing a spectral expression, arose from the front row and approached the lectern on the left side of the courtroom with a piece of paper in hand.

Barely audible, she said that she was going to read a prepared statement from Anna.

The revelation shook the courtroom like an unexpected crash of thunder.

While Anna, then 18, had been a central player throughout the trial, she never physically materialized—either in the gallery or on the stand.

Prosecutors feared that she might sway jurors with a tearful defense of her father and lie about what she had witnessed that night.

Gottlieb also resisted calling her to testify, knowing that it would allow Bogdanos to introduce Rod's attempt to have her pin a rape on his father.

Thanks to a restraining order issued after Rod's arrest, Anna had not seen or spoken to her father in four years. Observers had wondered if her once-unwavering support had perhaps weakened. Months prior, she had moved out of the Covlin home to attend college out of state and used an alias to distance herself from the lurid case. She would visit her father twice between his conviction and sentencing date but chose not to read the statement in person.

Speaking in a barely audible drone, Carol began her recitation.

"She did not get to watch me grow up, and I did not get to know her as a friend," Anna wrote. "I love my mom. I love my mom. I will always love my mom. I think about her every day. I just want to tell her everything and be in her arms. It's so incredibly painful to live each day without my mommy."

The letter went on to praise Carol and Dave for their undying devotion and support.

Any doubt as to Anna's position on her father was then swept away in an outpouring of praise and tenderness.

"My dad is one of the most caring and loving people I know," the letter said. "My dad has always been funny, strong, honest, kind, intelligent, loving and the most wonderful dad that any person could hope for and simply makes me happy. I struck the jackpot. Thankfully, my dad is still here. I still have one parent, another source of unconditional love, unconditionally trustworthy, and the third most important thing in my life: God, Myles and Daddy."

She said that before her mom died, Shele had mentioned in passing that she wanted to learn how to knit. Rod, Anna said, quietly taught himself the skill so he could pass it along to his wife.

"And some Sundays I'd wake up to little notes with drawings on them saying, 'Let Mommy sleep. Wake me,'" she recalled. "I have one parent that I cannot imagine my whole life without him. I know you are hearing this, Daddy, so please don't cry."

Anna's words triggered Rod's first overt display of emotion during the trial as he dabbed at his eyes with a tissue.

"I lost my mom already," Anna wrote. "Why should I have to lose my daddy too?"

The letter then shifted into a vehement defense of her father.

"I didn't get to tell my side of the story, being the only person in the apartment that night aside from Myles who was there, especially when the jurors haven't heard the truth," she wrote.

Anna said that she awoke in the middle of the night and noticed her mother's absence. She entered the bathroom three times and saw Shele in the bathtub on each trip.

"The third time, I couldn't continue denying what I knew to be true," she wrote. "This time I walked into the bathroom, I saw my mom in the fetal position not moving. I said, 'Mommy!' and tapped her on the shoulder, but she didn't move. I ran to the home phone and called my dad. The only words I could get out were, 'Mommy! Bathroom! Help!' My dad had told me not to call him without my mom's permission unless it was an emergency."

The curious phrase, which appeared to reference Shele's protective order against Rod, elicited disbelieving looks in the gallery—along with suspicions that the letter had more than one author.

Anna said that her dad then instructed her to unlock the door so he could enter.

"I held Myles in my arms and overheard my dad crying and yelling into the phone with the woman instructing him on how to perform CPR," she continued. "It was miserable. As I mentioned earlier, my dad is incredibly strong, so I was shaken by his wailing. I had never heard anything like it. My mom slipped, hit her head, fell unconscious and drowned, just like the medical examiner said when he found her."

Anna excoriated investigators for failing to take notes of her interviews the morning of Shele's death, which she said would have absolved her father.

"Was the prosecution's intention to keep my story out of the trial?" she asked. "I refused to read any of the articles or watch any of the news channels publicizing this injustice and false story, so I've heard about the trial from my paternal grandparents."

Anna's statement then took aim at the Danishefskys, casting them as insincere in their claims of devotion to her. Far worse, Anna said that they suspected her of helping to cover up her mother's murder.

"They think I'm complicit in the death of my mother," the letter stated. "I could not have been complicit in an accident, but how is it that they love me so much but are accusing me of helping to kill my own mother? There's a reason my paternal grandparents got custody of me and Myles."

The address concluded with a plea to Pickholz.

"I need my dad in my life," she begged. "I can't express to you how much I need my dad in my life. I have cried the entire time writing this letter because I just don't know how to put into words how much I need my dad. I need to know that this will end. I need to know that I will get to have my dad back one day and that despite everything that has happened, despite the people that have betrayed me and caused me so much emotional damage and psychological damage, that everything is okay. Please give him the lightest sentence so I can have my dad back in my life."

Her sniffles the only audible sounds in an otherwise silent courtroom, Carol carefully folded the letter and returned to her seat.

With the audience still digesting Anna's words, Gottlieb heightened the drama still further. He said that Myles was in the building and would address the court in person.

With all heads turned toward the courtroom entrance, in walked an apprehensive little boy.

Myles, 12, accompanied by his grandfather, timidly stepped to the lectern with his eyes downcast. The handsome, dark-haired child bore a striking resemblance to his father.

"I'm Myles Covlin," he said in a whisper. "I lost one parent and hope not to lose a second one: my dad. Unfortunately, my mother died when I was only three, and I have no memories of her. I do not believe that my dad murdered my mother, because I had multiple discussions with my sister. During these discussions she told me that my dad wasn't in the apartment the night my mom died, therefore could not have murdered my mom. Because of this I ask that you give my dad the minimum sentence possible."

In wrenchingly simple prose, Myles said he had suffered such awful bullying after his dad's arrest that he was forced to switch schools in the second grade. But the stress of that relentless abuse paled next to his fears for his imprisoned father's well-being.

"Some nights I can't fall asleep because I'm thinking about the fact that he could be stabbed to death at any moment," Myles said.

Amid the unfair chaos of his boyhood, Myles said he had always managed to find peace in building things. He begged Pickholz to give him back his father so they could assemble tree houses and go-karts together.

"I'm afraid that if he's given the maximum sentence, I may

not have the opportunity to do things with my dad," Myles said, drawing tears from several spectators. "I want to spend my childhood with my dad."

From jail, Rod had continued to help his son with his homework, teaching him algebra, geometry and physics. "My dad has done such a good job of being my teacher, guide and dad," he said. "I ask of you, for my mental health, education and basic rights, let me have a dad that I can spend time with not in jail."

After he completed his statement, Dave escorted Myles from the courtroom. He didn't look in the direction of Eve, Marc or their son, who sat just a few feet away, passing them like strangers.

It was Gottlieb's turn to address Pickholz. The attorney delivered a meandering statement discussing the depth of the "unfathomable tragedy" that had befallen the family— especially Rod's children.

"They have lost their mother. They are about to lose their father," Gottlieb said. "Their punishment will continue for years." He did not argue for mercy or suggest that Rod was deserving of it.

Rod, his eyes reddened from emotion, briefly addressed the court. "As my attorney said, I will be appealing and do maintain my innocence," he stated firmly. "Fortunately, my daughter, who slept in Shele's bed that night, knows the truth. She's the one person who could.

"My children are amazing people," he told the judge as his eyes welled with tears. "They're strong and courageous and wise, and they know that I love them infinitely."

Pickholz wasted little time in meting out her sentence.

"To both families, I wish I had the power to bring Shele back to you and to her children. I am rendering sentence based solely on the evidence that came forth during trial. I'm not considering any uncharged accusations against

Mr. Covlin in imposing the sentence. The evidence at trial was overwhelming. The jury spoke. I sentence Mr. Covlin to 25 years to life."

It was the maximum penalty available to her.

Rod remained largely stoic, registering the blow with no more than an extended blink. He rose and placed his hands behind his back before a court officer handcuffed him and escorted him from the courtroom.

The Danishefskys, tearful but ebullient, gathered on one side of the emptying gallery, smiling and chatting with at least a dozen friends and family. Carol, her white hair neatly parted down the middle, sat alone on a bench staring blankly at the floor, Anna's statement still in her hand.

CHAPTER TWENTY-EIGHT

Afterword

After his conviction, Rod was transferred to Green Haven Correctional Facility, a maximum-security compound in upstate New York. Set atop an imposing hillside in a depressed farming hamlet an hour from his childhood home, the fortress houses some of New York's most notorious convicts. About nine months after his conviction, Rod appeared in the visiting area but politely declined to be interviewed for this book. He wore a colorful, embroidered yarmulke, apparently having embraced his faith in full.

He jotted down a quick note and asked a guard to hand it over. "I don't want anything I say taken out of context—that's been done more than enough," he wrote.

Days earlier, we obtained a sealed affidavit from the inmate for whom Rod performed the alleged chokehold in the Brooklyn jail's law library. He had sent it to prosecutors on November 10, 2018, to notify them of the video. His name and signature are redacted. The cover letter, handwritten in clear block letters, informed the prosecution that there are video cameras in the law library "which recorded what Roderick Covlin did when he Murdered His Wife Shele." He told them to look for videos from November 9 and November 10 from 7 A.M. to 11 A.M.

Only the November 9 video was introduced at trial.

He politely signed the letter, "Thank You for Your Consideration. I look Forward To Hearing From your Office Soon."

The full contents of the typed affidavit are reproduced below:

1. On November 9, 2018, between the hours of 7–11am, while in the law library located at Brooklyn Detention Complex, 275 Atlantic Avenue, Brooklyn, NY 11201. Inmate Roderick Covlin admitted to me that he had came into his wife's bathroom (Shele) and placed her in a headlock squeezing her neck until she passed out and then placed her in the bathtub water making it seem as if she had drowned.

2. He demonstrated this by first drawing me a diagram of the inside of the bathroom and then telling me that he did not strangle her with his hands because it would have left finger marks. So he choked her by placing her in a chokehold. He stated that as he was choking her she tried to get his arm off her neck to no avail. (See also November 10, 2018 video of him demonstrating how she was clawing at his arm and scratching her own face).

3. He demonstrated this on video recording inside the law library on the above date November 9, 2018.

4. Roderick Covlin, has also admitted that he had taken his spouse's phone and then placed it in her bedroom, I believe connected to a charger and he placed it on the floor next to a picture frame.

5. He also stated to me, that he tried to make it seem as if a burglary occurred.

6. He removed some surveillance cameras he had hidden within some vents of the apartment to watch Shele and his daughter.

7. He showed me an insurance policy that his spouse Shele used to change the benefactors to her two children and he said that money belongs to him because he never signed the bottom part of the form. And that the money he had been given to his (sic) is free money and that he is owed interest on that money.

8. Asked him why is he worried about the money? He should be happy his children are the recipients' to that money, but he was very adamant about not being the administrator of those millions and that it was his money anyway.

9. He also stated that his children, were staying at his parents' and that he wanted [to] okay someone in Mexico to marry his daughter so that she could then be emancipated and could then move in with him and he would then manage her half of the inheritance money Shele left her. And that he could then make sure that his daughter does not testify against him.

10. Roderick Colvin [sic] also stated to me that he had taken some martial arts classes from some law enforcement officer. I did not get the person's name though.

The informant, a convicted murderer and rapist, later recanted the statement. It was unclear what he was looking to gain from penning the letter. Most of its contents could have been gleaned from media reports and packaged for prosecutors in a bid to negotiate a shortened sentence or some other reward. But details related to the reappearance of Shele's cell phone had never been made public.

Citing their distrust of the media and what they considered to be biased coverage of Rod's case, Dave and Carol declined to participate in this book. In their lone post-verdict interview with NBC's "Dateline," the couple vehemently defended their son's innocence and insisted that Shele's death was an accident.

As to Anna's and Myles' state after their father's conviction, Carol said, "They're holding it together the best they can."

Gottlieb refused to say why the defense never called Anna to the stand, given her support of her father. But the attorney expressed his admiration for the young girl. "I find her to be a remarkable person, considering everything she has gone through," he said. "She has stayed on course to do wonderful things with her life, with all the turmoil. She moved away, she's in college. Very few young children could do what she has done."

Acknowledgments

We would like to thank our parents for their indispensable support and their unconditional love. Our deepest gratitude to Jane Rosenberg, for watching our children every weekend for months on end so we could research and write this book. Thank you to Hamid Algar, for your masterful copyediting and keen interest.

We would also like to thank our editor at the *New York Post,* Michelle Gotthelf, for her unyielding support over the years.

To Jeanine Ferguson-Bridgwater, thank you for your help researching and fact-checking this book.